DISCARD

ROBERT GRAVES

Modern Critical Views

Henry Adams
Edward Albee
A. R. Ammons
Matthew Arnold
John Ashbery
W. H. Auden
Jane Austen
James Baldwin
Charles Baudelaire
Samuel Beckett
Saul Bellow
The Bible
Elizabeth Bishop
William Blake
Jorge Luis Borges
Elizabeth Bowen
Bertolt Brecht
The Brontës
Robert Browning
Anthony Burgess
George Gordon, Lord
   Byron
Thomas Carlyle
Lewis Carroll
Willa Cather
Cervantes
Geoffrey Chaucer
Kate Chopin
Samuel Taylor Coleridge
Joseph Conrad
Contemporary Poets
Hart Crane
Stephen Crane
Dante
Charles Dickens
Emily Dickinson
John Donne & the Seven-
   teenth-Century Meta-
   physical Poets
Elizabethan Dramatists
Theodore Dreiser
John Dryden
George Eliot
T. S. Eliot
Ralph Ellison
Ralph Waldo Emerson
William Faulkner
Henry Fielding
F. Scott Fitzgerald
Gustave Flaubert
E. M. Forster
Sigmund Freud
Robert Frost

Robert Graves
Graham Greene
Thomas Hardy
Nathaniel Hawthorne
William Hazlitt
Seamus Heaney
Ernest Hemingway
Geoffrey Hill
Friedrich Hölderlin
Homer
Gerard Manley Hopkins
William Dean Howells
Zora Neale Hurston
Henry James
Samuel Johnson and
   James Boswell
Ben Jonson
James Joyce
Franz Kafka
John Keats
Rudyard Kipling
D. H. Lawrence
John Le Carré
Ursula K. Le Guin
Doris Lessing
Sinclair Lewis
Robert Lowell
Norman Mailer
Bernard Malamud
Thomas Mann
Christopher Marlowe
Carson McCullers
Herman Melville
James Merrill
Arthur Miller
John Milton
Eugenio Montale
Marianne Moore
Iris Murdoch
Vladimir Nabokov
Joyce Carol Oates
Sean O'Casey
Flannery O'Connor
Eugene O'Neill
George Orwell
Cynthia Ozick
Walter Pater
Walker Percy
Harold Pinter
Plato
Edgar Allan Poe
Poets of Sensibility & the
   Sublime

Alexander Pope
Katherine Ann Porter
Ezra Pound
Pre-Raphaelite Poets
Marcel Proust
Thomas Pynchon
Arthur Rimbaud
Theodore Roethke
Philip Roth
John Ruskin
J. D. Salinger
Gershom Scholem
William Shakespeare
   (3 vols.)
   Histories & Poems
   Comedies
   Tragedies
George Bernard Shaw
Mary Wollstonecraft
   Shelley
Percy Bysshe Shelley
Edmund Spenser
Gertrude Stein
John Steinbeck
Laurence Sterne
Wallace Stevens
Tom Stoppard
Jonathan Swift
Alfred, Lord Tennyson
William Makepeace
   Thackeray
Henry David Thoreau
Leo Tolstoi
Anthony Trollope
Mark Twain
John Updike
Gore Vidal
Virgil
Robert Penn Warren
Evelyn Waugh
Eudora Welty
Nathanael West
Edith Wharton
Walt Whitman
Oscar Wilde
Tennessee Williams
William Carlos Williams
Thomas Wolfe
Virginia Woolf
William Wordsworth
Richard Wright
William Butler Yeats

These and other titles in preparation

Modern Critical Views

ROBERT GRAVES

Edited and with an introduction by
Harold Bloom
Sterling Professor of the Humanities
Yale University

CHELSEA HOUSE PUBLISHERS ◊ 1987
New York ◊ New Haven ◊ Philadelphia

© 1987 by Chelsea House Publishers, a division of Chelsea House
Educational Communications, Inc.,
    95 Madison Avenue, New York, NY 10016
    345 Whitney Avenue, New Haven, CT 06511
    5014 West Chester Pike, Edgemont, PA 19028

Introduction © 1987 by Harold Bloom

Library of Congress Cataloging-in-Publication Data
Robert Graves.
   (Modern critical views)
   Bibliography: p.
   Includes index.
   1. Graves, Robert, 1895–   —Criticism and
interpretation.   I. Bloom, Harold.   II. Series.
PR6013.R35Z76   1987   821'.912   86–24439
ISBN 0–87754–644–4 (alk. paper)

Contents

Editor's Note

This book gathers together what seems to me the most useful criticism available upon the work of the poet, novelist, and mythographer Robert Graves, reprinted here in the chronological order of its original publication. I am grateful to Peter Childers for his skill and erudition in helping me to edit this volume.

My introduction expresses some moderate disenchantment with *The White Goddess*, Graves's personal credo disguised as a history of poetic myth, and then proceeds to a consideration of *King Jesus* and of Graves's lasting achievement as a lyrist. The chronological sequence of criticism commences with Randall Jarrell's early and perceptive overview of Graves, and then is complemented by J. M. Cohen's integration of *Good-bye to All That* with the earlier novels and some significant poems.

Douglas Day traces the origins of the figure of the White Goddess in Graves's life and work, while the poet Daniel Hoffman analyzes how Graves's "significant wounds" helped generate the "barbarous knowledge" of his poetic mythology. The domesticated "Black Goddess of Wisdom," a rather less vivid Gravesian myth, is related by Michael Kirkham to some of Graves's most enduring poems.

John B. Vickery quests for the contours of Gravesian myth in his bringing together of *The White Goddess* and *King Jesus*, while Paul Fussell finds in Graves's autobiographical caricatures a significant instance of the effect of World War I upon the memory of modern literature.

The most synoptic and balanced of Graves's critics, Patrick J. Keane, sums up the poet's achievement in relation to his precursors in the Romantic tradition. Martin Seymour-Smith, Graves's biographer, usefully delineates the personal context of the Claudius novels, Graves's most popular works. In a fitting conclusion to this book, the novelist Anthony Burgess gives us a genial, overall estimate of Graves as a writer, and as a representative figure in modern culture.

Introduction

In 1948, I was one of many young enthusiasts for poetry who fell in love with *The White Goddess: A Historical Grammar of Poetic Myth* by the lyric poet and popular novelist Robert Graves. Graves died December 8, 1985, at his home in Deya, Majorca, and I began writing this introduction some seven months later, in July, 1986, after having reread *The White Goddess* for the first time in many years. Nearly four decades after first reading Graves's remarkable phantasmagoria, I cannot recover the enchantment that the book held for me when I was eighteen. What replaces mystery, and intellectual desire, is the puzzled impression I remember recording back in 1969, the last time I reread *The White Goddess*:

> The shamanism of Empedocles, so strangely reborn in Yeats's *A Vision*, Lawrence's *Fantasia of the Unconscious*, and Graves's *The White Goddess*, proposes a preternatural catharsis to heal a magical spirit in us. . . .
>
> Romantic poetry, in its long history, has been saved . . . by its sense of its own tradition, by the liberating burden of poetic influence. Yeats, Lawrence, Graves—despite their varied and real poetic successes—willfully placed their First Romantics too freely and too far away, and were saved from too crippling a freedom by the relative proximity of their true Romantic ancestors: Blake and Shelley for Yeats, Whitman and Hardy for Lawrence, Keats and Hardy for Graves. . . .
>
> When we turn to the major descendants of Romanticism in modern poetry, we behold a competition to drink of Circe's cup, with only a few notable exceptions. The *daimon* is our destiny, Yeats says, and our destiny is even a kind of justice, but then we discover that this justice means only the exhaustion of every possible illusion,

1

the completion of every possible emotional relationship. Or, to descend to a lower comedy, Graves tells us that Freud projected a private fantasy upon the world and then Graves offers us the assurance that true poetry worships a barbaric lunar Muse. Both Yeats and Graves show us the nightmare cyclic world of Blake's *The Mental Traveller*, but what Blake tells us is mere unnecessary masochism, Yeats and Graves affirm as imaginative truth, though only Graves insists also on the mutual rendings of poet and Muse as being true love.

Patrick J. Keane, who impresses me as Graves's most persuasive critical defender, argues against this judgment by observing, "it is equally true that Gravesian wildness is tempered by stoicism and a stress on limitation." Yet *ethos* or character does not seem to me the issue. What calls *The White Goddess* and many of the poems founded upon it into question is Graves's curious literalism, which prevents the reader from regarding the White Goddess or Muse as a metaphor for the Gravesian imagination. What cheerfully kept Graves a good minor poet, despite authentic genius, was his distrust of figurative language, and his powerfully reductive tendency to historicize and literalize every manifestation of the Goddess he could discover, whether in life or literature. Just before the end of *The White Goddess*, Graves states his credo, which I am afraid requires both critical correction and experiential skepticism:

> True poetic practice implies a mind so miraculously attuned and illuminated that it can form words, by a chain of more-than-coincidences, into a living entity—a poem that goes about on its own (for centuries after the author's death, perhaps) affecting readers with its stored magic. Since the source of poetry's creative power is not scientific intelligence, but inspiration—however this may be explained by scientists—one may surely attribute inspiration to the Lunar Muse, the oldest and most convenient European term for this source? By ancient tradition, the White Goddess becomes one with her human representative—a priestess, a prophetess, a queen-mother. No Muse-poet grows conscious of the Muse except by experience of a woman in whom the Goddess is to some degree resident; just as no Apollonian poet can perform his proper function unless he lives under a monarchy or a quasi-monarchy. A Muse-poet falls in love, absolutely, and his true love is for him the embodiment of the Muse. As a rule, the power of absolutely falling in love soon vanishes; and, as a rule, because the woman feels embarrassed by the spell she exercises over her poet-lover and repudiates it; he, in disillusion, turns to Apollo who, at least, can provide him with a livelihood and intelligent en-

tertainment, and reneges before his middle 'twenties. But the real, perpetually obsessed Muse-poet distinguishes between the Goddess as manifest in the supreme power, glory, wisdom and love of woman, and the individual woman whom the Goddess may make her instrument for a month, a year, seven years, or even more. The Goddess abides; and perhaps he will again have knowledge of her through his experience of another woman.

This is Gravesian autobiography, and as such has a certain limited authority. If the greatest poets in English include Milton, Blake, and Wordsworth, then we can imagine the grim comedy of their reactions to Graves's assurance that they were inspired by the Lunar Muse. Graves had a lifelong contempt for Milton, the butt of his nasty novel *Wife to Mr. Milton*, and had little liking also for Wordsworth, while he managed to so weakly misread Blake's *The Mental Traveller* as not to hear its horror at the dreadful cycle it depicted. "Muse-poets," as Graves describes them, are rather rare. John Keats certainly is the clearest instance of what Graves thinks he means, but that would be the Keats of *Endymion*, not the mature poet of *The Fall of Hyperion* and the great Odes. Graves's favorite lyric, Keats's "La Belle Dame sans Merci," is hardly a celebration of enchantment by the Muse, since the "wretched wight" is starving to death, and cannot be saved. But *The White Goddess*, as Keane admits, loses sight of the reality of human suffering, a loss totally un-Keatsian. Its dedicatory poem, marvelous with bravura, is the purest Graves:

In Dedication

All saints revile her, and all sober men
Ruled by the God Apollo's golden mean —
In scorn of which I sailed to find her
In distant regions likeliest to hold her
Whom I desired above all things to know,
Sister of the mirage and echo.

It was a virtue not to stay,
To go my headstrong and heroic way
Seeking her out at the volcano's head,
Among pack ice, or where the track had faded
Beyond the cavern of the seven sleepers:
Whose broad high brow was white as any leper's,
Whose eyes were blue, with rowan-berry lips,
With hair curled honey-coloured to white hips.

Green sap of Spring in the young wood a-stir
Will celebrate the Mountain Mother,

> And every song-bird shout awhile for her;
> But I am gifted, even in November
> Rawest of seasons, with so huge a sense
> Of her nakedly worn magnificence
> I forget cruelty and past betrayal,
> Careless of where the next bright bolt may fall.

When Graves reprinted this, under the title of "The White Goddess," as the first poem in *Poems and Satires 1951*, he changed its "I" and "my" to "we" and "our," rather ruining it, at least for me, since its point is the Keatsian assertion of poethood in one's own generation. Behind Graves is Keats's declaration to the scornful Muse, Moneta, in *The Fall of Hyperion*: "I sure should see / Other men here; but I am here alone." Yeats appropriated Keats's assertion for *A Full Moon in March*, and Yeats, as Keane rightly argues, is Graves's true rival as a Muse-poet in our century. To engage Yeats in a poetic *agon* simply was beyond Graves's powers, and led to some inadequate posturings, and a number of lyrics weaker than perhaps they had to be.

What survives rereading in *The White Goddess* is neither its spurious history nor its tendentious mythmaking, which increasingly seems Graves's romance with Laura Riding writ large (and according to Miss Riding, writ wrong indeed). Nor can many readers tolerate the book's interminable speculations on tree-alphabets, which read like John Ruskin gone even madder than in his weirdest phase:

> The thumb of Venus is connected with the palm-tree by its sacredness to the orgiastic goddess Isis, Latona or Lat. Lat was the mother of Nabatean Dusares the vine-god, worshipped in Egypt, and the lowest consonant on the thumb was the vine.
>
> The Jupiter-finger is connected with the furze, or gorse, by the Spring gorse-fires burned in his honour as god of shepherds.
>
> The connexion of the Mercury-finger with the yew is made by Mercury's conducting of souls to the place presided over by the death-goddess Hecate, *alias* his mother Maia, to whom the yew was sacred.

Fortunately there is a very different Graves who also inhabits the mythographic chapters of *The White Goddess*. Call his an authentic religious sensibility that writes best in negation, and you have him at his strongest:

> What ails Christianity today is that it is not a religion squarely based on a single myth; it is a complex of juridical decisions made under political pressure in an ancient law-suit about religious rights between adherents of the Mother-goddess who was once supreme in

the West, and those of the usurping Father-god. Different ecclesiastical courts have given different decisions, and there is no longer a supreme judicature. Now that even the Jews have been seduced into evading the Mosaic Law and whoring after false gods, the Christians have drifted farther away than ever from the ascetic holiness to which Ezekiel, his Essene successors, and Jesus, the last of the Hebrew prophets, hoped to draw the world. Though the West is still nominally Christian, we have come to be governed, in practice, by the unholy triumdivate of Pluto god of wealth, Apollo god of science, and Mercury god of thieves. To make matters worse, dissension and jealousy rage openly between these three, with Mercury and Pluto blackguarding each other, while Apollo wields the atomic bomb as if it were a thunderbolt; for since the Age of Reason was heralded by his eighteenth-century philosophers, he has seated himself on the vacant throne of Zeus (temporarily indisposed) as Triumdival Regent.

Two years before *The White Goddess* appeared, Graves published his most effective novel, *King Jesus* (1946), and eventually risked *The Nazarene Gospel Restored* (with Joshua Podro, 1953). Though the return of matriarchal religion, which is the positive program of Graves's polemic, is now a fashionable notion in certain sects and covens, Graves is not taken as a prophet by current literary feminists. His quest for his kind of historical Jesus may however prove more lasting and disturbing than his celebration of the White Goddess.

II

Graves's curious literalism, which weakens *The White Goddess* and all but a double handful of his poems, constitutes the strength of *King Jesus*. Certain that he tells us the story as it must have been, Graves persuades us at least that he has persuaded himself. Convinced that he had suspended time, Graves insisted that he had recovered the truth about Jesus, and therefore the truth about the origin and meaning of Christianity. Yet *The Nazarene Gospel Restored*, seven years after *King Jesus*, recovers a totally contrary truth, in a clean contradiction that Graves charmingly shrugged off. What *King Jesus* and the *Nazarene Gospel* have in common is a very Jewish, indeed properly Pharisaic Jesus, who takes the Law of Moses to be "sacred and immutable." Graves and Podro divide early Christianity into three factions: the Nazarenes, headed by James and the other surviving disciples of Jesus, who remained loyal to the normative Pharisees; the Alexandrians, essentially Gnostics; Paul and his Gentile churches, who circulated the slander that Jesus condemned the Pharisees rather than some charlatans pretending to be Pharisees. Whether the reader agrees with Graves and Podro that the Nazarenes, rather than the Gnostics or the triumphant Paulines, were the true Christians, is not likely to make much difference. Far more interesting is the authors' contention that Jesus survived the cross, an assertion they share with the ill-assorted literary company of George Moore, Samuel Butler, and D. H. Lawrence.

King Jesus, though hardly one of the neglected masterpieces of narrative in our time, remains far more vital than *The Nazarene Gospel Restored*. Its Jesus is a grandson of Herod the Great, which is at variance with the *Nazarene Gospel*, and indeed only can be called the Gospel according to Graves, since the Nazarenes hardly would have hailed as Messiah an abominable Edomite of the House of Herod. Yet the Herodian Jesus of Graves's novel is the only successful and attractive representation of a personality and moral character to appear anywhere in Graves's prose fiction. Claudius, though newly popular because of a recent television series, is merely a droning voice, scarcely distinguishable from Graves's own. King Jesus speaks a voice of his own, as in the dialogue with the synagogue elders of Capernaum:

> They asked him: "Do you dishonour the memory of the learned Hillel from whom we learned these 'absurd legal fictions', as you call them, these 'falsifications of the Law'?"
>
> "Hillel was a carpenter who never ceased to labour with his hands and remained a poor man to the last. If any man now pleads poverty as an excuse for not studying the Law, it is asked of him: 'Are you poorer even than Hillel was?' He interpreted the Law in the spirit of love and laid no burden on the people that he would not himself undertake with joy. It is written that when Moses died all the men of Israel mourned for him; but at the death of Hillel, as at Aaron's death, not only men but women and children also mourned. Honouring his memory, I say: Sell your profitable business, merchants, distribute the proceeds to the poor, return to the boats and nets that you foolishly abandoned, and as you labour on the waters of the Lake remember again your duty towards your neighbour! For is it not written: 'Six days *shalt* thou labour'? And the learned Shammai, who received from Simeon son of Shetach, said: 'Love work, and hate lordship.' And others of the wise have said: 'A man should hire himself out to a stranger rather than sit idle; let him flay a carcase in the street to earn his bread rather than say: "I am a priest", or "I am a great and learned man".' "
>
> "You are called Jesus the carpenter. Where then are your hammer, saw, chisel and mallet?"
>
> "From a carpenter I have become a shepherd." He displayed his

pastoral staff and mantle. "Let no man envy me my laborious new trade."

"And these idle disciples of yours?"

"Let no man envy them their laborious apprenticeship."

The elders took their leave of him without another word; and he received no more invitations to preach in any synagogue of Capernaum.

The vigorous, plain style is Graves at his best, and the portrayal of his Jesus carries dignity, persuasiveness, and an authentic ethical force. These are, I think, the virtues of Graves's poetry at its very best. The Muse-poems, celebrations of the sadistic and vengeful White Goddess, are less likely to live than what I take to be the best and most bitter love poems in the language since Hardy:

The Foreboding

Looking by chance in at the open window
   I saw my own self seated in his chair
With gaze abstracted, furrowed forehead,
   Unkempt hair.

I thought that I had suddenly come to die,
   That to a cold corpse this was my farewell,
Until the pen moved slowly upon paper
   And tears fell.

He had written a name, yours, in printed letters:
   One word on which bemusedly to pore—
No protest, no desire, your naked name,
   Nothing more.

Would it be to-morrow, would it be next year?
   But the vision was not false, this much I knew;
And I turned angrily from the open window
   Aghast at you.

Why never a warning, either by speech or look,
   That the love you cruelly gave me could not last?
Already it was too late: the bait swallowed,
   The hook fast.

RANDALL JARRELL

Graves and the White Goddess

At the beginning of Robert Graves's *Collected Poems* there is a list of thirty-three books and three translations. The list makes it seem foolish to talk only of the poems, and if you think of *Good-bye to All That* and *The White Goddess*, it seems foolish to talk only of the writing: there is a great deal of Graves's life in what he has written, and a great deal of his writing seems plausible—explicable, even—only in terms of his life. I want to write, [here] about what his poetry seems to me; and later, about how his life (all I know of it comes from him) has made his poetry and his understanding of the world into the inimitable, eccentric marvels that they are.

Looking along his list, I see that I have read two of the translations and twenty-nine-and-a-half of the books: three haven't got to me yet, and I quit in the middle of *Homer's Daughter*—but I have read three or four of the books Graves doesn't list. And I have read *I, Claudius* (a good book singular enough to be immortal) and its slightly inferior continuation three or four times; *King Jesus*, a wonderfully imagined, adequately written novel, three times; *The White Goddess*, that erudite, magical (or, as Eliot calls it, "prodigious, monstrous, stupefying, indescribable") masterwork of fantastic exposition, twice; the poems scores or hundreds of times. In two months I have had time to read *The Greek Myths* only once, but it is, both in matter and in manner, an odd rare classic that people will be rereading for many years. And they will be reading, I think, the book with which, in 1929, I began: the thirty-three-year-old Robert Graves's autobiography, *Good-bye to All That*. If you are interested in Graves—and how

From *The Yale Review* 45, no. 1 (September 1955), © 1955 by *The Yale Review*; and from *The Yale Review* 45, no. 3 (March 1956), © 1956 by *The Yale Review*.

can anyone help being interested in so good and so queer a writer?—there is no better place to begin. No better, except for the *Collected Poems*: that, with Graves, is where one begins and ends.

For Graves is, first and last, a poet: in between he is a Graves. "There is a coldness in the Graveses which is anti-sentimental to the point of insolence," he writes. The Graveses have good minds "for examinations . . . and solving puzzles"; are loquacious, eccentric individualists "inclined to petulance"; are subject to "most disconcerting spells of complete amnesia . . . and rely on their intuition and bluff to get them through"; and, no matter how disreputable their clothes and friends, are always taken for gentlemen. This is a fine partial summary of one side of Robert von Ranke Graves: of that professional, matter-of-fact-to-the-point-of-insolence, complacent, prosaic competence of style and imagination that weighs down most of his fiction, gives a terse, crusty, Defoe-esque plausibility to even his most imaginative nonfiction, and is present in most of his poetry only as a shell or skeleton, a hard lifeless something supporting or enclosing the poem's different life. Graves has spoken of the "conflict of rival sub-personalities," of warring halves or thirds or quarters, as what makes a man a poet. He differentiates the two sides of his own nature so sharply that he speaks of the first poem "I" wrote and the first poem "I wrote as a Graves"; he calls his prose "potboiling"—much of it is—and puts into his autobiography a number of his mother's sayings primarily to show how much more, as a poet, he owes to the von Rankes than to the Graveses. (One of these sayings was, "There was a man once, a Frenchman, who died of grief because he could never become a mother." I find it delightful to think of the mother bending to the child who was to become the excavator or resurrector of the White Goddess, and repeating to him this Delphic sentence.)

The sincere and generous von Rankes, with their castles, venison, blind trout, and black honey; their women who "were noble and patient, and always kept their eyes on the ground when out walking"; their great historian of whom Graves says, "To him I owe my historical method"—a tribute that must have made Leopold von Ranke's very bones grow pale—the von Rankes are certainly, as Graves considers them, the more attractive side of himself. He speaks of his "once acquiline, now crooked nose" as being "a vertical line of demarcation between the left and right sides of my face, which are naturally unassorted—my eyes, eyebrows, and ears all being notably crooked and my cheek-bones, which are rather high, being on different levels." I do not propose to tell you which is the Graves, and which the von Ranke, eye, eyebrow, ear, and cheekbone, but I am prepared to do as much for almost any sentence in Robert Graves—to tell you whether it was written by the cold, puzzle-solving, stamp-collecting, logic-chopping Regimental Explainer; or by the Babe, Lover, and Victim howling, in dreadful longing, for the Mother who bears, possesses, and destroys; or, as happens sometimes, by both. But I am being drawn, not much against my will, into the second part of this essay; let me get back to the poetry.

Graves's poems seem to divide naturally into six or seven types. These are: mythical-archaic poems, poems of the White Goddess; poems about extreme situations; expressive or magical landscapes; grotesques; observations—matter-of-fact, tightly organized, tersely penetrating observations of types of behavior, attitude, situation, of the processes and categories of existence; love poems; ballads or nursery rhymes.

These last are early poems, and disappear as soon as Graves can afford to leave "what I may call the folk-song period of my life," the time when "country sentiment," childlike romance, were a refuge from "my shellshocked condition." The best of these poems is his grotesquely and ambiguously moving, faintly Ransomesque ballad of the Blatant Beast, "Saint." Some others are "Frosty Night," "Apples and Water," "Richard Roe and John Doe," "Allie," "Henry and Mary," "Vain and Careless," "The Bed-Post," and the beautiful "Love without Hope":

> Love without hope, as when the young bird-catcher
> Swept off his tall hat to the Squire's own daughter,
> So let the imprisoned larks escape and fly
> Singing about her head, as she rode by.

The young bird-catcher might have stepped from "Under the Greenwood Tree" or "Winter Night in Woodland (Old Time)"—and in all Italy where is there a halo like his, made from such live and longing gold?

Graves has never forgotten the child's incommensurable joys; nor has he forgotten the child's and the man's incommensurable, irreducible agonies. He writes naturally and well—cannot keep himself from writing—about bad, and worse, and worst, the last extremities of existence:

> Walls, mounds, enclosing corrugations
> Of darkness, moonlight on dry grass.
> Walking this courtyard, sleepless, in fever;
> Planning to use—but by definition
> There's no way out, no way out—
> Rope-ladders, baulks of timber, pulleys,
> A rocket whizzing over the walls and moat—
> Machines easy to improvise.

> No escape,
> No such thing; to dream of new dimensions,
> Cheating checkmate by painting the king's robe
> So that he slides like a queen;
> Or to cry, "Nightmare, nightmare!"
> Like a corpse in the cholera-pit
> Under a load of corpses;
> Or to run the head against these blind walls,
> Enter the dungeon, torment the eyes
> With apparitions chained two and two,
> And go frantic with fear—
> To die and wake up sweating in moonlight
> In the same courtyard, sleepless as before.

This poem, "The Castle," and such poems as "Haunted House," "The Pier-Glass," "Down," "Sick Love," "Mermaid, Dragon, and Fiend," "The Suicide in the Copse," "The Survivor," "The Devil at Berry Pomeroy," "The Death Room," and "The Jealous Man" are enough to make any reader decide that Graves is a man to whom terrible things have happened.

At the end of the First World War, Graves says, "I could not use a telephone, I was sick every time I travelled in a train, and if I saw more than two new people in a single day it prevented me from sleeping. . . . Shells used to come bursting on my bed at midnight even when Nancy was sharing it with me; strangers in daytime would assume the faces of friends who had been killed." Graves has removed from his *Collected Poems* any poem directly about the war; only the generalized, decade-removed "Recalling War" remains. When he had said *Good-Bye to All That* he had meant it—meant it more than he had known, perhaps. The worst became for him, from then on, a civilian worst, and his thoughts about war dried and hardened into the routine, grotesque professionalism that is the best way of taking for granted, canceling out, the unbearable actualities of war. Who would have believed that the author who wrote about these, in *Good-bye to All That*, with plain truth, would in a few years be writing such a G. A. Henty book as *Count Belisarius*?

To Graves, often, the most extreme situation is truth, the mere seeing of reality; we can explain away or destroy the fabulous, traditional mermaids or dragons or devils of existence, but the real "mermaids will not be denied / The last bubbles of our shame, / The dragon flaunts an unpierced hide, / The true fiend governs in God's name." In "The Jealous Man" Graves writes with this truth about another war in which he has fought—writes about it in nightmarishly immediate, traditional, universal terms. The objectively summarizing, held-in, held-back lines seem, in Hopkins's phrase, to "wince and sing" under the hammering of this grotesque, obscene, intolerable anguish—an anguish that ends in untouched, indifferent air:

> To be homeless is a pride
> To the jealous man prowling
> Hungry down the night lanes,
>
> Who has no steel at his side,
> No drink hot in his mouth,
> But a mind dream-enlarged,
>
> Who witnesses warfare,
> Man with woman, hugely
> Raging from hedge to hedge:
>
> The raw knotted oak-club
> Clenched in the raw fist,
> The ivy-noose well flung,
>
> The thronged din of battle,
> Gaspings of the throat-snared,
> Snores of the battered dying,
>
> Tall corpses, braced together,
> Fallen in clammy furrows,
> Male and female,
>
> Or, among haulms of nettle
> Humped, in noisome heaps,
> Male and female.
>
> He glowers in the choked roadway
> Between twin churchyards,
> Like a turnip ghost.
>
> (Here, the rain-worn headstone,
> There, the Celtic cross
> In rank white marble.)
>
> This jealous man is smitten,
> His fear-jerked forehead
> Sweats a fine musk;

A score of bats bewitched
By the ruttish odor
Swoop singing at his head;

Nuns bricked up alive
Within the neighbouring wall
Wail in cat-like longing.

Crow, cocks, crow loud!
Reprieve the doomed devil,
Has he not died enough?

Now, out of careless sleep,
She wakes and greets him coldly,
The woman at home,

She, with a private wonder
At shoes bemired and bloody —
His war was not hers.

Often these poems of extreme situation, like those of observation, are grotesques — this neither by chance nor by choice, but by necessity. Much of life comes to Graves already sharpened into caricature: "another caricature scene" and "plenty of caricature scenes" are ordinary remarks in his autobiography. ("Another caricature scene to look back on," he writes of his wedding.) The best of his grotesques have a peculiar mesmeric power, shock when touched, since they are the charged caricatures of children, of dreams, of the unconscious:

All horses on the racecourse of Tralee
    Have four more legs in gallop than in trot —
    Two pairs fully extended, two pairs not;
And yet no thoroughbred with either three
    Or five legs but is mercilessly shot.
I watched a filly gnaw her fifth leg free,
Warned by a speaking mare since turned silentiary.

Somewhere in Kafka there is a man who is haunted by two bouncing balls; living with this poem is like being haunted by a Gestalt diagram changing from figure to ground, ground to figure, there in the silent darkness, until we get up and turn on the light and look at it, and go back to sleep with it ringing — high, hollow, sinister, yet somehow lyric and living — in our dream-enlarged ears. One can say about this poem of Graves's, as about others: "If I weren't looking at it I wouldn't believe it." According to Stalky and Company, the impassioned

Diderot burst forth, "O Richardson, thou singular genius!" When one reads "It Was All Very Tidy," "The Worms of History," "Ogres and Pygmies," "Lollocks," "The Laureate," "The Death Room," one feels just like Diderot; nor is one willing to dismiss grotesques like "Song: Lift-Boy," "The Suicide in the Copse," "Grotesques" II, "The Villagers and Death," "Welsh Incident," "Wm. Brazier," "General Bloodstock's Lament for England," "Vision in the Repair Shop," and "Front Door Soliloquy" with a mere "Singular, singular!"

Sometimes these grotesques are inspired hostile observations, highly organized outbursts of dislike, revulsion, or rejection: where these observations (and much else) are concerned, Graves is the true heir of Ben Jonson, and can give to his monstrosities, occasionally, the peculiar lyric magnificence Jonson gives them in "The Alchemist." It is easy for him to see God or Death as grotesque monsters; and the White Goddess, with all her calm, grave, archaic magnificence, is monstrous. But sometimes Graves writes grotesques of local color, traditional properties, comfortable-enough types, and these can be good-humored—are even, once, wistful:

> Even in hotel beds the hair tousles.
> But this is observation, not complaint—
> "Complaints should please be dropped in the complaint-box"—
> "Which courteously we beg you to vacate
> In that clean state as you should wish to find it."
>
> And the day after Carnival, today,
> I found, in the square, a crimson cardboard heart:
> "Anna Maria," it read. Otherwise, friends,
> No foreign news—unless that here they drink
> Red wine from china bowls; here anis-roots
> Are stewed like turnips; here funiculars
> Light up at dusk, two crooked constellations.
>
> . . . .
>
> "It is not yet the season," pleads the Porter,
> "That comes in April, when the rain most rains."
> Trilingual Switzer fish in Switzer lakes
> Pining for rain and bread-crumbs of the season,
> In thin reed-beds you pine!
>
>   In bed drowsing,
> (While the hair slowly tousles) uncomplaining.
>
> . . . .

Anna Maria's heart under my pillow
Evokes no furious dream. Who is this Anna?
A Switzer maiden among Switzer maidens,
Child of the children of that fox who never
Ate the sour grapes: her teeth not set on edge.

The reader can murmur: "Why—why, this is life." But Graves—as mercilessly good a critic of his own poetry as he is a mercilessly bad critic of everybody else's—has here had a most disconcerting spell of complete amnesia: "Hotel Bed" isn't included in his new *Collected Poems*. "My poetry-writing has always been a painful process of continual corrections and corrections on top of corrections and persistent dissatisfaction," he writes. He is the only one who can afford to be dissatisfied with the process or the poems it has produced: he is the best rewriter and corrector of his own poetry that I know. Lately I have gone over the new, and old, and very old versions of all the poems in *Collected Poems*, and I am still dazzled by the magical skill, the inspiration apparently just there for use when needed, with which Graves has saved a ruined poem or perfected a good one. Usually the changes are so exactly right, so thoroughly called for, that you're puzzled at his ever having written the original; it grieves me that I have no space in which to quote them.

About sixty of Graves's collected poems are what one might call Observations—observations of types, functions, states; of characteristic strategies and attitudes, people's "life-styles"; of families, genetic development in general; of the self; of well-known stories or characters; of good reasons and real reasons; of dilemmas; of many of the processes and categories of existence. Ordinarily these observations are witty, detailed, penetrating, disabused, tightly organized, logical sounding, matter-of-fact, terse: Graves sounds, often, as if he were Defoe attempting to get his Collected Works into the "Sayings of Spartans." Frequently an observation is put in terms of landscape or grotesque, organized as an approach to a limit or a *reductio ad absurdum*; sometimes a set of observations (for instance, "To Bring the Dead to Life" and "To Evoke Posterity") reminds one of a set of non-Euclidean geometries, differing assumptions rigorously worked out. Such a poem seems an organized, individual little world, this and no other. Finishing one we may feel, as in Graves's dry masterpiece, that It Was All Very Tidy—tidier, certainly, than life and our necessities; we feel about it a gnawing lack, the lack of anything lacking, of a way out—between the inside of the poem and the great outside there is no communication, and we long for an explosion or an implosion, we are not sure which. But these local actions, limited engagements, punitive expeditions; these poems which do, with elegance and dispatch, all that they set out to do; these bagatelles—on occasion Beethoven bagatelles; these complete, small-scale successes, are poems in which Graves excels. Few poets have written more pretty good poems: "Midway," "The Devil's Advice to Story Tellers," "The Fallen Tower of Siloam," "The Reader Over My Shoulder," "To Bring the Dead to Life," "To Walk on Hills," "The Persian Version," "The Furious Voyage," "The Climate of Thought," and "The Shot" are some examples of notably successful "observations," but there are many more; and the grotesques and landscapes and love-poems are full of such small successes.

Landscapes have always been of particular importance to Graves; shell-shocked, he spent an entire leave walking through some favorite country, and went back to France half-cured. When he writes about landscapes he puts into them or gets out of them meanings, attitudes, and emotions that poets rarely get from poetic landscapes; like Wordsworth, he is not interested in landscape as landscape. Some of the best of these poems describe magical landscapes—inside-out, box-inside-a-box, infinite regress—that seem to express, or correspond to, emotional or physiological states in Graves that I am not sure of, and that Graves may not be sure of: "Warning to Children," "Interruption," and, especially, "The Terraced Valley" are better than I can explain, and I listen to

> Neat outside-inside, neat below-above,
> Hermaphrodizing love.
> Neat this-way-that-way and without mistake:
> On the right hand could slide the left glove.
> Neat over-under: the young snake
> Through an unyielding shell his path could break.
> Singing of kettles, like a singing brook,
> Made out-of-doors a fireside nook.
>
> .   .   .   .
>
> I knew you near me in that strange region,
> So searched for you, in hope to see you stand
> On some near olive-terrace, in the heat,
> The left-hand glove drawn on your right hand,
> The empty snake's egg perfect at your feet—

with, at the climax, a kind of rapt uneasy satisfaction.

But Graves's richest, most moving, and most consistently beautiful poems —poems that almost deserve the literal *magical*—are his mythical-archaic pieces, all those the reader thinks of as "White Goddess poems": "To Juan at the Winter Solstice," "Theseus and Ariadne," "Lament for Pasiphae," "The Sirens' Welcome to Cronos," "A Love Story," "The Return of the Goddess," "Darien," and eight or ten others. The best of these are different from anything else in English; their whole meaning and texture and motion are different from anything we could have expected from Graves or from anybody else. "The Sirens' Welcome to Cronos," for instance, has a color or taste that is new because it has been lost for thousands of years. In the second part of this essay I mean to discuss exactly what these poems are, and how they got to be that, along with the more ordinary love-poems which form so large a part of Graves's work; but here I should like simply to quote the poem that represents them best, "To Juan at the Winter Solstice":

> There is one story and one story only
> That will prove worth your telling,
> Whether as learned bard or gifted child;
> To it all lines and lesser gauds belong
> That startle with their shining
> Such common stories as they stray into.

> Is it of trees you tell, their months and virtues,
> Or strange beasts that beset you,
> Of birds that croak at you the Triple will?
> Or of the Zodiac and how slow it turns
> Below the Boreal Crown,
> Prison of all true kings that ever reigned?

> Water to water, ark again to ark,
> From woman back to woman:
> So each new victim treads unfalteringly
> The never altered circuit of his fate,
> Bringing twelve peers as witness
> Both to his starry rise and starry fall.

> Or is it of the Virgin's silver beauty,
> All fish below the thighs?
> She in her left hand bears a leafy quince;
> When with her right she crooks a finger smiling,
> How may the King hold back?
> Royally then he barters life for love.

> Or of the undying snake from chaos hatched,
> Whose coils contain the ocean,
> Into whose chops with naked sword he springs,
> Then in black water, tangled by the reeds,

Battles three days and nights,
To be spewed up beside her scalloped shore?

Much snow is falling, winds roar hollowly,
The owl hoots from the elder,
Fear in your heart cries to the loving-cup:
Sorrow to sorrow as the sparks fly upward.
The log groans and confesses
There is one story and one story only.

Dwell on her graciousness, dwell on her smiling,
Do not forget what flowers
The great boar trampled down in ivy time.
Her brow was creamy as the crested wave,
Her sea-blue eyes were wild
But nothing promised that is not performed.

Graves's best poems, I think, are "To Juan at the Winter Solstice," "The Jealous Man," "Theseus and Ariadne," "Lament for Pasiphae," "The Sirens' Welcome to Cronos," "Ogres and Pygmies," "The Worms of History," "It Was All Very Tidy," "Saint," "The Terraced Valley," "The Devil at Berry Pomeroy," "Lollocks"; poems like "The Laureate," "The Castle," "Hotel Bed," "A Love Story," and "The Death Room" might end this list and begin a list of what seem to me Graves's next best poems: "Interruption," "Warning to Children," "The Young Cordwainer," "Down," "Reproach," "Recalling War," "Song: Lift-Boy" (with the old coda), "The Bards," and "The Survivor." Quite as good as some of these are the best of Graves's slighter poems, delicate or witty or beautiful pieces without much weight or extent of subject and movement: "Love Without Hope," "She Tells Her Love While Half Asleep," "Advocates," "Dawn Bombardment," "Sick Love," "Grotesques" sections 2 and 4, "The Suicide in the Copse," "Like Snow," "An English Wood," "The Shot," "On Dwelling," "The Portrait"; and I have already listed what seem to me some of his best grotesques and observations.

Graves is a poet of varied and consistent excellence. He has written scores, almost hundreds, of poems that are completely realized, different either from one another or from the poems of any other poet. His poems have to an extraordinary degree the feeling of one man's world, one man's life: what he loves and loathes; what he thinks and feels and doesn't know that he feels; the rhythms of his voice, his walk, his gestures. To meet Robert Graves is unnecessary: all his life has transformed itself into his poetry. The limitations of his poetic world come more from limitations of temperament than from limitations of gift or ability—anything Graves is really interested in he can do. He writes, always, with economical strength, with efficient distinction. Both the wording and the rhythm of his verse are full of personal force and impersonal skill: the poems have been made by a craftsman, but a craftsman whose heart was in his fingers. His wit; terseness; matter-of-factness; overmastering organizational and logical skill; penetrating observation; radical two-sidedness; gifts of skewness, wryness, catercorneredness, sweet-sourness, of "English eccentricity," of grotesque humor, of brotherly acceptance of the perverse random contingency of the world; feeling for landscapes and for Things; gifts of ecstasy, misery, and confident command; idiosyncratic encyclopedic knowledge of our world and the worlds that came before it; the fact that love—everyday, specific, good-and-bad, miraculous-and-disastrous love, not the Love most writers write about—is the element he is a native of; his—to put it in almost childish terms—invariable *interestingness*, are a few of the many qualities that make Graves extraordinary.

Later on I should like to discuss Graves's limitations, which are as interesting as any of his qualities—which are, so to speak, the grotesque shadow of his qualities. His poems seem to me in no sense the work of a great poet; when you compare Graves with Wordsworth or Rilke, you are comparing a rearrangement of the room with a subsidence of continents. But Graves's poems are a marvel and a delight, the work of a fine poet who has managed, by the strangest of processes, to make himself into an extraordinary one. In the "Fiend, Dragon, Mermaid" that is not included in this last *Collected Poems*, Graves tells how he escaped from the monstrous fiend, dragon, mermaid, each dying—and how, quit of them, "I turned my gaze to the encounter of / The later genius, who of my pride and fear / And love / No monster made but me." This is true: he is, now, somewhat of a monster, a marvelous and troubling one, and it is by means of this "later genius," the White Goddess, the monstrous Muse, that he has made himself into what he is. . . . I shall try to show how it was done.

"There is one story and one story only," Graves writes; all poems have the same theme. "The theme," as he says in *The White Goddess*,

> is the antique story . . . of the birth, life, death, and resurrection of the God of the Waxing Year; the central chapters concern the God's long battle with the God of the Waning Year for love of the capricious and all-powerful Threefold Goddess, their mother, bride, and layer-out. The poet identifies himself with the God of the Waxing Year and his muse with the Goddess; the rival is his blood-brother, his other self, his weird. All true poetry—true by Housman's practical test—celebrates some incident or scene in this very ancient story, and the main characters are so much a part of our racial inheritance that they not only assert themselves in poetry but recur on occasions

of emotional stress in the form of dreams, paranoiac visions and de-
lusions. . . . The Goddess is a lovely, slender woman with a hooked
nose, deathly pale face, lips red as rowanberries, startlingly blue eyes
and long fair hair; she will suddenly transform herself into sow, mare,
bitch, vixen, she-ass, weasel, serpent, owl, she-wolf, tigress, mermaid
or loathsome hag. . . . I cannot think of any true poet from Homer
on who has not independently recorded his experience of her. . . .
The reason why the hairs stand on end, the skin crawls and a shiver
runs down the spine when one writes or reads a true poem is that a
true poem is necessarily an Invocation of the White Goddess, or
Muse, the Mother of All Living, the ancient power of fright and
lust—the female spider or the queen-bee whose embrace is death.

. . . The true poet must always be original, but in a simpler sense:
he must address only the Muse—not the King or Chief Bard or the
people in general—and tell her the truth about himself and her in
his own passionate and peculiar words. . . . Not that the Muse is
ever completely satisfied. Laura Riding has summed her up in three
memorable lines:

> Forgive me, giver, if I destroy the gift:
> It is so nearly what would please me
> I cannot but perfect it.

The Muse or Triple Goddess "was a personification of primitive woman—
woman the creatress and destructress. As the New Moon or Spring she was girl;
as the Full Moon or Summer she was woman; as the Old Moon or Winter she
was hag. . . . The revolutionary institution of fatherhood, imported into Europe
from the East, brought with it the institution of individual marriage. . . . Once
this revolution had occurred, the social status of women altered: man took over
many of the sacred practices from which his sex had debarred him, and finally
declared himself head of the household." Graves describes with disgust the pro-
gressive degradation of this patriarchal world, as it moved farther and farther
from its matriarchal beginnings, and as the "female sense of orderliness" was
replaced by "the restless and arbitrary male will." This "female sense of orderliness" seems a rationalization or secondary elaboration: usually Graves speaks,
without any disguise, of "the cruel, capricious, incontinent White Goddess," and
values above all things the prospect of being destroyed by her. *Though she slay
me, yet will I trust in her* is his motto, almost; if one substitutes *if* and *then* for
though and *yet*, the sentence exactly fits his attitude.

One sees both from *The White Goddess* and the lectures recently published
in England that almost no poets seem "true poets" to Graves; most of the poets
of the past belonged to the Apollonian or "Classical homosexual" tradition, and

most modern poets have ceased "to make poetic, prosaic, or even pathological sense." Woman "is not a poet: she is either a Muse or she is nothing." (One of his poems to Laura Riding is dedicated "To the Sovereign Muse": of all the poets who erstwhile bore the name, he says, "none bore it clear, not one"; she is the first to do so.) A woman should "either be a silent Muse" or "she should be the Muse in a complete sense; she should be in turn Arianrhod, Blodenwedd and the Old Sow of Maenawr Penarrd who eats her farrow." For the poet "there is no other woman but Cerridwen and he desires one thing above all else in the world: her love. As Blodenwedd, she will gladly give him her love, but at only one price: his life. . . . Poetry began in the matriarchal age. . . . No poet can hope to understand the nature of poetry unless he has had a vision of the Naked King crucified to the lopped oak, and watched the dancers, red-eyed from the acrid smoke of the sacrificial fires, stamping out the measure of the dance, their bodies bent uncouthly forward, with a monotonous chant of 'Kill! kill! kill!' and 'Blood! blood! blood!' "

But the reader before now will have interrupted this summary of Graves's world-picture with an impatient, "Why repeat all this to me? It's an ordinary wish-fantasy reinforced with extraordinary erudition—a kind of family romance projected upon the universe. Having the loved one the mother is the usual thing. Of course, some of the details of this Mother-Muse, female spider, are unusual: she always *has* to kill, so that she is called cruel, capricious, incontinent, and yet is worshipped for being so; she—but case histories always are unusual. Let's admit that it's an unusual, an extraordinary fantasy; still, why quote it to me?"

I quote it for two reasons:

(1) It is the fantastic theory that has accompanied a marvelous practice: some of the best poems of our time have been written as a result of this (I think it fair to say) objectively grotesque account of reality. If the Principle of Indeterminacy had been discovered as a result of Schrödinger or Heisenberg's theory that the universe is a capricious, intuitive Great Mother whose behavior must always rightfully disappoint the predictions of her prying son—*a fingering slave, / One that would peep and botanize / Upon his mother's grave*—the theory would have an extrinsic interest that it now lacks. Because of the poems it enabled Yeats to write, many of us read *A Vision*. That Graves's astonishing theories should be so necessary to him, so right and proper for him, that by means of them he could write "To Juan at the Winter Solstice," "Theseus and Ariadne," "The Sirens' Welcome to Cronos," is a thing worthy of our admiration and observation.

(2) Graves's theories, so astonishing in themselves, are—when we compare them with Graves's life and with psychoanalytical observation of lives in general, of the Unconscious, of children, neurotics, savages, myths, fairy tales—not astonishing at all, but logical and predictable; are so *natural* that we say with a

tender smile, "Of course!" We see, or fancy that we see, why Graves believes them and why he is helped by believing them. Few poets have made better "pathological sense." I wish to try to explain these theories in terms of Graves's life; I shall try as far as possible to use Graves's own words.

In *Good-bye to All That* Graves cannot speak with enough emphasis of the difference between the side of him that is Graves and the side that is von Ranke. He writes with rather patronizing exactness of the Graveses, who are made to seem dry English eccentrics, excellent at puzzle solving, but writes with real warmth of the "goodness of heart" of his mother and the von Rankes; he seems to associate her idealism and *gemütlichkeit*, her *Children, as your mother I command you . . .* with all that is spontaneous and emotional in his own nature —he has a heartfelt sentence telling "how much more I owe, as a writer, to my mother than to my father." His father was a poet. Graves writes: "I am glad in a way that my father was a poet. This at least saved me from any false reverence for poets. . . . Some of his songs I sing without prejudice; when washing up after meals or shelling peas or on similar occasions. He never once tried to teach me how to write, or showed any understanding of my serious work; he was always more ready to ask advice about his own work than to offer it for mine." Graves also says that "we children saw practically nothing of him except during the holidays." It is not difficult to see why, in Graves's myth of the world, it is a shadowy left-handed "blood-brother" or "other self," and not the father in his own form, against whom the hero struggles for the possession of the mother.

Graves's mother was forty, his father forty-nine, when he was born; she "was so busy running the household and conscientiously carrying out her obligations as my father's wife that we did not see her continuously"; he writes about his nurse: "In a practical way she came to be more to us than our mother. I began to despise her at the age of twelve—she was then nurse to my younger brothers—when I found that my education was now in advance of hers, and that if I struggled with her I was able to trip her up and bruise her quite easily." Graves says that his religious training developed in him, as a child, "a great capacity for fear (I was perpetually tortured by the fear of hell), a superstitious conscience and a sexual embarrassment." Graves's reading was "carefully censored"; after two years of trench service he had still been to the theatre only twice, to children's plays; his mother "allowed us no hint of its [humanity's] dirtiness and intrigue and lustfulness, believing that innocence was the surest protection against them." Two of his earlier memories seem particularly important to him:

> And the headmaster had a little daughter with a little girl friend, and
> I was in a sweat of terror whenever I met them; because, having no
> brothers, they once tried to find out about male anatomy from me by

exploring down my shirt-neck when we were digging up pig-nuts in
the garden.

Another frightening experience of this part of my life was when I
once had to wait in the school cloakroom for my sisters. . . . I waited
about a quarter of an hour in the corner of the cloakroom. I suppose
I was about ten years old, and hundreds and hundreds of girls went
to and fro, and they all looked at me and giggled and whispered
things to each other. I knew they hated me, because I was a boy
sitting in the cloakroom of a girls' school, and when my sisters arrived they looked ashamed of me and quite different from the sisters
I knew at home. I realized that I had blundered into a secret world,
and for months and even years afterwards my worst nightmares were
of this girls' school, which was filled with coloured toy balloons.
"Very Freudian," as one says now.

My normal impulses were set back for years by these two experiences. When I was about seventeen we spent our Christmas holidays in Brussels. An Irish girl stopping at the same *pension* made
love to me in a way that I see now was really very sweet. I was so
frightened I could have killed her.

In English preparatory and public schools romance is necessarily
homosexual. The opposite sex is despised and hated, treated as something obscene. Many boys never recover from this perversion. I only
recovered by a shock at the age of twenty-one. For every born homosexual there are at least ten permanent pseudo-homo-sexuals made
by the public school system. And nine of these ten are as honorably
chaste and sentimental as I was.

His strained affection for Dick, a boy at his school, ended disastrously only after
two years of military service. Graves went directly from what seemed to him the
organized masculine nightmare of the public schools, into the organized masculine nightmare of the First World War. He was an excellent soldier. His sense of
professional tradition, of regimental loyalty, was extreme ("we all agreed that
regimental pride was the greatest force that kept a battalion going as an effective
fighting unit, contrasting it particularly with patriotism and religion"), but it led
him only into prolonged service at the front, murderous and routine violence,
wounds so serious that he was reported dead, shell-shock, neurosis, and an intense hatred for governments, civilians, the whole established order of the world.
Jung says, in a sentence that might have been written to apply specifically to
Graves: "It is no light matter to stand between a day-world of exploded ideals
and discredited values, and a night-world of apparently senseless fantasy. The
weirdness of this standpoint is in fact so great that there is nobody who does not

reach out for security, even though it be a reaching back to the mother who shielded his childhood from the terrors of night."

When, on sick leave, he met a young artist, Nancy Nicholson, Graves reached back. "Of course I also accepted the whole patriarchal system of things," he writes. "It is difficult now to recall how completely I believed in the natural supremacy of male over female. I never heard it even questioned until I met Nancy, when I was about twenty-two, towards the end of the war. *The surprising sense of ease* that I got from her frank statement of equality between the sexes was among my chief reasons for liking her. . . . Nancy's crude summary: 'God is a man, so it must be all rot,' *took a load off my shoulders*." [My italics.]

Champagne was scarce at their wedding:

Nancy said: 'Well, I'm going to get something out of this wedding, at any rate,' and grabbed a bottle. After three or four glasses she went off and changed into her land-girl's costume of breeches and smock. . . . The embarrassments of our wedding night were somewhat eased by an air-raid. . . . Nancy's mother was a far more important person to her than I was. . . . The most important thing to her was judicial equality of the sexes; she held that all the wrong in the world was caused by male domination and narrowness. She refused to see my experiences in the war as in any way comparable with the sufferings that millions of married women of the working-class went through. . . . Male stupidity and callousness became an obsession with her and she found it difficult not to include me in her universal condemnation of men.

In country cottages; living from hand to mouth; ashamed of himself "as a drag on Nancy"; a friend, rather than a father, to Nancy's children; helping with the housework, taking care of the babies; so hauntedly neurotic that he saw ghosts at noon, couldn't use a telephone, couldn't see more than two new faces without lying awake all that night; writing child-poems or "country sentiment" poems to escape from his everyday reality, or else haunted nightmare-ish poems to express that everyday reality—so Graves spent the next six or eight years. (The keenest sense of the pathetic strangeness of that household comes to me when I read Graves's "I realized too that I had a new loyalty, to Nancy and the baby, tending to overshadow regimental loyalty now that the war was over.") "I had bad nights," Graves writes. "I thought that perhaps I owed it to Nancy to go to a psychiatrist to be cured; yet I was not sure. Somehow I thought that the power of writing poetry, which was more important than anything else I did, would disappear if I allowed myself to get cured; my *Pier-Glass* haunting would end and I would become a dull easy writer. It seemed to me less important to be well than to be a good poet. I also had a strong repugnance against allowing anyone to have the power over me that psychiatrists always seem to win over their patients." *Anyone*, here, means *any man*, I think; in the end Graves decided that he "would read the modern psychological books and apply them to my case," and "cure myself."

Their marriage, regretted by both husband and wife, ended after the two read an American poem and invited its author to come and live with them. Its author was a violent feminist, an original poet, a more than original thinker, and a personality of seductive and overmastering force. Judging from what Graves has written about her (in many poems, in some novels, and in his ecstatic epilogue to *Good-bye to All That*, in which he tells how he and she "went together to the land where the dead parade the streets and there met with demons and returned with the demons still treading behind us," speaks of the "salvation" that, through her, he has neared, and calls her a being essentially different from all others, a mystic savior "living invisibly, against kind, as dead, beyond event"), I believe that it is simplest to think of her as, so to speak, the White Goddess incarnate, the Mother-Muse in contemporary flesh. She seems to have had a radical influence on Graves's life, poetry, and opinions until 1939; and it was only after Graves was no longer in a position to be dominated by her in specific practice that he worked out his general theory of the necessary dominance of the White Goddess, the Mother-Muse, over all men, all poets.

Graves's theoretical picture of what life necessarily must be is so clearly related to what his life actually has been that it is possible to make summaries or outlines of the two, to put these outlines side by side, and to see that they match in every detail: this is what I have tried to do. (If the reader feels that he understands no better than before how and why Graves's world-picture came into existence, either I have made very bad summaries or else I have deluded myself with an imaginary resemblance.) One does not need much of a psychoanalytical or anthropological background to see that Graves's world picture is a projection upon the universe of his own unconscious, of the compulsively repeated situation in which, alone, it is able to find satisfaction; or to see that this world picture is one familiar, in structure and in much detail, in the fantasies of children and neurotics, in dreams, in fairy tales, and, of course, in the myths and symbols of savages and of earlier cultures. Many details of case histories, much of Freud's theoretical analysis are so specifically illuminating about Graves's myth that I would have quoted or summarized them here, if it had been possible to do so without extending this essay into a third issue of the [Yale] *Review*. That all affect, libido, mana should be concentrated in this one figure of the Mother-Muse; that love and sexuality should be inseparably intermingled with fear, violence, destruction in this "female spider" —that the loved one should be, necessarily, the Bad Mother who, necessarily, deserts and destroys the child; that the child should permit against her no conscious aggression of any kind, and intend his *cruel, capricious, incontinent,* his *bitch, vixen, hag,* to be neither condemnation nor invective, but only fascinated description of the loved and worshipped Mother and Goddess, She-Who-Must-Be-Obeyed—all this is very interesting and very unoriginal. One encounters a rigorous, profound, and quite unparalleled understanding of such cases as Graves's in the many volumes of Freud; but one can read an excellent empirical, schematic description of them in volume 7 of Jung's *Collected Works,* in the second part of the essay entitled "The Relations Between the Ego and the Unconscious." Anyone familiar with what Jung has written about the *persona* and *anima,* and what happens when a man projects this *anima* upon the world and identifies himself with it, will more than once give a laugh of astonished recognition as he goes through *The White Goddess.*

The double-natured Graves has continually written about this split in himself—thought of it, once, as the poet's necessary condition: "I regarded poetry as, first, a personal cathartic for the poet suffering from some inner conflict, and then as a cathartic for readers in a similar conflict." One side of Robert Graves was—and is—the Graves or Father of the Regiment side: the dry, matter-of-fact, pot-boiling, puzzle-solving, stamp-collecting, "anti-sentimental to the point of insolence" side, which notes, counts, orders, explains, explains away, which removes all affect from the world and replaces it by professional technique, pigeon-holing, logic-chopping. When this side is haunted or possessed by the childish, womanly, disorderly, emotional night-side of things, by the irresistible or inconsequential Unconscious—when *the dusty-featured Lollocks, by sloth on sorrow fathered, play hide and seek* among the *unanswered letters, empty medicine bottles* of *disordered drawers; plague little children* who cannot sleep; *are nasty together in the bed's shadow,* when *the imbecile aged are over-long in dying;* are invisible to, denied by, the men they torment; are visible to women, *naughty wives* who *slily allow them* to lick their *honey-sticky fingers*—when all this happens, the dry masculine Ego can protect itself from them only by *hard broom and soft broom, To well comb the hair, To well brush the shoe, And to pay every debt So soon as it's due.* These measures—so Graves says—*are sovereign against Lollocks.*

And so they are, much of the day, a little of the night; that they are ever sovereign against "the Mother of All Living, the ancient power of fright and lust—the female spider or the queen-bee whose embrace is death," I doubt. The whole Tory, saddle-soap, regimental-song-singing side of Graves can only drug, quiet temporarily, disregard as long as routine and common sense have power, the demands, manifestations, and existence of Graves's other side, the side that says: "Oh, *him*! He's just something I fool people with in the daytime."

Yet we should be foolish to believe its remark—to insist, with Graves's unconscious, that the male principle is without all affect, libido, mana. (We can see from Graves's early life, from his public school experiences, why it is necessary for *him* to insist that this is so.) It would be equally foolish to believe that the White Goddess does not exist: she is as real as the Unconscious which she inhabits and from which she has been projected, first upon actual women and later upon the universe. (A car's headlights can rest upon a deer until the deer moves away, but then the beam of light goes out to the sky beyond.) The usefulness of this projection, the therapeutic value of Graves's myth, is obvious: it has been able to bring into efficient and fairly amiable symbiosis the antagonistic halves of his nature.

Graves understands men far better than he understands women; has taken as his own *persona* or mask or lifestyle the terse, professional, matter-of-fact, learned Head of the Regiment—Colonel Ben Jonson of the Royal Welch Fusiliers, so to speak. Men are as dry and as known to him as his own Ego; women are as unknown, and therefore as all-powerful and as all-attractive, as his own Id. Salvation, Graves has to believe, comes through Woman alone; regimented masculinity can work only for, by means of, everyday routine, unless it is *put into the service of Woman*. Graves is willing to have the Ego do anything for the Id except notice that it *is* the Id, analyze it, explain it as subjective necessity; instead the Ego completely accepts the Id and then, most ingeniously and logically and disingenuously, works out an endless explanation of, justification for, every aspect of what it insists is objective necessity. (All of Graves's readers must have felt: "Here is a man who can explain anything.") Graves's Ego can dismiss any rebellion against the reign of Woman with a hearty matter-of-fact—next to the White Goddess, matter-of-factness is the most important thing in the world to Graves—"Nonsense! nonsense!"; can dryly, grotesquely, and cruelly satirize those who rebel; can pigeonhole them, explain them, explain them away—and all in the service of the Mother! No wonder that the once-torn-in-two Graves becomes sure, calm, unquestioning; lives in the satisfied certainty that he is right, and the world wrong, about anything, anything! He has become, so to speak, his own Laura Riding. *There is only one Goddess, and Graves is her prophet*—and isn't the prophet of the White Goddess the nearest thing to the White Goddess?

If you break your neck every time you climb over a stile, soon you will be saying that the necessary condition of all men is to break, not rib, not thigh, not arm, not shin, but always, without fail, THE NECK, when climbing over stiles; by making the accidental circumstances of your life the necessary conditions of all lives, you have transformed yourself from an accident-prone analysand into an emblematic Oedipus. Instead of going on thinking of himself, with shaky hope, as an abnormal eccentric, a "spiritual Quixote" better than the world, perhaps, in his own queer way, Graves now can think of himself as representing the norm, as being the one surviving citizen of that original matriarchal, normal state from which the abnormal, eccentric world has departed. The Mother whom he once clung to in personal shame ("childishly / I dart to Mother-skirts of love and peace / To play with toys until those horrors leave me")—what will the Fathers of the Regiment say?—turns out to be, as he can show with impersonal historical objectivity, the "real" Father of the Regiment: the Father-Principle, if you trace it back far enough, is really the Mother-Principle, and has inherited from the Primal Mother what legitimacy it has. Graves wants all ends to be Woman, and Man no more than the means to them. Everything has an original matriarchal core; all Life (and all "good" Death) comes from Woman. Authority is extremely important to Graves: by means of his myth he is able to get rid of the dry, lifeless, external authority of the father, the public school, the regiment, and to replace it with the wet, live, internal authority of the mother. All that is finally important to Graves is condensed in the one figure of the Mother-Mistress-Muse, she who creates, nourishes, seduces, destroys; she who saves us —or, as good as saving, destroys us—as long as we love her, write poems to her, submit to her without question, use all our professional, Regimental, masculine qualities in her service. Death is swallowed up in victory, said St. Paul; for Graves Life, Death, everything that exists is swallowed up in the White Goddess.

Graves's poems (the first half of this essay devoted itself to them) will certainly seem to the reader, as they seem to me, a great deal more interesting than any explanation of their origin. This account is no more than a sketch: the psychoanalytically or anthropologically minded reader will find in the poems, in *Good-bye to All That*, in *The White Goddess*, many things that I should have liked to discuss, many that I should have liked to understand. Because of the White Goddess, some of the most beautiful poems of our time have come into existence. But our gratitude to her need not stop there: as we read Graves's account of her we can say to ourselves, "We *are* the ancients," for it furnishes an almost incomparably beautiful illustration of the truth of Freud's "The power of creating myths is not extinct, but still produces in the neuroses the same psychical products as in the most ancient times."

J. M. COHEN

Autobiography, Historical Novels, and Some Poems

Good-bye to All That was published in 1929, at that point when public interest in the events of the war had suddenly revived. Remarque's *All Quiet on the Western Front* was the best-seller of the year. Among Graves's friends and fellow poets, Edmund Blunden had already had some success with his moving and personal memories of the fighting in France, *Undertones of War*, and Siegfried Sassoon was about to publish *Memoirs of an Infantry Officer*, the sequel to his *Memoirs of a Fox-Hunting Man*. In contrast to these last two books, which presented the war in some retrospect, Graves's autobiography was harshly actual, and its writing careless. Even in the revised edition of 1957, *Good-bye to All That* is not a shapely book; nor is its prose that of a poet. It is however remarkable for the clarity with which scenes, situations, and conversations of long ago are called to life. There seems to be no lapse of time between event and description, and there is no attempt on the writer's part to put the past into perspective. Graves explains the manner of the book's composition in his prologue to the 1957 edition:

> I partly wrote, partly dictated, this book twenty-eight years ago during a complicated domestic crisis, and with very little time for revision. It was my bitter leave-taking of England where I had recently broken a good many conventions; quarrelled with, or been disowned by most of my friends . . . and ceased to care what anyone thought of me.

It is this last factor that gives the book its special quality. It is the work of a man who is not trying to create an effect. Graves's experience of prose-writing was so

---

From *Robert Graves*. © 1960 by J. M. Cohen. Barnes & Noble, 1960.

far not great. Apart from his critical essays, he had written a popular life of his friend T. E. Lawrence, and two engaging and light-hearted contributions to the brilliant Today and Tomorrow Series, *Lars Porsena, or The Future of Swearing*, and *Mrs Fisher, or The Future of Humour*. In these not very important works he had, however, put into practice the advice given him long ago by a preparatory school master, and recorded in his autobiography, to eliminate all phrases that could be done without, and to use verbs and nouns instead of adjectives and adverbs whenever possible. Graves, in fact, despite his classical interests and influences, writes in a style that descends, like that of his contemporaries David Garnett and Rex Warner, rather from Bunyan and Defoe than from the more conscious stylists. This manner was particularly suitable to the direct and factual autobiography; it contributed even more, however, to the achievement of the Claudius novels and their successors, providing the leaven of modernity that made these historical reconstructions light and appetising.

Good-bye to All That is a tolerant book, that reveals in its author a reluctant sympathy with tradition even in its most fossilised state. His early descriptions of life at Charterhouse, while reinforcing the current criticisms of the prewar public school system, is not a piece of special pleading. Graves came through with a considerable respect for the philistines among whom he had lived, and even for the absurd rituals and taboos to which all alike were subjected. He had a similar respect for the niceties of life in a battalion which still preserved some of the hide-bound customs of the peace-time army, instructing its officers and men in the minutiae of regimental history, even though as the war went on the ranks were almost entirely refilled after each disastrous battle with fresh drafts of conscripts from home.

Graves's account of his boyhood is extremely objective. On such a subject as his early religious belief, expressed in the poem "In the Wilderness," and his subsequent lapse into agnosticism, he does not describe any emotional stress; and though in the revised edition he adds a little to his previously somewhat skimpy account of the difficulties arising from his partially German extraction — his mother was a von Ranke, a relative of the historian — the substance of his remarks is no more than that it made him insist all the more indignantly on his being Irish, taking his self-protective stand on the technical point that solely the father's nationality counted. There is throughout the book no appeal for the reader's sympathy. Even such a statement as "At least one in three of my generation at school died . . . The average life expectancy of an infantry subaltern on the Western Front was, at some stages of the war, only about three months; by which time he had been either killed or wounded," is made dry-eyed.

Graves's descriptions of climbing on Snowdon with George Mallory, who was afterwards lost on Everest, of his brief military training, and of trench life in

France gain much from their accurate documentation. He seems to have taken as much care in collecting this material from his own early life as afterwards in collating the Roman historians for his Claudius books, or regimental records for those devoted to Sergeant Lamb. But even more is gained by his lifelike reconstruction of conversations. The welcome given to Graves on his first arrival in the trenches by Captain Dunn, a veteran who eventually proved to be two months younger than himself, recreates the whole rhythm of the man and his conversation in a manner that was later to prove most effective in the evocation of Graves's Roman figures:

> Dunn did not let the war affect his morale at all. He greeted me very easily with: "Well, what's the news from England? Oh, sorry, first I must introduce you. This is Walker—clever chap from Cambridge, fancies himself as an athlete. This is Jenkins, one of these elder patriots who chucked up their jobs to come here. This is Price— joined us yesterday, but we liked him at once: he brought some damn good whisky with him. Well, how long is the war going to last, and who's winning? We don't know a thing out here."

Similar rhythms, though perhaps a little more formal, will be noticed in the conversations of Claudius and his Imperial relations.

The later chapters of *Good-bye to All That*, despite their telling sketches of T. E. Lawrence, Thomas Hardy, and other friends of Graves's postwar years, suffer from the fact that he is extremely reluctant to speak of private matters. Of his marriage, his children and their upbringing, his Oxford studies, his war neurosis, and the writing of his poems he tells us something. His brief stay in Egypt as Professor of English Literature at Cairo is the last event fully and amusingly recorded. The book leads up to a moment of unexplained crisis in the year of its writing, when Graves left England for Majorca. Among the things to which he here said good-bye was the habit of even guarded self-revelation. Unlike some of his contemporaries, he was henceforth unwilling to make his life the subject matter of his books. In describing the war, he could speak without revealing secrets. But postwar life was a private matter, and Graves had therefore to abandon autobiography.

Good-bye to All That introduced Graves's name to a vast new public that had never read his poetry. It revealed moreover certain qualities of the novelist in him. He had already written one or two melodramatic stories, of which one "The Shout," was subsequently published; and had attempted a war novel some parts of which had been incorporated in his autobiography, but had been defeated by the necessity of introducing an artificial plot. The making of plots has never come easily to Graves. Fortunately in his next venture, the two Claudius novels, history itself provided the framework. All that was necessary was to fill in plausible events and characters, the hints for which were already provided by the Roman historians.

Graves's attitude to the classical past is that of one bored by fourteen years of conventional linguistic training who wished to make a fresh approach for himself and was not afraid of iconoclasm. The decadence of the Roman Empire fascinated him because of the parallel situation in which he seemed to be living. The theme had been treated in several of his poems; it was to be restated even more determinedly in "The Fallen Tower of Siloam" and "The Cuirassiers of the Frontier." Graves saw himself somewhat as the Alexander of "The Clipped Stater," a frontier guard on the border of a lost Empire, already half-oblivious of the values for which it had once stood, and certain to be overwhelmed by the next onrush of barbarians. Similarly Claudius in his novel was the last civilised man in a world of criminal intriguers. Though he succeeded by guile in keeping himself alive, he was none the less certain to be overwhelmed in the end.

I, Claudius was published in May 1934, and went through six editions before the end of the year. It was translated into seventeen languages, and received two literary prizes. The first of his series of historical novels, it exploited all the nonpoetic talents of its author, while stealing nothing from the poetry. This was a matter of deliberate choice on Graves's part. Having decided that poetry could not be made to pay for itself, and that if he was not to take a teaching or journalistic post some secondary form of production must be attempted, he was resolved to use his lesser talents as money-makers that would leave him free to write the few poems that came to him in as many drafts as they might require.

I, Claudius is not in the modern sense a novel. It is a careful reconstruction from all available sources of the Rome of Augustus, Tiberius, and Claudius himself, and to this end Graves made use of all his interests: in the history and archaeology of the classical world, in military and political matters, and in the psychology of violence and crime. A novel is by definition concerned with character and motive; and the tendency since Henry James has been towards an ever greater emphasis on fluctuations in the consciousness of a few persons. *A la Recherche du temps perdu*, *Ulysses*, *To the Lighthouse* were the outstanding novels of the time. But just as in his poetry Graves largely ignored the experiments of the European avant-garde, making almost no use of the innovations which derived from Baudelaire and Rimbaud, so in his novels he refused to notice the examples of his contemporaries. Never in his writings had he shown any insight into character, and the people in *I, Claudius* remain as flat as the portrait of Captain Dunn already referred to. Graves is interested in the tissue of events, in what follows from what, and in the solving of historical enigmas. This saves him from indulging in the long descriptions that make such novels as *Salâmbbo* dull reading. It saves him also from the artificial attempt to create atmosphere. Compared with the greatest writer of historical novels in English, Sir Walter Scott, Graves is a historical theorist before he is a novelist, and Scott primarily a novelist who chooses his subjects from the past because life seemed to him to have been more dramatic before the Napoleonic wars and the onset of industrialism. In the same way *I Promessi Sposi* is primarily concerned with character and adventure; its setting at the end of the sixteenth century is unimportant; it is merely chosen as a time when the psychological conflicts which interested Manzoni were most clearly exposed. Graves on the other hand is captivated by the past. He is not, however, concerned with the differences in psychology between one age and another. His characters, like Bernard Shaw's, are actuated by purely modern motives. In fact, Graves is not greatly concerned with subtlety of motive or introspection. When the actions of his characters are explained it is usually by reference to thought and theory, never to illogical impulse. His attitude is that of the detective story writer; one master idea, be it poisoning by mushroom, or the prevalence of incest in the Imperial family, or, in the later novel *King Jesus*, Our Lord's actual descent from the Jewish royal house, is made to provide all the clues.

Graves's Roman world is in decay, stricken by the Punic Curse, of which the Sibyl of Cumae speaks to the deaf, lame, and stuttering Claudius in the first chapter of *I, Claudius*. This, perhaps, sufficiently explains the unrelieved criminality of Livia, Agrippina, Tiberius, Caligula, and the rest of the royal house. With the exception of Claudius himself, and Germanicus, who has the virtues of a good military leader, only Claudius's shadowy mistress Calpurnia seems to possess any virtues. Graves has projected his new-found distrust of society and its motives to which he refers in the prologue to the revised edition of *Good-bye to All That* on to the ancient world that he called to life. But he brought several ingredients of his own age to his evocation of Imperial Rome. The young Claudius, wary and self-protective in the dangerous company of his elders, bears some resemblance to the young Graves among the philistines at Charterhouse. Again, as an amateur military leader with more reliable insights than the professionals, Robert Graves the infantry officer reappears as the Emperor Claudius conducting his campaign in Britain; and the greatest virtue that he attributes to Livy in his novel is the very one that he has himself most persistently striven for: "He makes the people of Ancient Rome behave and talk as if they were alive now"; to which the ancient and carping Pollio replies in words that apply equally to Graves: "You credit the Romans of seven centuries ago with impossibly modern motives and habits and speeches. Yes, it's readable all right, but it's not history."

The Claudius novels are very readable comedies of evil, interspersed with often entertaining and sometimes learned digressions. While the characters' actions follow the events of their own day, in so far as they can be reconstructed from the historians, their speech, beliefs, and reasonings are those of witty and disillusioned modern persons. At their best they remind one of the early Aldous Huxley. But the conversation at the Empress Livia's dining table is closer to Noel Coward. Claudius begins by asking that great lady who is his grandmother why, despite his unattractive physical habits, she has on this occasion allowed him to dine with her:

> She smiled: "Well, I admit that your presence at table still causes me a certain amount of . . . But never mind. If I have broken one of my oldest rules that is my affair, not yours. Do you dislike me, Claudius? Be frank."
>
> "Probably as much as you dislike me, Grandmother." (Could this be my own voice speaking?)
>
> Caligula sniggered. Urgulania tittered. Livia laughed: "Frank enough! By the way, have you noticed that monster there? He's been keeping unusually quiet during the meal."
>
> "Who, Grandmother?"
>
> "That nephew of yours."
>
> "Is he a monster?"
>
> "Don't pretend you don't know it. You *are* a monster, aren't you, Caligula?"
>
> "Whatever you say, Great-grandmother," Caligula said with downcast eyes.
>
> "Well, Claudius, that monster there, your nephew—I'll tell you about him. *He's going to be the next Emperor!*"
>
> I thought it was a joke. I said smilingly: "If you tell me so, Grandmother, it is so. But what are his recommendations? He's the youngest of the family and though he has given evidence of great natural talent."

Claudius's last remarks provide a clue to Graves's attitude that has persisted even in his recent Penguin translations of Latin authors. "Recommendations" and "great natural talents" convey a double irony: that of Claudius who can see only negative qualities in his seemingly demure nephew, and the irony of the twentieth-century writer displaying by the use of strikingly modern language his disrespect for the monuments of the ancient world as erected for him by his schoolmasters. Graves at moments amuses himself by crowning the bust of Caesar with the steel helmet of a later Gallic War.

The Claudius novels owe much of their success to Graves's irreverence. But they benefit also by the compensating virtue, that he explains the past in terms of present-day knowledge or plausible theory. Sometimes, however, theory tips over into implausibility. Claudius's campaign for the conquest of Britain is brilliantly and imaginatively described. The Britons are entrenched on Brentwood Hill, with one flank protected by a marsh, the other by a thicket. Claudius, without military experience, is anxious to avoid a frontal attack, and the eunuch Posides, entrusted with the turning of the marsh flank, works out a ruse that is both anachronistic and incredible:

> Posides answered: "You have given me the easier flank, Caesar. There is, as it happens, a track through the marshes. One would have to go along it in single file, but there is a track. I met a man in London yesterday, a travelling Spanish oculist who goes about the country curing the people of marsh-opthalmia. He's in the Camp now, and he says he knows that marsh well, and the track—which he always uses to avoid the toll-gate on the hill. Since Cymbeline's death they have been levying no fixed toll, but a traveller must pay according to the amount of money he has in his saddle-bags, and the oculist got tired of being skinned.

The use of London for Londonium and the introduction of an occasional word of modern German into the mouth of a soldier from beyond the Rhine are no doubt legitimate devices. But it is doubtful whether any person in the first century would describe a disease in any terms that could reasonably be translated "marsh-opthalmia," or would describe himself as an "oculist." Nor is a tollgate on an ancient British track very easy to believe in.

The Claudius novels continue and develop in an original way a tendency in the movement of historical fiction of which Lion Feuchtwanger with his *Ugly Duchess* (*Die hässliche Herzogin*, 1923, transl. 1927) and *Jew Süss* (*Jud Süss*, 1925, trans. 1926) was so far the leading practitioner. But whereas Feuchtwanger's originality lay in the application of modern psychological analysis to characters in the past, Graves achieves a similar effect by the mere use of modern language. "Advisory assistant to the Chief Vestal in moral matters"; "to avoid the scandal Livia paid up"; "a dreadful old woman with a cleft chin and hair kept black with lamp-soot (the grey showing plainly at the roots)": all these touches taken from a single page cumulatively build up the impression that the Romans of the Empire were no more than twentieth-century people in period costume. Whereas the tradition of the novel from Sir Walter Scott and Alexandre

Dumas to the many minor practitioners of the generation of Conan Doyle and Stanley Weyman had been to present the characters of the past as more admirable and heroic or more villainous than those of the present, the new historical novel stressed rather the unchangingness of human motive and action.

In *Count Belisarius*, Graves's next important novel of 1938, he retreated from the extreme position to which he had advanced in the Claudius books. Here the historical and military interest is subordinated to the personal drama, yet even the Belisarius—Antonina—Theodosius love-triangle, the central intrigue of the book, follows the narrative of Procopius. Graves claims that only one character in this teeming book is of his own invention. For the rest hints at least were provided by the sixth-century Byzantine historian in his *Secret History* (Historia Arcana), in which he attacked the Emperor Justinian and his Empress Theodora, or in his account of Justinian's campaigns and of his building activities. Graves had in fact as much material to draw on for this little-known period of Byzantine history as he had had for the better-known Claudian epoch. Here, however, his concern with military campaigns, his detached interest in religious heresies, his power of presenting the clashes of people and factions, combine to make this essay in fictionalised history as dramatic, though rather more slow-moving, than his two previous exercises in historical fiction. It is also better constructed. For whereas the excursus on the Druids in *Claudius the God* is clearly a digression, the various accounts of military training and organisation in *Count Belisarius* form an intrinsic part of the story. Belisarius is, like Claudius, "the one good man in a wholly bad world." He is indeed described in these words in the horoscope that is cast for his future wife Antonina. The Emperor Justinian, by contrast, is characterised, in the horoscope of his Empress-to-be, Theodora, then a cheap actress and prostitute, as "the King of the Demons." For the world of Belisarius is, as Graves sees it, like that of Claudius, in decay, the prey to Goths, Huns, Vandals, Moors, and Gepids, and to the inner corruption of the Byzantine capital with its faction feuds, which affected even the most stalwart barbarians who fought it or took service with it. But Belisarius, the cavalry commander who preserved his loyalty to Justinian even though ill-treated by him, redeems the book, which does not present the picture of unrelieved evil of its predecessors. Belisarius, in fact, seems to offer a Christian forgiveness to his royal master, for in the last words given by Graves to the scribe whom he credits with the writing of his story, "Belisarius pitied Justinian for wishing to be a Christian and yet wanting the knowledge of how to set about it."

The style of *Count Belisarius* is more sober than that of the Claudius novels. Except in certain comic passages, like that in which the Empress makes fun of the old senator Hippobates, who had scorned her in her humble days, there is little of the levity either of description or conversation that Graves allowed himself in the Claudius novels. The conversation too is less modish than that round the Empress Livia's table, and the anachronisms far less blatant than in the description of the battle of Brentwood Hill.

The two books about the American Revolution which follow, *Sergeant Lamb of the Ninth* and *Proceed, Sergeant Lamb,* apply the same process of research and reconstruction to a soldier of whom Graves had first heard when instructing his men in 1915 in the history of their regiment. This same Lamb, once of the Ninth, later became a sergeant in the Twenty-third regiment of the line, or Royal Welch Fusiliers. Here again no major characters were invented, and no opinions expressed that were not current at the time. Graves took advantage of a brief visit to America to sketch in his background, and adopted a style with slight eighteenth-century echoes to suit the tongue of his fictitious narrator, who was the sergeant himself. Again, as in his classical novels, Graves has taken great pains to ensure the accuracy of his historical detail. On the subject of scalping, for instance, he is most circumstantial while the campaigns are meticulously recorded, and the habits of Indians, French, New Englanders, Rebels, and Loyalists carefully distinguished.

The last of this series of historical novels, *Wife to Mr. Milton,* tells in the first person the tale of the sixteen-year-old girl who married the then thirty-three-year-old poet. It constructs, with care equal to that of any of the previous books, a picture of England in the 1640s. It was an age that contained many features which attracted Graves: a plethora of religious cranks and creeds and of historical controversies, and a considerable campaigning interest. The setting of the book also was in that Oxfordshire country which he knew so well. Graves was, however, deflected into the writing of a type of pastiche that now brought him far closer to the conventional writer of historical fiction. The conversation of his characters is stiff; the narrative follows seventeenth-century rhythms, and uses the vocabulary of the time. Graves's attitude in this novel is more ambivalent than that in the Claudius books or in *Count Belisarius.* At bottom, he does not care much for Milton or for his age. Though willing to ape his language and expound his thought, he comes rather to mock than to worship.

DOUGLAS DAY

The Coming of the Goddess

Robert Graves, who had been forced to leave Majorca in 1936 by the outbreak of the Civil War, wandered around Europe in Miss Riding's company
until the spring of 1938, when they went to live in Pennsylvania. They soon
parted company and have never met since. A month before the outbreak of
World War II, Graves returned to England, remarried, and, after being rejected
for active service because of age, settled in a small Devonshire village, Galmpton-
Brixton, where he continued writing as prolifically as ever. His work during the
war years was primarily given to prose: *Sergeant Lamb of the Ninth* (1940) and
Proceed, Sergeant Lamb (1941) were historical novels about a member of the
Royal Welch Fusiliers during the Revolutionary War in America; *The Long
Week-End* (1940), written with Alan Hodge, was a "Social History of Great
Britain, 1918-1939"; *The Reader over Your Shoulder* (1943), also with Hodge,
was a "Handbook for Writers of English Prose"; and *Wife to Mr. Milton* (1943)
was an iconoclastic study of the relationship between Milton and Marie Powell
from which—characteristically, for Graves—Milton emerged as the villainous
oppressor of young womanhood. He wrote fewer poems during this time than
he had in the five preceding years. *No More Ghosts* (London: Faber and Faber,
1940) consisted chiefly of pieces previously published in *Collected Poems* (1938)
and contained only four new poems; and fourteen new pieces were printed in
Work in Hand (London: The Hogarth Press, 1942), a small volume in which
Graves's work appeared side-by-side with poems by Norman Cameron and Alan
Hodge.

From *Swifter than Reason: The Poetry and Criticism of Robert Graves.* © 1963 by the
University of North Carolina Press.

Two of the new poems in *No More Ghosts* reveal that Graves's tranquil mood of the late thirties was already beginning to dissipate, and that once again the more violent emotions were controlling his imagination. Both of these poems indicate, moreover, that Graves now chose to give a freer rein to his fondness for magic and myth than he had heretofore done. In "The Beast," for example, we find what seems to be a myth created for the purpose of the poem:

> Beyond the Atlas roams a love-beast.
> The Aborigines harry it with darts;
> Its flesh is esteemed, though of a fishy tang
> Tainting the eater's mouth and lips.
> Ourselves once, wandering in mid-wilderness
> And by despair drawn to this diet,
> Before the meal was over sat apart
> Loathing each other's carrion company.

The Beast is, of course, Graves's old enemy, Lust; and here it is depicted as a loathsome creature whose flesh is attractive to savages, but repellent to the poet and his lover, who, though compelled to eat, yet despise each other for having eaten. The whole poem is thus no more than a vivid recasting, in a framework of myth, of Graves's old theme of love versus lust.

The second poem, "A Love Story" (*No More Ghosts*), finds Graves once again using landscape as a symbol for emotional states. We are first given the sort of highly charged setting which was shortly to become a dominant characteristic of Graves's "magical" poems:

> The full moon easterly rising, furious,
> Against a winter sky ragged with red;
> The hedges high in snow, and owls raving—
> Solemnities not easy to withstand:
> A shiver wakes the spine.

This frightening scene recalls to the poet a similar one in his youth, when he had

> fetched the moon home
> With owls and snow, to nurse in my head
> Throughout the trials of a new Spring,
> Famine unassuaged.

Thus internalized, the Moon symbolized for the youthful poet an ideal, unattainable love; in the midst of spring his hunger for love went unrelieved, and the coldness of winter persisted in his heart. But, we learn in the third stanza, the youth did at last fall in love; and, while he retained the image of the moon as the "ensign" of his love,

> snows melted,
> Hedges sprouted, the moon tenderly shone,
> The owls trilled with tongues of nightingale.

In the fourth stanza, however, the poet admits that the spring his new love had awakened was illusory, that it was "all lies": the woman's image had soon "turned beldamish," the nightingales had become once again only owls, and

> Back again came Winter on me with a bound,
> The pallid sky heaved with a moon-quake.

It had been dangerous, he concludes, to "serenade Queen Famine"; for now he was compelled to surrender the warmth and happiness that his illusory love had brought him, and to return to the bleak emptiness of his first setting.

> In tears I recomposed the former scene,
> Let the snow lie, watched the moon rise, suffered the owls,
> Paid homage to them of unevent.

Graves had by now ceased for the most part to generalize in his poetry, so it is probable that he is here not speaking of the inevitable course of all love affairs, but only of one ill-fated experience. The poem is effective enough as it stands, but the central figures in it—the moon, the owls, and the snow—will all take on added significance when we consider them as integral parts of the symbolic system Graves was shortly to develop.

In "Mid-Winter Waking" (*Work in Hand*), one of Graves's best love poems, we find a happy sequel to "A Love Story"—and also perhaps a symbolic recognition of his recovered poetic powers. Here there is the same struggle between spring and winter in the poet; but now we find the poet, again in love, rejoicing that he has awakened from "long hibernation" to find himself "once more a poet," and looking forward eagerly to the spring which he is to enjoy with his lover, his new muse:

> Be witness that on waking this mid-winter,
> I found her hand in mine laid closely
> Who shall watch out the Spring with me.
> We stared in silence all around us
> But found no winter anywhere to see.

The overall theme of the few poems that Graves wrote during the period between 1939 and 1942 was love between man and woman, sometimes happy, sometimes not; and, despite the foreshadowing that we detect here, and that which we had discerned in the final poems of Graves's third period, it was not until 1944 that this theme became specifically related to the love of a special man — the Poet — for a special woman — the Muse.

The origins of this metamorphosis lie in Graves's *Hercules, My Shipmate*, his 1944 novel about Jason and the Argonauts in their quest for the Golden Fleece. His research for this work, like that for all his historical novels, was exhaustive: before he began writing, he consulted the works of Homer, Hesiod, Hecataeus, Aeschylus, Sophocles, Euripides, Herodotus, Pindar, Apollonius Rhodius, Diodorus Siculus, Strabo, Pausanias, and many other Greek and Roman poets and historians. By the time Graves had finished this research, he was able to trace in *Hercules, My Shipmate* the complete voyage of the Argo; to provide a complete roster of the Argonauts, with full biographies of each man present; and to determine — to his own satisfaction, at least — everything that had occurred during the adventure, from the initial loss of the Fleece by King Athamas of Minya, to the death of Jason years after the voyage. But Graves found something in his investigations of ancient Mediterranean history that seemed far more interesting to him than the story of the Argonauts: in every source he consulted, there were frequent references to a Mother-Goddess who appeared to have been worshipped, in any number of her varying forms, throughout all of the then known world. This was not Graves's first acquaintance with the Goddess: he had known of her since his schoolboy exposure to the Homeric epics, had encountered her often in his reading of the anthropological investigations of Jane Harrison and Sir James Frazer — and most especially in his encounters with her as Isis in *The Golden Ass* of Apuleius, in which she is described with great attention to detail:

> I had scarcely closed my eyes before the apparition of a woman began to rise from the middle of the sea with so lovely a face that the gods themselves would have fallen down in adoration of it. First the head, then the whole shining body gradually emerged and stood before me poised on the surface of the waves. . . . Her long thick hair fell in tapering ringlets on her lovely neck, and was crowned with an intricate chaplet in which was woven every kind of flower. Just above her brow shone a round disc, like a mirror, or like the bright face of the moon, which told me who she was. Vipers rising from the left-hand and right-hand partings of her hair supported this disc, with ears of corn bristling between them. Her many-coloured robe was of finest linen; part was glistening white, part crocus-yellow,

part glowing red and along the entire hem a woven bordure of flowers and fruit clung swaying in the breeze. But what caught and held my eye more than anything else was the deep black lustre of her mantle. She wore it slung across her body from the right hip to the left shoulder, where it was caught in a knot resembling the boss of a shield; but part of it hung in innumerable folds, the tasselled fringe quivering. It was embroidered with glittering stars on the hem and everywhere else, and in the middle beamed a full and fiery moon.

In her right hand she held a bronze rattle, of the sort used to frighten away the God of the Sirocco; its narrow rim was curved like a sword-belt and three little rods, which sang shrilly when she shook the handle, passed horizontally through it. A boat-shaped gold dish hung from her left hand, and along the upper surface of the handle writhed an asp with puffed throat and head raised ready to strike. On her divine feet were slippers of palm leaves, the emblem of victory.

But in spite of such striking descriptions, it was in his fiction about the Argonauts that she first fully captured his imagination; and *Hercules, My Shipmate* soon became not so much the story of Jason and his adventures as it was a study of the Goddess cults in the second and first millennia B.C.

Following generally the theses of Frazer and Miss Harrison, Graves proposes in his novel that all religious systems prior to the middle of the second millennium were entirely matriarchal—that male deities were unknown until the thirteenth century B.C., when the Achaean and Dorian invaders of what is now Greece brought with them their patriarchal religion, dethroned the Goddess, occupied her temples, and set up the familiar Olympic pantheon, presided over by Zeus. From this time on, according to Graves, Goddess-worship was broken into isolated cults which were, over the centuries, gradually hunted down and destroyed by the followers of the patriarchal religions, until the once-supreme Goddess became almost totally replaced by the new gods.

Hercules, My Shipmate is set in time about two generations before the fall of Troy, in a period when, according to Graves, the White Goddess was by no means yet evicted from the Mediterranean; and Graves sees the adventures of Jason and the Argonauts as a series of clashes between the old and new religions, in which the forces of the Goddess consistently triumph over the forces of the Olympians. The Fleece is stolen because King Athamas insists on venerating Zeus; Jason is invulnerable only because he is championed by the White Goddess of Pelion; and the Fleece is regained because the Argonauts are aided by Medea, the Goddess's priestess at Colchis. At the conclusion of the novel, the Goddess is still all-powerful, although she continues to suffer the indignities imposed on her by Zeus, whom she regards as a foolish and wayward son.

The precise nature of this Goddess is only hinted at in *Hercules, My Shipmate*; but Graves devotes himself to a study of her in *The White Goddess*, the exotic, often bewildering, but undeniably brilliant "Historical Grammar of Poetic Myth" he wrote this same year. This work, which "will take its place beside *The Anatomy of Melancholy* as an eccentric classic of English literature," is a curious blend of fact and fancy, an often impenetrable wilderness of cryptology, obscure learning, and apparently *non sequitur* reasoning brought to bear on a thesis that has its roots partly in historic fact, partly in generally accepted anthropological hypotheses, and partly in pure poetic intuition. The most careful reader of *The White Goddess* will have difficulty in determining where fact leaves off and imagination begins, and it is perhaps for this reason that scholars have refused to treat the work seriously. But this neglect appears not to have disturbed Graves very deeply: in *5 Pens in Hand* he states that *The White Goddess* was intended not as a scholarly document, but as a manifestation of poetic faith; and that, as a poet, he was seeking neither to compete with professional scholars, nor to solicit sympathy from them.

In this same essay Graves recalls the genesis of *The White Goddess*:

> In 1944 . . . I was working against time on a historical novel about the Argonauts and the Golden Fleece, when a sudden overwhelming obsession interrupted me. It took the form of an unsolicited enlightenment on a subject I knew almost nothing of. . . . I began speculating on a mysterious "Battle of the Trees," allegedly fought in prehistoric Britain, and my mind worked at such a furious rate all night, as well as all the next day, that my pen found it difficult to keep pace with the flow of thought. . . . within three weeks, I had written a 70,000-word book about the ancient Mediterranean Moon-Goddess whom Homer invoked in the *Iliad* . . . and to whom most traditional poets ever since have paid at any rate lip-service.
>
> (*5 Pens in Hand*)

This mysterious enlightenment, Graves goes on to say, began one morning when he was rereading Lady Charlotte Guest's translation of *The Mabinogion*, and came across "a hitherto despised minstrel poem" called *Hanes Taliesin* (*The Song of Taliesin*).

> I suddenly knew (don't ask me how) that the lines of the poem, which has always been dismissed as deliberate nonsense, formed a

series of early medieval riddles, and that I knew the answer to them
all, although I was neither a Welsh scholar, nor a medievalist, and
although many of the lines had been deliberately transposed by the
author (or his successors) for security reasons.

He knew also (again, without knowing how) that the answer to these riddles
must in some way be linked with an ancient Welsh poetic tradition of a *Câd
Goddeu* ("Battle of Trees"), the subject of a thirteenth-century poem recorded in
The Red Book of Hergest, a collection of early Welsh verse. The story of the
Argonauts now temporarily forgotten, Graves dove into his father's collection of
Celtic literature, and in a short time came up with the "facts" that supported his
intuition. The *Câd Goddeu* and *The Song of Taliesin* were both, he concluded,
intentionally garbled accounts of an ancient struggle between rival priesthoods
in Celtic Britain for control of the national learning. These priesthoods were
those which worshipped respectively the Goddess Danu (the Celtic version of
Danäe of Argos) and the solar god Beli (originally the Egyptian god Bel). Danu-
worship had been brought to Ireland and Britain in the middle Bronze Age by
the Tuatha dé Danaan, a tribe of nomadic Grecians; and Beli-worship had been
imposed on the British Isles by the Celtic invaders of the first millennium B.C.
Thus, Graves concluded, the *Câd Goddeu* and *The Song of Taliesin* were symbolic accounts of a conflict between matriarchal and patriarchal religions—the
same conflict that had begun hundreds of years earlier in the Mediterranean.

The bulk of *The White Goddess* is given to Graves's intricate explanation
of the reasoning that had brought him to this conclusion, and deals chiefly with
the nature of a pair of secret Druidic alphabets and the ways in which they
served as sacred calendars for the old religion. It seems that these alphabet-
calendars were, like the eighteen-letter Greek Orphic alphabet which preceded
that of the Classical Greek period, tied in with tree-worship; and that tree-
worship was throughout the Bronze Age, from Palestine to Ireland, associated
everywhere with veneration of the pre-Aryan Triple Moon-Goddess. Once he
had made this connection between the religions of the British Isles and the Mediterranean, Graves could proceed with great confidence to draw a multitude of
correspondences between Greek and Celtic myth, and to assert that both of
these mythic systems were, like his mysterious Welsh poems, nothing more or
less than symbolic representations of the ancient battle between the Goddess and
the usurping male deities.

Although most modern anthropologists would agree that goddess-worship
was the earliest form of western religion, there is much about Graves's audacious
thesis that seems, even to the anthropological layman, to rest on shaky founda-
tions. There is little reason to believe, for example, that the Tuatha dé Danaan

were ever more than supernatural characters in Irish fairy-tales; or that Graves is correct in asserting that the Picts were originally from Thrace, and were driven from their original homes by the Achaean invaders. When discussing gnosticism, Graves does not make it clear that this earlier heresy was not held by a single sect, but sprang from at least three sources: Jewish (Essene and Kabbalist), Greek, and Oriental. In several places he seems to rely on information derived from sections of *The Golden Bough* which have since been disproved by anthropologists—as in his assumption that the Egyptian god Osiris was a less powerful and important personage than his spouse, Isis. There is, apparently, no evidence to link the Druids with any pre-Celtic element in British prehistory, as Graves does; and there is even some question that the earlier of Graves's Druidic alphabets—on the authenticity of which much of the argument of *The White Goddess* depends—is in fact authentic. But if the work has caused academicians to view Graves as "a dangerous amateur, possibly even a charlatan, who imposes upon reality a world of private fantasies," it is still of immense value to the reader who is content to accept it as a supremely imaginative attempt to define the precise nature of poetic inspiration by relating it to classical and preclassical myth, and specifically to the ancient veneration of the great Triple Goddess, the Magna Mater.

In the prehistoric matriarchal societies, says Graves, a queen who was the temporary incarnation of the Goddess took to herself periodically a king, who had to be sacrificed before his strength decayed, to preserve the fertility of the land. This Goddess is that familiar and traditional figure, the Muse, the religious invocation of whom is the function of all true (that is, "inspired") poetry. She is the female principle in its three archetypal aspects: as the Mother who bears man, the Nymph who mates with him, and the Old Crone who presides over his burial. She is thus instrumental in effecting man's creation, fulfilment, and destruction. She is simultaneously the Goddess of Happiness and Life, and of Pain and Death, and to ignore her in any of her manifestations, is impious and dangerous. Her ambivalent nature is reflected in the adjective "White" which is often part of her title: "In one sense it is the pleasant whiteness of pearl-barley, or a woman's body, or milk, or unsmutched snow; in another it is the horrifying whiteness of a corpse, or a spectre, or leprosy" (*The White Goddess*). Thus she may appear in Welsh mythology as Olwen, the lily-white May-queen, or as Cerridwen, the fearsome white sow-goddess. In Greek myth she may be Hera, the mother; or Aphrodite, the love-nymph; or Hecate, the crone—or Cotytto, or Demeter, or Cybele, or Persephone, or Pasiphaë, or any of countless other figures. In Ireland she is Bride; in Egypt, Isis; in Syria, Ishtar; and in Jerusalem, Rahab.

Whatever she calls herself, however, she is almost always represented in mythic iconography as "a lovely, slender woman with a hooked nose, deathly pale face, lips red as rowan-berries, startlingly blue eyes, and long fair hair," who is capable of transforming herself suddenly into "sow, mare, bitch, vixen, she-ass, weasel, serpent, owl, she-wolf, tigress, mermaid, or loathsome hag." She is often referred to as the "Triple Goddess" not only because of her concern with birth, procreation, and death, but also because as Goddess of the Earth she is involved in the three seasons of spring, summer, and winter, and because as Goddess of the Sky she is the Moon, in her three phases of New Moon, Full Moon, and Waning Moon. Most importantly, for Graves, she is also the Muse of Poetry.

In many mythic icons she is represented as granting her favors alternately to a pair of lovers—the God of the Waning Year, and the God of the Waxing Year. In the more violent Goddess-cults, the parts in this seasonal drama were originally taken by the chief priestess and two men chosen from the tribe; and at the midsummer celebrations the man acting as the God of the Waxing Year was lamed, crucified, dismembered, and ultimately eaten, in order to insure the health of the crops; and the man acting as the God of the Waning Year then became the consort of the priestess—until the mid-winter rites, when he in turn was sacrificed.

For Graves, all "true" poetry (which he now defines by citing A. E. Housman's famous test: does it make the skin bristle and the hairs stand on end if one repeats it silently while shaving?) is religious invocation of the Muse-goddess, and as such it may have only one theme.

> The theme, briefly, is the antique story, which falls into thirteen chapters and an epilogue, of the birth, life, death, and resurrection of the God of the Waxing Year; the central chapters contain the God's losing battle with the God of the Waning Year for love of the capricious and all-powerful Threefold Goddess, their mother, bride, and layerout. The poet identifies himself with the God of the Waxing Year and his Muse with the Goddess; the rival is his blood-brother, his other self, his weird. All true poetry—true by Housman's practical test—celebrates some incident or scene in this very ancient story, and the three main characters are so much a part of our racial inheritance that they not only assert themselves in poetry but recur on occasions of emotional stress in the form of dreams, paranoiac visions, and delusions. The weird, or rival, often appears in nightmare as the tall, lean, dark-faced bed-side spectre, or Prince of the Air, who tries to drag the dreamer out through the window, so that he looks back and sees his body still lying rigid in bed, but he takes countless other

malevolent or diabolic or serpent-like forms. . . . The test of a poet's vision, one might say, is the accuracy of his portrayal of the White Goddess and of the island over which she rules. The reason why the hairs stand on end, the eyes water, the throat is constricted, the skin crawls, and a shiver runs down the spine when one writes or reads a true poem is that a true poem is necessarily an invocation of the White Goddess, or Muse, the Mother of All Living, the ancient power of fright or lust—the female spider or the queen-bee whose embrace is death.

(The White Goddess)

When the Goddess-cults, which had spread across the Mediterranean into the Iberian Peninsula, and thence to Northwest Europe, were forced to go underground, her faith survived for a time among the peasants (who continued to celebrate her traditional festivals at the summer and winter solstices, as well as at May Day and Hallowe'en) and later among the anti-Christian witch-cults which persisted until the eighteenth century. Since then, however, except among certain primitive and isolated matrilineal societies, the Goddess has been venerated only by the few poets who have chosen to make her their Muse. These are, for Graves, the only true poets: their imagery is drawn either consciously or unconsciously from the symbols of the Goddess-cults, and the magical quality of their poems largely depends on their familiarity with her mysteries. They may be called "romantic" poets, but Graves is careful to state that all members of the Romantic Movement in England were not necessarily true poets:

"Romantic," a useful word while it covered the reintroduction into Western Europe by the writers of verse-romances of a mystical reverence for woman, has become tainted by indiscriminate use. The typical Romantic poet of the nineteenth century was physically degenerate, or ailing, addicted to drugs and melancholia, critically unbalanced, and a true poet only in his fatalistic regard for the Goddess as the mistress who commanded his destiny.

(The White Goddess)

In English literary history, there have been few really true poets. Among them are John Skelton, "who wore the Muse-name 'Calliope' embroidered on his cassock in silk and gold"; John Donne, whose Songs and Sonets are the record of his love affair with the woman who served as his Muse; John Clare, who believed in "a beautiful presence, a woman deity"; John Keats, who saw the White Goddess as his "Belle Dame sans Merci"; and Samuel Coleridge, "whose description in the *Ancient Mariner* of the woman dicing with Death in the phantom ship is as faithful a record of the White Goddess as exists."

Shakespeare, too, knew and feared the Goddess. In *Macbeth* he introduced her as the Triple Hecate presiding over the witches' cauldron, and as Lady Macbeth inspiring her husband to murder Duncan (just as the ancient queens presided over the ritual murder of *their* kings). The "magnificent and wanton" Cleopatra, too, was a type of the Goddess (and, fittingly, died from the bite of an asp—the serpent sacred to Isis); as was "the damned witch Sycorax" in *The Tempest*.

True poets have been rare in England chiefly because they have been forced to live in a patriarchal society; and a patriarchal society favors a different sort of poetry. Under Apollo, who became the God of Poetry after the suppression of the Goddess, an era of classicism arose, which has flourished whenever a society becomes rigid and academic and ruled by logic and by manners. According to classical, Apollonian doctrine, the test of a good poet is "his ability to express time-proved sentiments in time-honored forms with greater fluency, charm, sonorousness, and learning than his rivals." The classical poets use "old-fashioned diction, formal ornament, and regular, sober, well-polished metre, as a means of upholding the dignity of their office."

The true poet, according to Graves, must always be original, but in a simpler sense than his classical counterpart. He must address only the Muse—not the King or Chief Bard or the people in general—and tell her the truth about himself and her in his own impassioned and distinctive manner: "The Muse is a deity, but she is also a woman, and if her celebrant makes love to her with the secondhand phrases and ingenious verbal tricks that he uses to flatter her son Apollo she rejects him more decisively even than she rejects the tongue-tied or cowardly bungler." If he is sincere in his protestations of love, the Goddess may smile on him for a time; but the poet is the God of the Waxing Year, and he must expect that the Goddess will ultimately destroy him, savagely and remorselessly. The poet's "death" is, of course, a metaphoric one; what really happens is that he loses his vision of the Goddess, which means that his poetic inspiration must die: "The woman whom he took to be a Muse, or who was a Muse, turns into a domestic woman and would have him turn similarly into a domesticated man. Loyalty prevents him from parting company with her, especially if she is the mother of his children and is proud to be reckoned a good housewife; and as the Muse fades out, so does the poet."

Graves's attitude toward the Goddess is an ambiguous one. At one level in *The White Goddess* he is completely a rationalist: myth, for him, is primarily a dramatic shorthand record of such matters as invasions, migrations, dynastic changes, admission of foreign cults, and social reforms; and with disinterested precision he goes about making historical sense of them, and tracing the ancient Goddess-worship through its vicissitudes. As archetypes of central human experiences and emotions—in spite of what he says about the Prince of the Air in the passage quoted above—myths appear not to interest him at all. Jungian psychology, he has insisted, has no place in his concept of the Goddess and her importance to society and the individual man.

On another level, however, the poet in Graves prevails; his Goddess is all-powerful, and he is capable of such passages as this:

> Cerridwen abides. Poetry began in the matriarchal age, and derives its magic from the moon, not the sun. No poet can hope to understand the nature of poetry unless he has had a vision of the Naked King crucified to the lopped oak, and watched the dancers, red-eyed from the acrid smoke of the sacrificial fires, their bodies bent uncouthly forward, with a monotonous chant of "Kill! kill! kill!" and "Blood! blood! blood!"

> (*The White Goddess*)

To a generation of readers who have been conditioned to this sort of thing by Sir James Frazer, Jane Harrison, Jessie Weston, and other cultural anthropologists, the theories expressed in *The White Goddess* will not necessarily appear absurd. We may, like Randall Jarrell, choose to see the whole work as a monumental sublimation on Graves's part of his personal experiences with women, especially with Laura Riding. Although Graves has emphatically denied this (*5 Pens in Hand*), readers of his poetry and his autobiography may feel that Jarrell is at least partially correct. But Graves is very much a part of the literary environment of his childhood: he was brought up on the algolagnic heroines of Swinburne, the wan, hypnotic beauties of the romantic poets, and the Fatal Women of Elizabethan tragedy; and his vision of the Goddess corresponds so closely to these stereotypes that it is impossible to see her solely as the product of his personal experience. What seems most probable is that Graves, in constructing his concept of the Muse, took the familiar female stereotype he inherited from centuries of romantic literature, and associated it with the antique Goddess who killed and devoured her lovers. He was seeking a name for the abstract concept which he felt lay behind all poetic inspiration, and he found the White Goddess, in all her awesome ferocity. Whether or not Graves believes in her as a true Goddess is irrelevant: what is important for us to realize from *The White Goddess* is that, for Graves, no poet is a true poet until he devotes himself utterly to the expression of his love for her. If he does not do this, then he will find himself writing the artificial, uninspired poetry of classicism. Once we have recognized this, we see that the fundamental ideas of Graves have not altered a great deal since the time of *On English Poetry*. The chief difference is that, in *On English Poetry* and *Poetic Unreason*, his defence of romanticism and his dislike for classicism were dressed in semi-Freudian attire; and that, in *The White Goddess*, the same points of view are expressed in a mythological, religious framework. He has simply traded one nonliterary technique for another, and his basic beliefs have remained unchanged except in one respect: as he was to say one year after the publication of *The White Goddess*, "I now regard the poet as independent of fashion and public service, a servant only of the true Muse, committed on her behalf to continuous personal variations on a single pre-historic, or post-historic theme; and have thus ceased to feel the frantic strain of swimming against the stream of time." The disdain for the public that he had felt during his second and third periods continues, then; poetry is for Robert Graves in the fourth period of his career still a purely personal matter—a private dialogue between the poet and his Muse, in which the reader can only be an eavesdropper.

DANIEL HOFFMAN

Significant Wounds

In a slightly sententious preface to one of his thirty-six books of verse, Robert
Graves writes,

> A volume of collected poems should form a sequence of the intenser
> moments of the poet's spiritual autobiography, moments for which
> prose is insufficient: as in the ancient Welsh and Irish prose tales the
> lyric is reserved for the emotional crises.

Here is a poet who has never subscribed to T. S. Eliot's encyclicals about the
need for poetry to express the extinction of personality. Indeed, the personality
expressed in Graves's poems is one that takes a wry zest in the knowledge of its
own peculiar individuality. In a poem ostensibly about a butterfly who "Will
never master the art of flying straight," he praises the creature that has the knowledge, not of flight, but "of how not to fly." The diction in the poem is precise,
yet the effect of its precision is to leave us, like the poet, giving thanks for the
"flying-crooked gift" of lurching "by guess" as well as by "God and hope and
hopelessness." This backlash of gratefulness upon unaptitude is typical of Graves,
as is a more frequent paradox, the backlash of terror upon ecstasy. But as one
reads Graves with greater familiarity both paradoxes are resolved into still a
third, one's recognition that his "flying-crooked" *is* his gift, that his terror is intrinsic to his joy. And his beloved

> is wild and innocent, pledged to love
> Through all disaster
> .   .   .   .   .   .

From *Barbarous Knowledge: Myth in the Poetry of Yeats, Graves, and Muir.* © 1967 by
Daniel Hoffman. Oxford University Press, 1967.

> Here is her portrait, gazing sidelong at me,
> The hair in disarray, the young eyes pleading:
> 'And you, love? As unlike other men
> As I those other women?'

He is unlike them, and his poems are unlike other men's. Once, he wrote,

> The lost, the freakish, the unspelt
> Drew me: for simple sights I had no eye.
> And did I swear allegiance then
> To wildness, not (as I thought) to truth—

But in latter days he has learned "There is one story and one story only / That will prove worth your telling." This story is the theme of his stupefying and exhilarating book *The White Goddess*, which ransacks the mythology of the ancient world and the literature and scholarship of the modern to refashion its hidden yet absolute truth:

> The theme, briefly, is the antique story, which falls into thirteen chapters and an epilogue, of the birth, life, death and resurrection of the God of the Waxing Year; the central chapters concern the God's losing battle with the God of the Waning Year for the love of the capricious and all-powerful Threefold Goddess, their mother, bride and layer-out. The poet identifies himself with the God of the Waxing Year and his Muse with the Goddess; the rival is his blood-brother, his other self, his weird. All true poetry . . . celebrates some incident or scene in this very ancient story, and the three main characters are so much a part of our racial inheritance that they not only assert themselves in poetry but recur on occasions of emotional stress in the form of dreams, paranoiac visions and delusions.

Let us defer an examination of the argument in detail, and instead seek out some obvious implications from this brief summary. Graves finds the meaning of life in a monomyth, the contemporary recurrences of an eternal pattern of conflict. Yet this monomythic net swings wide, containing, in the conflicts already described, the struggles between increase and diminution, life and death, and the seasons, as well as the contention between the sexes, and the division of the self into the lover and the rival, his "bloodbrother" and "weird." Further, these characters and the action of this theme are graven upon our souls from birth, in the manner that Jung ascribes to inherent archetypes. Conditions of emotional stress, dream, paranoia, and delusion offer the materials of true poetry, if not the finality of poetic statement. Graves found his own poetic materials in such emotional stresses long before he recognized their universality in myths. Or did he find in myths a way to universalize his own "paranoiac visions"? As the loquacious narrator of his poem, "Welsh Incident" says, "I was coming to that." But first we can notice that Graves, following Freud's *Totem and Taboo* and Otto Rank's *Myth of the Birth of the Hero*, considers dreams the individual's access to myths, and he considers myths the dreams of the race.

Graves maintains that his discovery of this theme made obsolete and super-fluous many of the poems he wrote before *The White Goddess*. He feels, and many of his critics agree, that until then his work was unfocussed, disunified, and he has accordingly excised most of this early work from successive volumes of collected poems. The early work he retains, however, is among his very best, and, as I hope to show, not only compels admiration for its own excellences but forms an intrinsic part of his achievement. Graves's poems accorded with his "grammar of poetic myth" even before he spelled its laws, and the myth is but another set of metaphors for solving contradictions he has always been rent by.

Since Graves directs us to his own "spiritual autobiography" in his poems, we may approach the poet and his chosen theme by seeking evidence of his divided self. Despite the particularity with which the passage from *The White Goddess* describes this division, Graves does not, as Yeats did, elaborate his opposites in charts and tables. Yet the opposed *personae* of his poems and prose are self-revealing. "In Broken Images" reveals them:

> He continues quick and dull in his clear images;
> I continue slow and sharp in my broken images.
>
> He in a new confusion of his understanding;
> I in a new understanding of my confusion.

From childhood Graves has been aware of his dual nature. In his auto-biography he traces the conflict between the complementary strains of his inheritance. His mother's father's people were von Rankes, "not anciently noble. Leopold von Ranke, the first modern historian, my great-uncle, introduced the von. I owe something to him. He wrote, to the scandal of his contemporaries: 'I am a historian before I am a Christian; my object is simply to find out how the things actually occurred.'" His grand-nephew's like compulsion would equally have scandalized Leopold's contemporaries. To his grandmother Graves attributes his "gentler characteristics," which abounded in his "gemütlich" mother. "Our busy and absent-minded father would never worry about us children" (there were ten children, five by the father's previous marriage). But "our mother did worry." She looms over the Graves brood, "noble and patient," protective, Germanic.

Father was Albert Percival Graves, "a very busy man, an inspector of schools for the Southwark district in London. . . . He occasionally played games with us, but for the most part, when not busy with educational work, was writing poems, or being president of literary or temperance societies." Robert Graves takes a rather ironical tone about his father's literary activities, which, in fact, were far more extensive than a reader of *Good-bye to All That* would suppose. A. P. Graves was a minor figure in the Irish literary renaissance that Yeats, AE, and Douglas Hyde had led. Dr. Hyde, in fact, wrote an appreciative foreword to one of A. P. Graves's books of translations from early Irish poetry. All told, the elder Graves published forty-three books—translations from Welsh as well as Irish verse, his own facile poems on traditional Irish themes, anthologies of Irish fairy tales and Irish poetry, four plays, and sixteen volumes of songs. Of all this Robert Graves comments, "That my father is a poet has, at least, saved me from any false reverence for poets. I am even delighted when I meet people who know of him and not of me. I sing some of his songs while washing up after meals, or shelling peas." No doubt Albert Percival Graves will in the end, as his son predicted, be chiefly remembered for writing the one popular song, "Father O'Flynn." His prolix career, however, made certain courses of action probable for Robert Graves, and certain others impossible. The literary tendency, though in part from the historian von Ranke, comes more strongly from father Graves and from various antecedent Graveses, minor poets of the eighteenth and early nineteenth centuries. As the poetry-writing son of a poetry-writing father who was besides a professional Man of Irish Letters—even were Robert Graves interested in Ireland, how could he have written a line about Diarmuid and Grainne or Cuchulain?

By leaving Dublin for London and Harlech, his father "broke the geographical connection with Ireland, for which I cannot be too grateful to him." Young Graves grew up in a home library of Celtic scholarship, which he would one day put to his own uses. But the Celtic land he made his own would not be Ireland. Wales became the adoptive home of the poet who found in *The Mabinogion* the threads through the labyrinth of myths that led him at last to the White Goddess. In a poem (since dropped from his *Collected Poems*) he once acknowledged his ambiguous patrimony. Graves's father, in an anthology, *The Book of Irish Poetry*, had translated twenty-two triads from the Gaelic, but not this one:

> Poetry is, I said, my father's trade,
> Familiar since my childhood; I have tried
> Always to annul the curse of that grim triad

> Which holds it death to mock and leave a poet
> In mockery, death likewise to love a poet,
> But death above all deaths to live a poet.

As for the rest of his inheritance: "The Graves's have good minds for such purposes as examinations, writing graceful Latin verse, filling in forms, and solving puzzles. There is a coldness in the Graves's which is anti-sentimental to the point of insolence, a necessary check to the goodness of heart from which my mother's family suffers." The qualities of all the antecedent Graveses live again, in varying degrees, in Robert. He claims there is a turbulence in his blood between the Graves intellectuality, coldness, and orderliness, and the von Ranke goodness of heart. Pulled in both directions at once, he is both quick and dull, slow and sharp, an intuitive rationalist distrusting reason, yet using it to justify the hegemony of the imagination. . . .

Graves's early verses show the influence of many models: the nonsense rhymes of Edward Lear appear in his earliest poems, published in his father's autobiography, as well as in the zany logic of his later satires and grotesques; the lyrical sweetness and facility of Ralph Hodgson, the fantasy of de la Mare, and the simple structures and stock symbols of old ballads and nursery rhymes are also evident. These enthusiasms were appropriate to a young Georgian poet whose first book, *Over the Brazier*, was published in 1916 by Harold Munro.

Graves has confessed to a still more important influence:

Skelton has had a stronger influence on my work than any other poet alive or dead: particularly I have admired in him his mixture of scholarship and extravaganza, his honest outspokenness and unconventionality in life and writings, his humour, his poetic craftsmanship, and, in spite of appearances, his deep religious sense. . . . Time and time again . . . I have caught myself playing at being Skelton, in literary affections, in choice of metre and handling of words particularly: always admitting my hero's faults (by twentieth-century standards, that is) of long-windedness, over-exuberance, crabbedness and occasional formlessness; his vindictive attitude towards [his rivals], his childish conceit . . . and other by no means admirable examples of poetic conduct. I certainly quite often identify myself with him.

This confession is half-jocular, yet true; for everything, except the final fault, which Graves says of Skelton is in good measure true of himself. In some poems in *Fairies and Fusiliers* (1917), Graves imitated the Skeltonic line, with its stumbling rhymes and metrical freedom. William Nelson in his study of this neglected Tudor poet observes that the Skeltonic "constituted a deliberate refusal to obey the rules he had learned in school. . . . The style he invented had the liberty of prose and the sharpness of poetry," and "It gave him room for the flow of his imagination and the torrent of his anger. . . . It gave him liberty to speak." For Graves these qualities, both personal and poetic, were extremely attractive. To resurrect Skelton in 1917, when criticism as yet had done little to mitigate Pope's scornful jape that "Beastly Skelton heads of houses quote," took a bit of nerve. Already Graves was determinedly going his own way, against the grain of the literary establishment and equally against the counter-establishment of the avant-garde. To put his discovery of Skelton into perspective we must recall that the literary ancestor of the hour was John Donne. Professor Grierson's edition had appeared only in 1912 with an immediate effect upon young poets as different from one another as Rupert Brooke, Isaac Rosenberg, and T. S. Eliot. Donne had an effect on Graves too—the tortuous quality of intellectualized passion, the boldness of his wit, struck a response in the young poet already torn between his romantic and his classical selves. But Graves would not accept everyone else's metaphysical ancestor as his own. He practically invented Skelton to be his own peculiar forebear and familiar.

It was a lucky discovery, for it helped Graves to jack himself out of the slough of too easy sentiment, too facile rhyming, which his early won mastery of late Victorian poetic convention had made a temptation. Skelton gave him an example of a bold metrical irregularity, a heavily accentual line taking its movement from common speech. His influence helped Graves to develop a craggy individualistic personal meter. Many of his best poems could not have been written without the aid of Skelton's ghost. Yet even Skelton's admirers—and I am one—may have been surprised when, forty-five years after the poems in *Fairies and Fusiliers*, Graves praised Skelton in his *Oxford Addresses* as a Muse poet:

> Muse poetry is composed at the back of the mind: an unaccountable product of a trance in which the emotions of love, fear, anger, or grief, are profoundly engaged, though at the same time powerfully disciplined; in which intuitive thought reigns supralogically, and personal rhythm subdues metre to its purposes.

In the next lecture in 1961 Graves defined the Anti-Poet, Skelton's opposite. He avoids taverns, is girlishly shy, has a facility for versification, but writes on themes suggested by his patrons. He divorces poetry from common sense, uses poetic license and grammatical inversions, never lampoons those in power, and maintains style to be more important than subject. Where Skelton joked in church about his illegitimate children, the Apollonian Anti-Poet is incapable of loving any woman, much less of adoring the Muse with whose powers a particular woman might attract him. Indeed, he may be a pederast. In time of war he does not bear arms.

The Anti-Poet of course is Graves's anti-self, the reverse image in the mirror that he would exorcise. In his Oxford lecture he told us that this specter goes by the name of Virgil.

Such dichotomies cleave all of Graves's poetry and theories. In *Poetic Unreason* he proposed to

> show Poetry as a record of the conflicts between various pairs of Jekyll and Hyde, or as a record of the solution of these conflicts. In the period of conflict, poetry may be either a partisan statement in the emotional or in the intellectual mode of thought of one side of the conflict; or else a double statement of both sides of the conflict, one side appearing in the manifest statement, that is, in the intellectual mode, the other in the latent content, that is, in the emotional mode, with neither side intelligible to the other. In the period of solution there will be no discrepancy between latent content and manifest statement.

Graves further characterizes his doppelgängers:

> The terms Jekyll and Hyde . . . are rather more than synonyms for 'deliberate' and 'unwitting' because Jekyll is always used in the restricted sense of action in conformity with the dominant social code of the community, while Hyde is the outlaw. When Jekyll appears, Hyde is the 'unwitting,' but it must not be forgotten that Jekyll is the 'unwitting' when Hyde appears.

The terms as well as the logic of this argument derive from Rivers, who proposed "unwitting" as descriptive of what Freud calls the unconscious. In Graves's later work we see the doubling and redoubling of these antagonistic selves, striving to be reconciled. His Muse hands him a double-bladed axe: he writes only "poems for poets and satires for wits" —the poetry of Unreason, the wit the work of Reason. The conflict between romanticism and classicism is unassuaged in Graves; yet, he wrote in 1925, "The interaction of the two bodies of literature has been so fruitful that pure Classicism and pure Romanticism are nowadays far to seek in English poetry."

Much later, when he found the reinterpretation of myths essential to validate his theories, Graves again showed both sides of his nature: the irrational (romantic) in requiring myth, and the rational (classicist) in requiring its validation. As readers of *The Greek Myths* are aware, his retellings combine a Dionysian compulsion to belief with an Apollonian clarity of presentation. Yet again in the *Oxford Addresses* he proposed the achieving of paradisal visions by use of a hallucinogenic mushroom to produce "a controlled schizophrenia." Graves would split the self by narcosis—yet never forgets the need for "control." While he would make "intuitive thought reign supreme," it must nonetheless be "profoundly disciplined." His poetic theories attempt to show us how the interaction of these dichotomous states comprises both the origin and the function of poetry. His poems demonstrate their interaction.

The divided selves of Robert Graves early found their homes in different countries. The rationalist recognized his in a mild and quiet valley, where nothing alters "the set shape of things." This place is called "An English Wood." Here the dread creatures—harpies, rocs, gryphons—which haunt the imaginative man are quite unknown. Here "No bardic tongues unfold / Satires or charms," and "Small pathways idly tend / Toward no fearful end." A bland little spot, recalling D. H. Lawrence's descriptions of Crèvecoeur's farm, of Ben Franklin's neat little moral garden, fencing off the wilderness and the terrors of the soul. Graves's other self inhabits the opposite landscape from "An English Wood," places where "Mermaid, Dragon, Fiend" abound and difficult paths are followed compulsively toward fearful ends. His *paysage moralisé* appears as "Rocky Acres":

> This is a wild land, country of my choice,
> With harsh craggy mountains, moor ample and bare.
> Seldom in these acres is heard any voice
> But voice of cold water that runs here and there
> Through rocks and lank heather growing without care.
> No mice in the heath run, no song-birds fly
> For fear of the buzzard that floats in the sky.
>
> He soars and he hovers, rocking on his wings,
> He scans his wide parish with a sharp eye,
> He catches the trembling of small hidden things,
> He tears them in pieces, dropping them from the sky;
> Tenderness and pity the heart will deny,
> Where life is but nourished by water and rock—
> A hardy adventure, full of fear and shock.

These acres are surely the "desolate, rocky hill-country" where Robert and his sisters used to wander in their teens. "Above Harlech I found a personal peace independent of history or geography. The first poem I wrote as myself concerned those hills. (The first poem I wrote as a Graves was a neat translation of one of Catullus's satires.)" But I doubt that "Rocky Acres" was this poem, for it first appeared in *Country Sentiment*, his fifth book, in 1920. By then he had been through the war, had endured and outlasted unmitigated disasters and useless battles which could not be won. "Is this joy? to be doubtless alive again, / And the others dead?" he asked in "The Survivor." It was Wales he went to when sent home on sick leave, and it was then he found his "personal peace" among its rocky acres. That "peace independent of history or geography" is a paradigm of the state of being for which Graves in his poems is continually searching. As is true in "Rocky Acres," that peace, when found, offers a landscape more of menace than of comfort:

> Time has never journeyed to this lost land,
> Crakeberry and heather bloom out of date,
> The rocks jut, the streams flow singing on either hand,
> Careless if the season be early or late,
> The skies wander overhead, now blue, now slate;
> Winter would be known by his cutting snow
> If June did not borrow his armour also.

> Yet this is my country, beloved by me best,
> The first land that rose from Chaos and the Flood,
> Nursing no valleys for comfort and rest,
> Trampled by no shod hooves, bought with no blood.
> Sempiternal country whose barrows have stood
> Stronghold for demigods when on earth they go,
> Terror for fat burghers on far plains below.

Here is a primordial landscape outside of time where the seasons turn anarch against the calendar. We exchange the poised, calm elementals of England for the fearsome buzzard who "scans his wide parish." In this land of no valleys one feels newly delivered "from Chaos and the Flood," beside the ruined temples to the earliest forces that knew man's frightened gratitude and worship. "The country of my choice" is of course a psychological landscape. This is the country of man's mind, of forces whose atavistic power Graves cannot and would not control with consciousness. Here, "bardic tongues unfold / Satires or charms," the only verses Graves admits as poems. But why charms? Because charms are magical incantations arraigning the power of the spirit to obey the importunate will of the poet. In *On English Poetry* Graves had argued for the magical authority of poetry. This is the burden of his poem "The Bards."

The scene in this poem suggests the court of an early medieval Welsh king, where the bards entertaining at dinner are pelted with bones by the "drunken diners": pelted for stumbling in their song, stumbling for fear of "an unknown grief"—and the rest of Graves's poem is an invocation of that grief which "like a churl / Goes commonplace in cowskins." This churl, "by a gross enchantment," razes the palace, where twelve kings play at chess, and leads away their beautiful daughters.

Any reader familiar with medieval romance literature will recognize the traditional properties on which Graves draws, true though it is that he has put these familiar materials together in a new way and for a new purpose. This churl with his "unpilled holly-club" is surely of the same breed as the Ugly Herdsman in such well-known romances as *Aucassin and Nicolette* or, to approach the rocky acres, Chrétien's *Yvain*, where, near Arthur's court at Carduel in Wales, Sir Calogrenant met such a shepherd guarding a sacred spring. Graves has disclosed his source as an old Irish legend which probably lies at the root of this tradition, "The Pursuit of the Gilla Dacker," a farcical yarn of an ugly giant of the Fomor who carries away sixteen Fenian warriors on his magical, hideous horse. Graves takes from this tale merely the key motif of the invasion of a royal castle by an ugly giant; his churl "by a gross enchantment" destroys the palace and kidnaps the beautiful queens. The luxuriousness of the palace, J. M. Cohen has suggested, may be a deprecatory allusion to Yeats's Byzantine artificialities; I think it far more probable, however, that Graves has in mind the lapidary splendors described in a Welsh romance of the early thirteenth century, "The Dream of Rhonabwy," which he knew from Lady Charlotte Guest's translation of *The Mabinogion*. In this romance Rhonabwy comes to a mean and filthy cottage where an old crone grudgingly lets his party sleep on flea-covered skins on a floor of cow urine and dung; once asleep, he dreams of a game of chess between Arthur and King Owein, played while Owein's ravens fight dire battles against Arthur's men. The action is subordinate to the enameled beauty of the court and costumes; regal splendor and disdain are in contrast to both the slaughter of battle and the meanness of the real world from which Rhonabwy's dream is a magical escape.

Graves analogously creates a reduplicated escape from the conditions of life through incantation. First he evokes the banquet scene, brutal and primitive in the diners' hurling bones at the failure of the bards' spell. This first spell has been broken by a stronger one, that of "unknown grief," which both overmasters the "running verse" of the bards and supplants, for us, the drunken rage of the diners. But this churl intensifies the rage of the drunkards. Being pelted by bones had made the bards stumble in their song, but the blows of the churl magically transform the faltering song into an unanticipated legend of disaster, as he leads the queenly beauties off "to stir his black pots and to bed on straw." We are made to take literally this churl, who was introduced only in a metaphorical comparison—he is not even a character, but merely what the "unknown grief" is compared to. Wholly a figment, a specter, he arrogates in the poem the psychic energy that compels our belief; from unreality the poet creates a reality.

This is the reality of imagination, linked, here and in such other poems as "Outlaws" and "Rocky Acres," with the primordial figures and features of pre-history. Thus far—through the 1920s—Graves had not attempted to synthesize or systematize his fearful fascination with a reality "independent of geography or history." No need to wonder at this time at his emphasis upon an imaginary reality or his suspicion of the world of appearances. For some years after the war Graves was in a state of serious traumatic disorientation:

> Shells used to come bursting on my bed at midnight, even though Nancy shared it with me; strangers in daytime would assume the faces of friends who had been killed. When strong enough to climb the hill behind Harlech and revisit my favourite country . . . I would find myself working out tactical problems . . . where to place a Lewis gun if I were trying to rush Dolwreiddiog Farm.

One surcease from such exigencies was to retreat into the assurance of childhood. In the books of these years—*Fairies and Fusiliers* (1917) and *Country Sentiment* (1920)—Graves wrote charming and seemingly carefree nursery rhymes and ballads, some of them for and about his own children. But even childlike ballads had a way of being haunted.

To a man who could not bear to use a telephone or ride on trains, whose daylit life was peopled by the reappearing dead, it was not possible to look directly at life, or to find reality other than in the confusion of his own dreams. The title poem of his 1921 volume is "The Pier-Glass," a mirror in which a murderess, haunted by her guilt and trapped by her past, vainly looks for a freedom it cannot give:

> Ah, mirror, for Christ's love
> Give me one token that there still abides
> Remote—beyond this island mystery,
> So be it only this side Hope, somewhere,
> In streams, on sun-warm mountain pasturage—
> True life, natural breath; not this phantasma.

In time Graves rejected the child's-eye view of reality, repressing most of his poems of escape to the nursery from the successive volumes of collected poems. By 1929 he could, both as a recuperated veteran and as a parent, write a "Warning to Children,"—and in a dreamlike iteration and reiteration he admonishes them to beware of unwrapping the appearances of things, for appearance encloses appearance in boxes within boxes. If this is reality, the truth revealed by the poem is in its pattern of compulsive repetition. This is one of Graves's most convincing poems about dream-states, in which the rhythms of feeling well up from the unconscious. "Warning to Children" might be taken as a statement, or a demonstration, of the futility of consciousness and reason to discern the shapes of reality. He wrote it to repeat and display the confusion of his understanding, and so to understand his confusion.

In "Alice" (1926), another mirror poem, Graves finds a symbolic *persona* (like that of "The Pier-Glass," feminine), whom he can make a mediator between the "unwitting" and the "deliberate" in life. Alice, "that prime heroine of our nation," can represent the English mind's fascination with mind. But as a child she is exempt from the bland rationalism of older dwellers in an English wood. Courageously she follows her "speculative bent" into the topsy-turvy world beyond the Looking Glass, where, playing the game with "simple faith in simple stratagem," she wins her crown.

> But her greater feat
> Was rounding these adventures off complete:
> Accepting them, when safe returned again,
> As queer but true—not only in the main
> True, but as true as anything you'd swear to,
> The usual three dimensions you are heir to.

Alice could understand that neither did Looking Glass logic affect

> the clean
> Dull round of mid-Victorian routine,
> Nor did Victoria's golden rule extend
> Beyond the glass: it came to the dead end
> Where empty hearses turn about: thereafter
> Begins that lubberland of dreams and laughter.

Whereas the lady gazing in the pier-glass was trapped by her own reflection, Alice is able not only to live among the creatures of Unreason but to keep her conscious and unconscious knowledge sorted out:

> Though a secure and easy reference
> Between Red Queen and Kitten could be found—
> She made no false assumption on that ground
> (A trap in which the scientist would fall)
> That queens and kittens are identical.

Alice's resolution is complete; but most of Graves's poems in the mid-1920s do not manage such a mediation between Hyde and Jekyll. For instance, "In Procession" begins as an attempt to celebrate "that lubberland of dreams and laughter" he would mention in "Alice."

> Often, half-way to sleep
> Not yet sunken deep—
> The sudden moment on me comes

—a procession of "coloured pomps," "Carnival wagons" from which he harangues a crowd "in strange tongues" while "the sun leaps in the sky." When he awakens, however, he longs for the courage "To renew my speech" and summon back the marvels of legend and imagination from "the land where none grows old":

> But cowardly I tell,
> Rather, of the Town of Hell—
> A huddle of dirty woes
> And houses in fading rows
> Straggled through space:
> Hell has no market place,
> Nor place where four roads meet,
> Nor principal street . . .
> Neither ends nor begins,
> Rambling, limitless, hated well
> This Town of Hell
> Where between sleep and sleep I dwell.

Graves cannot escape into a "lake isle" of imagery, for he knows it to be a dream. Yet it is clear that the distortion of reality into "This Town of Hell" is also a dream-illusion. At this time, for Graves, reality is as illusory as is the hope of escaping from it. In such poems as "The Witches' Cauldron," "Welsh Incident," "The Castle," he recognizes entrapment without hope of release. Self-knowledge may be rendered humorously, as when the Welsh storyteller embellishes his tale of mythological creatures coming in from the sea, leaving out all the details that his interlocutor (obviously an English rationalist) wants to know. There may be the rage and aggression of the misdirected traveler moving through the mountain mist in ever-widening circles, coming always to the one sign, "The Witches' Cauldron / One mile." And in "The Castle," "by definition / There's no way out, no way out—." All machinery of escape is futile, even

> Cheating checkmate by painting the king's robe
> So that he slides like a queen

for imagined sexual reversal is ominous, and, as we know from "The Bards," the
chess game can be blasted by disaster—

> Or to cry, 'Nightmare, nightmare!'
> Like a corpse in the cholera-pit
> Under a load of corpses.

In this recrudescence of the war-born fear of death, Alice's logic—playing the
game by the rules of the game—can be of no avail. There is no recourse in this
castle but "To die and wake up sweating by moonlight / In the same courtyard,
sleepless as before."

Here, and in such poems as "Down," the form of the feeling is that of
rebirth—into the same death. It is this pattern of action which produces the
haunting effect of these poems upon the reader. Incantatory and repetitive rhythms
heighten the normative iambic meter and phrasal line. The imagery, as in "The
Castle," is chiefly visual, rendered with staccato emphasis and great clarity of
definition: "Walls, mounds, enclosing corrugations / Of darkness, moonlight on
dry grass." These descriptive notations set the scene; the main work of the poem
is borne by the hallucinatory images of balked escape, the wild stratagems
(painting the king's robes, escape by rope ladders or rockets) all coming to
naught. Fear is the essence of the poem, defined by the inability of either speaker
or reader really to abandon hope of escape. Therefore, despite the knowledge
given at the start that "by definition / There's no way out, no way out—" to
have the poem end "With apparitions chained two and two, / And go frantic
with fear . . . In the same courtyard," comes as an unexpected shock. The
inevitability of movement toward nonmovement has the logic of hallucination or
dream, the understanding of a reality revealed by the unconscious mind.

In a chapter of *On English Poetry* called "The Pattern Underneath," Graves
discusses this movement in which the reversal of implication discloses the meaning. It is a movement characteristic of his poems:

> The power of surprise which marks all true poetry seems to result
> from a foreknowledge of certain unwitting processes of the reader's
> mind, for which the poet more or less deliberately provides. . . . The
> poet may be compared with a father piecing together a picture-block
> puzzle for his children. He surprises them at last by turning over the
> completed picture, and showing them that by the act of assembling
> the scattered parts of 'Red Riding Hood with the Basket of Food' he
> has all the while been building up unnoticed underneath another
> scene of the tragedy—'The Wolf eating the Grandmother.'

To this passage he adds that "The underlying associations of each word in a
poem form close combinations of emotion unexpressed by the bare verbal pat-

tern." In addition, then, to the thematic movement which contains the surprise played by the unwitting upon the conscious mind, there is the further concentration of meanings inhering in the associations of words. This property of language (which Ernst Cassirer and Susanne Langer have linked to the liberating powers of myth) is, for Graves, an aspect of associative thinking. It comprises one of the most important of the illogical elements which he values in poetry. "The creative side of poetry," he wrote almost forty years later, "consists in treating words as if they were living things—in coupling them and making them breed new life."

Before the convergence, in *The White Goddess*, of these and other latent conceptions, Graves had already partially articulated the organizing structure of his thought. Thus far his work was more unified than has generally been supposed, and his view of life had constancy if not coherence. At this time—until about his thirty-third year and the clarifications that followed his writing an autobiography and moving from England—he conceived of poetry as therapeutic magic, creating from the unconscious a reality that reason could not discover. The external world is unreal; in it, appearance and conventional society are Dr. Hydes. But they are really Jekylls in disguise, and only the unwitting can discern this truth. By turning topsy-turvy the pleasant picture-puzzle that reason puts together as its image of the world, the unwitting reveals the latent meaning hidden in the picture: Wolf Eating Grandmother.

The unwitting meaning of life, which appears latently in the symbols of poems that derive from the unconscious mind, are contained and revealed in the language and the structure of the poem. Graves believes that the vocabulary of poetry should be drawn from the "ordinary spoken language of the day"; each word should be used with full awareness of its implications and meanings; and, by juxtaposition of language, the copulative power of words can breed new "life"—which is to say, can create a new realization of reality.

Obviously, diction and form—what Graves's friend John Crowe Ransom would call texture and structure—must complement one another. In Graves's work we find an inherent conservatism of both diction and structure as compared with the contemporaneous experiments of Pound, Cummings, Marianne Moore, and Eliot. The means by which he divines the truth of Unreason do not—as in the case of Pound, whose work Graves has always detested—abandon such appurtenances of logic as normal syntax or causal relationships.

Although Graves's practices, like his theories, seem often conformable with symbolist assumptions, he has never knowingly been influenced by the French tradition which Eliot, Pound, Stevens, and Williams brought into the mainstream of poetic modernism. It is principally the symbolist renunciation of syntax which Graves renounces. He has no interest in verbal copulars without connectives, in the *disjecta membra* of the imagination undisciplined by the inherent order of language. One might compare with Graves's poem "In Procession," in which the images are those that occur to him as he falls asleep, a poem by Pierre Reverdy presenting an analogous condition (though to a different end). Reverdy's "Et Maintenant" is, like Graves's poem, three pages long, but it is unpunctuated and contains not one completed sentence. This is to his purpose, of course, for a completed sentence expresses a beginning, a middle, and an end, and contains a subject, an action, and often an object. The trance-like dissociated state his poem evokes is not so much illogical as pre-logical. But when Graves brings up from his unwitting mind the material of the unconscious, this material is always subjected to that "secondary elaboration" described by Rivers, and the illogical element is revealed rather in the elaborated pattern than by an unelaborated lack of pattern. Graves combines a reverence for the truth of unreason with a reverence for the logic of language. The former must reveal itself to him, the latter he knows he must never relinquish. This is the last bastion to which intellect can cling, and it is from this assumption that the poet as rationalist can join the poet as daemon in their common attack across the treacherous terrain of the seeming world. For the poet of unreason is also the traditionalist captain and the classical scholar who abides no willful inaccuracy in translation. He is in fact the Dr. Syntax who so roundly thwacks the knuckles of schoolboy Pound. These dual sides of Graves's nature of course operate simultaneously. Dr. Syntax is forever taking hold of the incantations of the Medicine Man.

In his own poetic rhythms, too, we see the interrelation of reason and unreason. Graves has been dogmatic in his insistence on the need for a formal rhythm in poetry. At first he explained this by the hypnotic quality of rhythm, needed to put the reader's logical mind into a trance-state and impose upon him the compelling magic of the poet-witch doctor. Later he acknowledged the need to individuate meter (the traditional element) by a personal rhythm. He has always found rhythm to be accentual, in the nature of the English language, and has rejected alike such deviations as Marianne Moore's syllabic line and the complete abandonment of meter by the vers-librists. Graves does use a phrasal rather than a metronomic rhythm in such poems as "To Walk on Hills" and "To Bring the Dead to Life," but his most characteristic line is strongly accentual, often incorporating a variable number of unaccented syllables, sometimes rhyming accented syllables with unaccented. Thus in "Rocky Acres,"

This is a wild land, country of my choice,

an anapest is followed by a spondee, then after the caesura an anapest is followed by an iamb. J. M. Cohen has suggested the influence of Skeltonic meter in this highly individual personal rhythm. There is probably also a touch of Hopkins in the rhythm of this poem, particularly in the description of the buzzard's flight.

A poem that brings together in a single net these concerns of Graves, articulated in one of his most profound and fully realized forms, is "The Cool Web." This appeared on the final page of *Poems (1914–1926)* and, with some minor revisions, has remained in Graves's successive books of *Collected Poems*. In "The Cool Web," the innocent child-protagonists of "Alice," "Warning to Children," and the early ballads are now menaced by the scent of roses, the "black wastes of evening sky," and the "tall soldiers drumming by"—that is to say, they are endangered by the indifference of nature, the fury of the elements, and the terror of war. The children in this poem have only speech to protect themselves: "We spell away the soldiers and the fright." As though we were fish, we are safeguarded by "a cool web of language" that "winds us in." In this poem, as Martin Seymour-Smith has observed, Graves conceives of language as itself the network of relationships that holds culture together. "In that sense it is the sea, what we swim in, where we move and live and have our being." The consolation Graves offers us, however, is minimal, for we must "retreat from too much joy" as well as from "too much fear," and in the end we shall "grow sea-green" and "coldly die." We perish into "brininess and volubility." The alternative, however, is to throw off "language and its watery clasp." Without the power of incantation to protect us from the "wide glare" of inchoate experience, we would "go mad no doubt and die that way."

There are, then, two conceptions of experience in this poem. Life without articulation is terrifying to the impotent observers, helpless as children. Given the power of language, however, the child-protagonists are caught in the protective web of incantation and immersed in the cool sea. It is not maintained that the reality of the cruelly indifferent rose, the menacing sky, and the tall soldiers is in the least altered by the cool web of language. The children have the power only to "chill the angry day" and spell away their fright. The ultimate manifestation of language's incantatory power to keep brutal reality in check appears in this poem to be the identification of the cold sea—colder than the merely cool web—with death.

> We grow sea-green at last and coldly die
> In brininess and volubility.

This is the final triumph of language over the heat of the war-torn waste land. Until it comes, Graves offers a stoicism abjuring the extremes of fright and ecstasy alike. In midcareer he summed it up in another poem, "Midway":

> Between insufferable monstrosities
> And exiguities insufferable,
> Midway is man's station.

Such a poet is in worse state than the authors of "Dejection" or "Ode to Melancholy," who at least could be passionate in their despairs. Graves's position had become so narrowed by the numbness of his feelings that the sources of poetry were in danger of being blocked. His life as well as his art was at a turning point. "Midway" was written in 1929, the year in which he also wrote *Good-bye to All That*. As its title implies, this autobiography is a farewell to the world whose values had been blasted by senseless wars and could not be reassembled in the haunted souls of the survivors. The book completed, Graves left England for Majorca where, except for intervals during the Spanish Civil War and the Second World War, he has made his home ever since. The world he rejected was modern life, industrial society, English rationalism, contemporary political activity, bureaucratic materialism, hidebound academia — in short, everything in the twentieth century which threatened his own poetic vision.

This withdrawal, or retreat, or victorious reestablishment of himself on a then remote island, corresponded with a personal crisis about which Graves has little to say in his autobiography. His marriage to Nancy Nicholson, whose opinions seemed so like his own, proved in a few years to have been a mistake. In an epilogue to the first edition of *Good-bye to All That*, dedicated to Laura Riding (and since dropped from later editions), Graves wrote,

> For could the story of your coming be told . . . ? How she and I
> happening by seeming accident upon your teasing *Quids*, were drawn
> to write to you, who were in America, asking you to come to us.
> How, though you knew no more of us than we of you . . . you
> forthwith came. And how there was thereupon a unity to which you
> and I pledged our faith and she her pleasure. How we went together
> to the land where the dead parade the streets and there met with
> demons and returned with the demons still treading behind. And
> how they drove us up and down the land.

Like Graves himself, Laura Riding had been given up for dead (after a spinal injury), but had survived. Her poems have a terse, gnomic intellectuality in a style determinedly flat, from which all romantic abandon has been excised. Like Graves, she has a sensibility in which passion is haunted by fear, and every romantic feeling straightened by a puritanical restraint. She went off to Majorca with Graves, whose marriage was soon terminated, and Laura Riding was for the next ten years Graves's companion, collaborator, instructress, and indeed his Muse. Together they wrote several polemical books of criticism — *A Survey of Modernist Poetry* (1927), *A Pamphlet Against Anthologies* (1928) — and published through the Seizin Press annual miscellanies of criticism and verse as well as limited editions of their own writings. Under Laura Riding's influence Graves redefined the theoretical bases of his poetry, but not until after their separation in 1939 could he consider his new position objectively and conceive of it as a contemporary example of an eternal, archetypal pattern. Since that pattern, as we know, identifies the Muse with the beloved, and the beloved appears in her threefold role as mother, bride, and layer-out, it may be that not until the breaking-off of their actual relationship, in which the poet would find his identity changed from God of the Waxing to God of the Waning Year and his beloved's changed, by her rejection of him, from lover to the goddess exacting vengeance, could Graves recognize that he had been reliving this myth, the "one story and one story only."

MICHAEL KIRKHAM

The Black Goddess of Wisdom

In the first five years of the sixties Graves had already published four volumes of poetry—*More Poems 1961, New Poems 1962, Man Does, Woman Is* (1964), and in a limited edition *Love Respelt* (1965)—and another collection. His astonishing productivity in these years is one sign that he has entered a new period in his writing. It is not the only sign: from the vantage point of his most recent work it can be seen that these poems are a progression of moods and attitudes leading to a new experience and a new conception of love; to this conception he has given the name of the Black Goddess. While the most complete embodiment of this experience is in *Love Respelt*, there are hints of it in the preceding volumes; the poem actually entitled "The Black Goddess" appears in *Man Does, Woman Is*, and several other poems in that volume use imagery peculiarly descriptive of her; the beginning of these images are to be traced in *More Poems 1961* and *New Poems 1962*.

In all the poems of the sixties, theme and manner express, more than anything else, the poet's ability to survive and then to transcend suffering. *Poems 1953* heralded this development; but angry robustness gives place in *More Poems 1961* to a different kind of robustness. The poet-lover neither resists his fate nor submits despairingly to it; both would be more demonstrative postures than these poems generally allow. Both, too, would indicate a flaw in the quality of the poet's acceptance of his experience: underlying the attitude of this volume is the tight-lipped acknowledgment, more unquestioning than ever before, that the lover's fate is irrevocable and that protest would be irrelevant—acknowledgment of, in the words of an earlier poem, "the thing's necessity" ("Despite and Still"). All the poems start from the curt assumption that love necessarily involves suf-

From *The Poetry of Robert Graves*. © 1969 by Michael Kirkham. Athlone, 1969.

fering; the only uncertainty is whether the lover can bear it. The poet asks in
"Patience":

> Must it be my task
> To assume the mask
> Of not desiring what I may not ask?

The answer being implicitly affirmative, what is really in question is the poet's
ability to maintain such an attitude of stoical self-denial. His cry is not to be
released from his "task" but for the patience to carry it out: "O, to be patient /
As you would have me patient." The question is the same in "Symptoms of
Love": can the lover "*endure* such grief?" (my italics). This word is, as it were,
the *leitmotif* in *More Poems 1961*. To his usual romantic list of epithets for love
Graves can now, in "Under the Olives," add one more: "Innocent, gentle, bold,
enduring, proud" (my italics).

The style of these poems is a more extreme development of the spare terse
style of *Poems 1953*. In keeping with the stated theme of several of them,
refraining from protest they express a tighter self-restraint than do the poems of
the earlier volume. Emotion is not excluded but held in check, so that it is felt as
a constant pressure behind the verse; the characteristic tone implies a severely
curbed pain. The poems are frequently brief; either they run to no more than
seven, eight or ten lines a piece, or if longer the lines themselves are short,
composed sometimes of five and six syllables each. Their syntactical simplicity
and the baldness of their statements, or the fact that occasionally a poem consists
of but a single sentence, add to the effect of brevity. "The Cure," a poem of
seven lines, is typically short, swift in movement and direct. It opens brusquely,
"No lover ever found a cure for love"; except, it continues, by the inflicting of
such a painful wound, killing hope, that it was worse than love itself. Here
abruptly the poet breaks off, adding only the summary dismissive verdict, "More
tolerable the infection than its cure." We are left with an impression of the poet's
fierce taciturnity, of an incipient rebelliousness cut short.

In "Symptoms of Love" the economy of the means employed to make the
poem's effect is as conspicuous as in "Counting the Beats."

> Love is a universal migraine,
> A bright stain on the vision
> Blotting out reason.
> Symptoms of true love
> Are leanness, jealousy

In lines so clipped much of the poem's intention is contained in the curt rhythms,
expressing a self-punishing naked truthfulness—in, for example, the brutal stress

on "blotting." Every word has the maximum impact: the telescoping of the two images in "bright stain," for example, gives to the phrase a compressed, complex power: "bright," implying instantaneous illumination and immediate pain (the brightness of a migraine flash), conflicts—the contrast is heightened by the contrasting vowel sounds—and combines with the suggestion of something slow, dark and indelible (as a migraine is not) in "stain," to epitomize the paradox of love.

Most striking of all, Graves has in these poems carried to its limit the discipline of leaving unsaid what it is not absolutely necessary to say. "Under the Olives" is in this respect representative.

> We never should have loved had love not struck
> Swifter than reason, and despite reason:
> Under the olives, our hands interlocked,
> We both fell silent:
> Each listened for the other's answering
> Sigh of unreasonableness—
> Innocent, gentle, bold, enduring, proud.

What we have is the plainest of statements, but one which at every point connotes an ambience of unstated feeling. The last line gives us the most definite clue—though it is still only a hint—to its character. It is a mixture of pain and satisfaction; while love induces gentleness in its subjects, it also requires from them the tougher qualities of boldness and endurance. The epithet "enduring," in particular, raises nearer to the surface of the poem a sense of the difficulty of the lovers' relationship: points to the element of pain in "struck," for example, and of conflict in "despite." It explains the resoluteness enacted in the verse-movement, which is made thereby to carry the further implications of cruelties survived and obstructions overcome. There is an intimation of something un-simple and laborious in love in the mere doubling of negatives in the first line. Even the pause after "We both fell silent" is eloquent—enacting the ensuing silence and the fullness of the moment that cannot be expressed; in the pause, as again in the line division between "answering" and "sigh," we fell happiness, awe, uncertainty and an awareness of difficulty.

Stoicism is not the only attitude communicated in these poems but it is the central one, out of which the attitudes of the next two volumes seem to have developed and which prepared the ground for the affirmation of *Love Respelt*. Graves's practice in the majority of these poems of keeping very close to an actual human relationship, using the mythology only sparingly and simply, is also indicative of the direction in which he is now moving. This new approach to his theme and the tone of resolute stoicism are evidently related phenomena, each expressions of the poet's now more naked exposure to his experience. In "Intimations of the Black Goddess," a lecture given in 1963, Graves wrote: "Only during the past three years have I ventured to dramatize, truthfully and factually, the vicissitudes of a poet's dealings with the White Goddess, the Muse, the perpetual Other Woman." The stress is on "dramatize" and "factually": it is not in the subject matter of his latest poems that he found evidence of a new daring—the "vicissitudes" of love was his theme throughout the White Goddess period—but in the bare, unmetaphorical treatment of it. This preoccupation with the literal human experience of love goes with, and perhaps derives from, the poet's concentration on love as a joint venture: woman is man's partner, though still the dominant one, rather than his conscience or the impartial administrator of justice. In "The Sharp Ridge," for example, the poet at a crisis in their relationship pleads with her to

> Have pity on us both: choose well
> On this sharp ridge dividing death from hell.

The theme is now more often the "difficult achievement" of love ("The Starred Coverlet"), an achievement towards which *both* struggle and which involves them *both* in suffering, than the cruelty and mystery of womanhood. In doing what she must do, periodically withdrawing her love, she is not exempt from the pain she inflicts. The lover who, in "The Intrusion," recoils with horror from the picture of "her white motionless face and folded hands / Framed in such thunderclouds of sorrow," at the same time is made to realize that this is an image of her suffering. He is urged to "give her no word of consolation" because her grief is "Divine mourning for what cannot be," but nevertheless her evident need of "consolation" accents her purely human plight; she is in the same position as the man—of having to suffer the fate of which she is only the involuntary instrument. It is a fate they share in common, and the separate roles they play are each as difficult as the other's. In "The Falcon Woman" Graves, for the first time, considers the woman's role from her point of view. To be a man who honourably keeps his promises and builds too much upon the loved woman's promises, made in "carelessness of spirit," to which she cannot be held, is, he admits, hard; but is it less hard for *such* a woman "in carelessness of spirit / To love such a man"?

In his third period, Graves was concerned with, separately or as a whole, the phases of love and the pattern of events in the man-woman relationship; each position taken was in answer to this preoccupation. Implied or stated in many of the poems now is a more fundamental question: not "what experiences must the lover undergo?" but "what *is* love, what makes it as a *single* experience different from any other?" The exclusive concentration on the essence of this reality accounts, in part, for the spareness and brevity of most of these poems.

The opening poem of *More Poems 1961*, "Lyceia," sets the tone, indicates the sort of interest that Graves now has in his theme. Lyceia is the wolf-goddess, and "All the wolves of the forest / Howl for Lyceia"; they compete for her love but she keeps them at a distance. The poet therefore asks: "What do the wolves *learn?*" (my italics). Love is regarded as offering a *schooling* in a radically different outlook than is available to the ordinary person. This view of love had to wait until *Love Respelt* for its complete expression. As yet, according to Lyceia, they learn nothing but "Envy and hope, / Hope and chagrin." But that there is more to be learned is the import of other poems in this volume: in "The Starred Coverlet" lovers are enjoined on different occasions to learn patience, to endure, and

> to lie mute, without embrace or kiss,
> Without a rustle or a smothered sigh,
> Basking each in the other's glory.

The "glory" is that of a distinct reality, the nature of which is the theme of several poems. They agree precisely on their definition: it strikes "Swifter than reason and despite reason" ("Under the Olives"). Graves presents this life of unreason as a positive and rare achievement: he explains in "The Laugh" that he had been at first baffled by it because "the identity of opposites / Had so confused my all too sober wits." The *marriage* of opposites—of two people "unyielding in / Their honest, first reluctance to agree" ("Joan and Darby")— has gained for them entry to this special world, which defies and is inaccessible to reason and logic: if they were "birds of similar plumage caged / In the peace of every day," he asks in "Seldom Yet Now,"

> Would we still conjure wildfire up
> From common earth, as now?

Not obeying known laws love is unpredictable, incalculable—to be "Neither foretold, cajoled, nor counted on" ("Turn of the Moon")—and is the more precious for being so. The most intensely romantic expression of this reality, "Two Children," comes the nearest to portraying the new kind of love celebrated in *Love Respelt*. In his youth, the poet records, it was "a fugitive beacon" chased by him in his dreams; it "set a nap on the plum, a haze on the rose"; it is "Child of the wave, child of the morning dew": the stress here is on the elusiveness, the apparent insubstantiality, and the almost *miraculous* nature of love.

New Poems 1962 is the crucial volume for the understanding of the development of Graves's new faith. Primarily it is the "factual" record of a period of despair and disillusionment with the never-ending cycle of death and rebirth— some of these poems are more bleak than anything else Graves has written. But in two or three memorable poems it introduces us to a new mood of ecstasy and "certitude" that signifies his release from the cycle and the discovery of the Black Goddess, and grew in the course of the next three years to be the dominant mood of his poetry.

"A bitter year it was," the poet says in "The Wreath," and asks: "What woman ever / Cared for me so, yet so ill-used me . . . ?" "Trance at a Distance" announces with stark matter-of-factness that "She has raised a wall of nothing-ness in between" them. The gesture of weary helplessness, despairing resigna-tion, which "Hedges Freaked with Snow" makes, epitomizes the prevailing mood of this volume: the poet decides that there shall be "No argument, no anger, no remorse . . . no grief for our dead love," only "the smile of sorrow." In "Possessed" he advises the lover, though he is certain that his love is returned, to "Build nothing on it." The themes of unreason and endurance recur—"Unrea-sonable love becomes you / And mute endurance"—but the emphasis is on "mute"; it is a more passive endurance than that urged and reflected in *More Poems 1961*. The poet responds to his suffering no longer even with the tones and rhythms of a strongly curbed pain but with the dead tone and flat rhythms of one who, while still having the strength to suffer, is withered by his knowledge of what must happen time and time again. "Horizon" presents such a moment of withered self-knowledge:

> Do as you will tonight,
> Said she, and so he did
> .   .   .   .
>
> Knowing-not-knowing that such deeds must end
> In a curse that lovers long past weeping for
> Had heaped upon him.

There is bitter awareness of the inevitability of betrayal in the bald "and so he did," and a soured tiredness in the falling movement, like a sigh, of "lovers long past weeping for," both of which express the final defeat of hope. Even his assertion of a revived faith, in "Uncalendared Love," has the same bleak inflec-tions. Those, he says, whose love is ruled by time are subject to the continuous seasonal death and rebirth. But he lays claim for himself and his beloved to a love unchanged by time:

> But you with me together, together, together,
> Survive ordeals never before endured
> .   .   .   .
>
> Ours is uncalendared love, whole life,

> As long or brief as befalls. Alone, together,
> Recalling little, prophesying less.

The triumph of "ours is uncalendared love" is immediately qualified by what
follows, which creates the impression rather that the lovers had no choice in the
matter; it is more their doom than their achievement, an ordeal rather than a
privilege. "Recalling little, prophesying less" is a grimly negative statement of
that living-in-the-present celebrated with such simple confidence at the beginning
of the White Goddess period in "Theseus and Ariadne" and "Worms of History." Here it is a state of being without the comfort of roots in the past or any
sort of promise for the future: the lovers inhabit a vacuum of loneliness. The
verse has a kind of resoluteness about it but the movement is curiously unvibrant.
With its frequent pauses it seems only to twitch with life; in "together, together,
together" rhythm breaks down completely—expressing the numbed exhaustion
of a state beyond suffering and opening up vistas of possible emptiness.

The return to the idea of togetherness in the fourth line quoted indicates
the poem's centre of interest. In "Possessed" the message is, as in *More Poems
1961*, that woman too suffers: the lover is told that she,

> no less vulnerable than you,
> Suffers the dire pangs
> Of your self-defeat.

In "Ibycus in Samos," where the emotion is a feverish ecstasy ("Sprigs of the
olive-trees are touched with fire"), the stress is, more positively, on the man and
woman's oneness in suffering:

> She whom I honour has turned her face away
> A whole year now, and in pride more than royal
> Lacerates my heart and hers as one.

"Uncalendared Love," however, while insisting that their union is an indissoluble
one, yet hints at depths of ambiguous feeling about the fact: "together" is a
neutral word and points to what may be either joy or despair.

The transition from the numbness of despair, the final consequence of the
White Goddess experience, to faith in a new kind of love—and, in fact, the
closeness of that despair to the freedom of the new love—are to be seen in the
most startling of these poems, "A Restless Ghost." In his affliction the poet no
longer yearns to be restored to the Goddess's favour but to be absolved once and
for all from his love of her. Out of the exhaustion of the old experience the new
love will be born; the poet anticipates different and, it seems, more intense joy:
the hills and coast will shine as never before

> when she is gone indeed,
> Her divine elements disbanded, disembodied
> And through the misty orchards in love spread.

It is as though the despair were a prerequisite of this state of ecstasy. Though not precisely defined, the nature of its difference from the old love is suggested in the carefully chosen "disembodied": it is the joy of a love that will perhaps transcend physical existence.

The results of this new experience are best studied in "The Winged Heart." The poem starts from the moment of a suddenly felt release, a sense of miraculous powers bestowed—his "heart suddenly sprouting feathers." He then reports how (in an image for their past estrangement) the season's drought had concluded in a four-day sirocco, and how this at last had been broken by the coming of "the full honest rain." The two symbols for spiritual renewal, the beneficent rain bringing freshness and the sudden winged lightness of the heart, lie as it were casually alongside each other—Graves makes no attempt to interweave them. The poem has elegance but not the neatness which has in the past been the hallmark of so much of his verse. The "open" kind of poem is a departure from his usual form that reflects most distinctively the new mood. The manner is correspondingly relaxed:

> How it hissed, how the leaves of the olives shook!
> We had suffered drought since earliest April;
> Here we were already in October.
> I have nothing more to tell you.

This has the ease and simplicity of informal conversation. The fact of their estrangement is accepted, easily and simply, as something inexplicable. The poet's abstention from questioning, reasoning about or protesting against the fact indicates on this occasion neither pain nor despair but contentment; the last sentence says—"there it is, a fact; that is all you can say about it."

The poet has come to a point where he can surrender himself completely to the unreason of this new "certitude" in love—careless of the practicalities, improvident for the future. The symbolic description, in "The Winged Heart," of their transfiguring experience resembles that in "A Restless Ghost": "the tranquil blaze of sky etherializing / The circle of rocks and our rain-wet faces." "Etherializing" carries the same message as "disembodied." The encirclement of the lovers, the enclosing of them within the impregnable security of their miraculous love, is an image that anticipates several images in the later Black Goddess poems. And "tranquil blaze" renders the fusion of pain and ecstasy that is the essential characteristic of the Black Goddess experience. Other images for it occur in "Ruby and Amethyst" and "An Unnamed Spell," the first and last poem in this volume. In the former its mystery is compared to the "rose-amethyst," which

> Has such a garden in it
> Your eye could wander there for hours
> And wonder, and be lost.

In "An Unnamed Spell" likenesses to the later poems abound. It leaves no doubt that the paradigm of the lovers' "royal certitude" mentioned in it is to be found in the illumination vouchsafed to those few who in the Orphic, Jewish and Sufi cults worshipped the Black Goddess of Wisdom. It has been evident for some time now that Graves is a serious student of Sufi lore, and it has been put beyond question by the introduction he contributed to Idries Shah's book on the subject. The language of this poem confirms it: the woman is the possessor of a "headlong wisdom," and their love harbours a nameless Truth which is the

> Secret of secrets disclosed only
> To who already share it,
> Who themselves have sometime raised an arch —
> Pillared with honour; its lintel love —
> And passed silently through —

secrecy and silence are the necessary accompaniments to the revelation of this new mystery.

Man Does, Woman Is is the third volume in what, according to his announcement in the brief foreword, Graves now sees as "a three-book sequence dramatizing the vicissitudes of poetic love." Poetic love is love that acknowledges its origin in the Muse, the White Goddess. No mention is made in the foreword of the Black Goddess, though the volume includes a poem dedicated to her; but his recognition that *Man Does, Woman Is* brought to a close a phase in his writing probably arose from a presentiment that in any poetry he should write in the future she would have a major role to play.

The theme of the man and woman's common fate is in a number of poems taken a stage further. Although the title of one poem, "Expect Nothing," and, indeed, the poem itself communicate as bleak a message as any in *New Poems 1962*, yet the tone expresses a dour strength which has its source in a perception also informing the more romantically confident "An Unnamed Spell": that, while the crumbs of comfort that she scatters are meagre, the diet is one on which she as well as he must subsist "while the *lonely truth / Of love* is honoured and her word pledged" (my italics).

The poet has taken heart from the knowledge that despite repeated estrangements the bond between them still holds and presumably will always hold: there is a "truth" in love apart from, and unendangered by, the sequence of actual events, painful or not; he has found a new pride in this knowledge. It is a pride in the privileged uniqueness of their fate; this is the feeling that governs the opening lines of "That Other World":

> Fatedly alone with you once more
> As before Time first creaked.

The poet's pride finds more urgent expression in "Eurydice":

> My own dear heart, dare you so war on me
> As to strangle love in a mad perversity?
> Is ours a fate can ever be forsworn
> Though my lopped head sing to the yet unborn?

Here his vowed allegiance to their joint fate, whether or not it should bring about the paradisal perfection prophesied by the hero's singing head, is religious in its absoluteness.

The vigorous life in the rhythms of that stanza is characteristic of this volume as a whole. The manner changes from poem to poem but, where the theme is the lover's suffering, the attitude of stoicism reflected in it invariably goes beyond the expression merely of the will to endure, as in *More Poems 1961*, or of exhausted tenacity, as in *More Poems 1962*; it has more of a *positive* strength in it. There is a steely quality in the poet's voice, for instance, when, in "Bank Account," he peremptorily refuses to consider the possibility of protest against the woman's cruel treatment of him:

> Never again remind me of it:
> There are no debts between us.

The manner of "Deed of Gift" is in sharp contrast with this but similarly testifies to the poet's assurance. It describes how, after "unembittered meditation," the loved woman "gave herself to herself, this time for good." Forswearing promises of love and friendship that she deemed it unnecessary to keep, she turned now to the accomplishment of her own private truth. But, the poet asks, though to have returned to her true path

> From which by misadventure she had strayed,
> So that her journey was that much delayed,
> Justified the default of duties owed,
> What debt of true love did she leave unpaid?

The tone emulates her "unembittered," quiet performance of her task. The movement's gentle, measured pace and the unruffled propriety of the diction take from the last line's hint of pain any suggestion of a reproachful intonation; it is mild, uncomplaining, almost neutral in its implications.

Yet it does cause a faint ripple of unease to pass over the calm surface of the poem; the mere use of the question form makes this inevitable. It has been Graves's occasional practice at every stage in his development to conclude poems with an unresolved question. "Children of Darkness" ended in this fashion; it played an important part in the effect of some of the very best poems of his second period, such as "Time" and "Certain Mercies"; and it was a feature of a number of fine poems written in the latter half of the third period—"The Survivor," "The Portrait" and "The Straw" are notable examples. The increased frequency of his use of it in the sixties confirms its importance to Graves as a technique; in *Man Does, Woman Is* alone sixteen poems end on the questioning note. It seems that in this way of organizing a poem he has discovered a form that captures the quintessence of his outlook on life: it represents his recognition that hardship and, especially, uncertainty are intrinsic to the way of life on which he sets supreme value. Here, for example, in "Deed of Gift," the question, without modifying the absoluteness of the poet's assent to the woman's behaviour, her withdrawal of her love, yet registers a sense of puzzlement at the difficulty of reconciling the different facets of their relationship—his need of her love, her conflicting loyalties on the one hand to him and on the other to herself. The uncertainty is not in the poet's fidelity but in the love-situation itself. The effect produced by this procedure is akin to irony: it sets against the view of the situation the poem is chiefly concerned to present simultaneous hints of opposite views and other considerations that would have to be taken into account before a final estimate could be calculated.

The explanation for the frequency of the question form in the poems of *Man Does, Woman Is* is not that the poet's awareness of uncertainty has intensified but that he has arrived at a new conception of "doubt," as something quietly positive—protective, beneficent, bringing luck. It is a state of mind not merely to be endured but to be cultivated by the poet, as spiritually nourishing as (and a kind of) certitude. The first poem in this volume, "Time of Waiting," is one that announces the attitude which informs the manner of most of these poems. The theme, as Graves describes it in *Mammon and the Black Goddess*, is the poet's "resolve not to prejudice the future by hasty action": to

> Conclude no rash decisions, enter into
> No random friendships, check the runaway tongue
> And fix my mind in a close caul of doubt.

This may be the moment that precedes the conception of a poem, or that precedes any important action. "Doubt" here is a state of mind that guarantees, by sealing from extraneous influence, the utter freshness of the newborn poem, or ensures that the new action is in spontaneous accord with the deepest needs of the personality. It is more difficult to maintain than "to face / Night-long assaults of lurking furies" but it is a pain that generates new life. Comparison of this with the lines on doubt in an early poem like "Children of Darkness" or those on the illusion of "certitude" in "Vanity" will quickly reveal the distance Graves has travelled.

"The Oleaster" illustrates at its finest the firm, challenging stance characteristic of this volume—in this respect recalling *Poems 1953*. Its verse has an aggressive, "impudent" robustness, for example, in these lines which compare the poet, appropriately, to the tough wild olive—

> The savage, inexpugnable oleaster
> Whose roots and bole bunching from limestone crannies
> Sprout impudent shoots born only to be lopped.

The poem, furthermore, develops the "open," relaxed form of "The Winged Heart." It has two narrative strands. Firstly the poet describes a night's storm and the munificent rain that just before dawn followed upon it. He breaks off, in a diffident manner, and begins to make an apparently unrelated observation about the Majorcan practice of grafting the sweet olive on to the oleaster instead of planting it separately. Again he breaks off suddenly and resumes the first narrative, proceeding to recount how when the rain had stopped he and his love walked out on the road. But here the two strands loosely, as it were casually, twine: they gaze at the waterfalls and the surf but chiefly at the olive trees—

> Whose elegant branches rain has duly blackened
> And pressed their crowns to a sparkling silver.

As the day has been refreshed by storm and rain so has the bark of the olive trees been cleansed by the New Year snows. The narrative is interrupted for the last time: the poet turns with awkward humility to the woman and compares her to the sweet olive and himself with the oleaster. His is the toughness of the wild olive that enables them to survive storm and is strengthened by winter snows; hers is the sweetness, promising a new miraculous love, of the sweet olive.

"The Oleaster" is also a vivid, suggestive celebration of a near-mystical state of being, akin to the positive doubt soberly rendered in "Time of Waiting." Longer than most of its neighbours, the poem is without their terseness yet, paradoxically, like them it leaves an impression of spareness. This is a result of the disjointed progress of the narrative: it is as though each change of direction —signified by punctuation dots—is an involuntary betrayal by the poet of his sense that what he has to say, though simple, is not fully communicable in words, that it is necessary to stop short at a certain point. What Graves *is* saying, eluding direct statement, is not only that suffering is a refining agent directly responsible for the purity and radiance of this new world inhabited by the lovers (one recalls the imagery of "The Winged Heart" and "A Restless Ghost"), but also that the pain and the ecstasy (like "doubt" and "certitude") are in some way identical. This is conveyed in the description of the olive trees: the same rain that has "blackened" (implying sorrow) the elegance of the branches has "pressed" (implying an intenser pain) the uppermost leaves to a dazzling brilliance. Darkness and illumination somehow go together. This identification is furthered by the association of "blackened," "pressed" (a word suggesting not only pain but a shaping activity) and "silver" with the creative processes of heating and moulding metal.

While "The Oleaster" is the most successful example of the *dominant* mood of *Man Does, Woman Is*, in these lines it also shows a close relationship with a small group of poems which are the first to present, fervently, rapturously, what for a want of a better word must be called the "mystical" Black Goddess experience. There are three distinct stages of love, writes Graves in "Intimations of the Black Goddess": first, the old-fashioned "affection and companionship"; next, the "experience of death and recreation at the White Goddess's hand"; and lastly, "a miraculous certitude in love," "a new pacific bond between man and woman corresponding to a final reality of love," represented in the Myth as the Black Goddess. "The Hearth," after summarizing the first two stages, describes the third as a place

> Where an unveiled woman, black as Mother Night,
> Teaches him a new degree of love
> And the tongues and songs of birds.

At Hierapolis, Jerusalem, and Rome she was acknowledged as the dark sister of the reigning White Goddess. Her devotees were few and select, for "she ordained that the poet who seeks her must pass uncomplaining through all the passionate ordeals to which the White Goddess may subject him" before he is admitted to an understanding of her mysteries. Blackness symbolized Wisdom, but in the Orphic Wisdom-cult the Sun was chosen as their "metaphor of illumination." "Throughout the Orient, Night was regarded as a positive power, not as a mere absence of daylight; and Black as a prime colour, not as absence of colour, was prized for capturing the Sun's virtue more than any other." This may account for the association of blackness with brightness in "The Oleaster."

These images belong to a larger complex of images, the burden of which is the ineffableness of the experience they aim to realize. It is the ultimate, wordless truth, the final secret: depicted in turn as intensity of dark and light, silence, the dark forest's centre, reality stripped of false appearances. Love, says the poet in

"The Metaphor," was a "dead metaphor / For love itself" until it became "numinous," pervaded everywhere. Then it became a forest enclosing them, and they dared to bring the metaphor to life, to discard its merely temporal garments, and

> So at last understood true nakedness
> And the long debt to silence owed.

Again, in "The Green Castle," their love is envisaged as a self complete reality, an enclosing silence. As distinct on the one hand from the innocent imagination, "unclouded / By prescience of death or change / Or the blood-sports of desire," and on the other from the Christian heaven, attainable by prudence, discipline and mortification of the body, this "seventh heaven" of love, effortlessly beyond desire, is

> a green castle
> Girdled with ramparts of blue sea
> And silent but for the waves' leisured wash.
> There Adam rediscovered Eve.

Green is for rebirth and blue is for eternity.

But the supreme evocation of this experience is the poem entitled "The Black Goddess":

> Silence, words into foolishness fading,
> Silence prolonged, of thought so secret
> We hush the sheep-bells and the loud cicada.
> And your black agate eyes, wide open, mirror
> The released firebird beating his way
> Down a whirled avenue of blues and yellows.
>
> Should I not weep? Profuse the berries of love,
> The speckled fish, the filberts and white ivy
> Which you, with a half-smile, bestow
> On your delectable broad land of promise
> For me, who never before went gay in plumes.

The new love is presented here as such a perfection of reciprocal understanding between the lovers that it can be greeted only with silence, a silence denoting thought beyond the scope of words. They own a secret knowledge of a mental state so deep, so unconnected with the external world, that it cannot coexist with —or exist below the consciousness of —even the everyday sounds of the sheep-bells and the cicadas, so incesssant that they form an uninterrupting accompaniment to all more ordinary, shallow thoughts. The poet's soul, released from time and space, finds its home in the "*black* agate eyes" of the Goddess, which are both a deep reflecting pool and a forest avenue of trees leading to the heart of the mystery. The treasures that the Goddess bestows in such profusion —they represent love, poetry and wisdom—belong one to each of the seasons, to Winter, Spring, Summer and Autumn, respectively: there is no hint here that the turning of the seasons imprisons the poet in a temporal cycle of creation, destruction and recreation.

The poem is an astonishing combination of clear, bare, simple expression and richness of thought. Each statement expands with multiple implications—I have attempted to identify some of those latent in the first stanza. Consider also in those lines the consummate skill with which the verse enacts the meaning: the way in which, with the pauses—each phrase threatening to bring the line to a standstill—and the falling rhythms within and at the end of each line, it seems to drift towards the silence it describes; and how the sibilant consonants have the effect of intensifying the quality of that silence. Economically and unostentatiously these sensations together create the powerful impression of movement towards a central, inexpressible reality. The extreme spareness of the writing, as in "The Oleaster," now serves the function for which, it seems, it was ultimately if unconsciously intended—to reflect the poet's humble awareness of just how inexpressible except by bare hints the "final reality of love" is. Again Graves uses the technique of disjointed progression, but less noticeably and with perhaps a finer effect. The poem does not pursue a consecutive argument but, as it were, walks round the subject, presenting in turn three separate approaches, each of which, however—a pointer merely to a meaning that cannot be fully revealed— penetrates so far and no further. The gap between each view, each stanza, is a tacit acknowledgment of all that it is not possible to say. The connection, for instance, between what is represented as silence in the first stanza and as spiritual release in the second is left mysterious: they may be regarded as nearly alternative versions of the same reality. The transition from the second to the third stanza— "Should I not weep?"—records the poet's awed bewilderment, simple relief, and gratitude for this illumination but not the desire for rational explanation.

The possession of this reality, it can be seen now, has all along been the goal of Graves's poetic efforts. It is that "Promise of glory, not yet known / In full perfection" of "Sullen Moods," and then the state beyond conflict which he attempted to define in *Whipperginny*, *The Feather Bed*, and *Mock Beggar Hall*; again, it is the Looking Glass world, outside the usual three dimensions and obeying other than logical laws, gaily celebrated in "Alice"; it is the realization of the desire, expressed in "The Felloe'd Year," that the year should "Be a fixed compass, not a turning wheel"—an experience rendered by a similar image, in

"Instructions to the Orphic Adept," as the "still, spokeless wheel: —Persephone"; and it is Darien, "guardian of the hid treasures" of the poet's world. The final possession of this reality is the culmination of Graves's development in this three-volume sequence of the sixties: signifying the reward of endurance, the conversion of love's "difficult achievement" into the accomplishment of the impossible, and the uncontested rule of unreason.

JOHN B. VICKERY

The White Goddess *and* King Jesus

In tracing the lineaments of the mature Graves's basic myth-motif and its relation to *The Golden Bough*, two complementary works stand out. These are *The
White Goddess* and *King Jesus*, which first appeared around the same time and
which are far more important in this respect than *Hercules, My Shipmate*, the
work whose research Graves claims first made him aware of the ubiquity of the
White Goddess. Actually his preparations for a full-scale study of myth antedate
the Hercules novel by at least ten years and probably longer. Thus, to look at his
first novels *I, Claudius* and *Claudius the God* is to see the measure of his interest
in the worlds explored by Frazer and others. The first of these novels contains no
explicit references to *The Golden Bough* or its themes and seems to be a quite
ordinary historical novel drawing on classical sources. Still, it does suggest unequivocally that history is the record of infamy and the historian a dispassionate
chronicler. This same attitude is one that dominates much of *The Golden Bough*
particularly when it discusses the rise of the priest-king to a position of power or
the efforts of organized religions to hold and extend their power.

In its sequel, published in the same year, Graves is more explicit about his
anthropological knowledge. He says, for instance, that his ideas about British
Druidism were aided by "borrowings from archaeological works, from ancient
Celtic literature and from accounts of modern megalithic culture in the New
Hebrides, where the dolmen and menhir are still ceremoniously used." Among
the ideas discussed in the course of the novel are those dealing with rituals for
producing rain, the importance of the oak and mistletoe in primitive religions,

From *Robert Graves and the White Goddess*. © 1972 by the University of Nebraska
Press.

the nature of the Saturnalia, the practice of women worshippers having sexual intercourse with their gods, the cult of Cybele with its eunuch priests, and the centrality of Jesus' resurrection and reappearance to the success of Christianity. As he himself avers, Graves likely drew on a number of sources for his information. It is, however, also true that all of these points are made, sometimes in copious detail, in *The Golden Bough*. And though he has not yet evolved the White Goddess, Graves does have Claudius use the cult of Cybele, the great orgiastic fertility goddess of Phrygia, as the basis for a kind of comparative study of religion from the standpoint of a practical politician and ruler. Similar adumbrations of the motifs of *The White Goddess* emerge in the notion of the god Osiris as a triple figure, in a human being annually serving as the god's representative and having the right to all human pleasures before being sacrificed, and in the importance attached to the number thirteen, as well as the significance of natural analogies as argumentative support and a method of reasoning. In *Claudius the God* these have become the triple goddess, her sacrificial consort, the ancient lunar year, and the book's essential logic respectively.

While *Hercules, My Shipmate* shows a number of these developments as full blown and adds others, such as the matriarchal stress, it can be bypassed in favor of *The White Goddess* if only because it is the latter book which has been most influential and which perhaps best sums up Graves's approach to myth and anthropology. Trying to summarize the leading concerns of a book that at first glance is as maddening as Yeats's *A Vision* is difficult. Yet in a general sense it is possible to isolate three recurring strands which stand out as central. These are the nature of poetry and modes of human thought, the myth of the White Goddess and her consort, and what might be called the religious symbolism of language. Of these it is obviously the second that is most closely linked with *The Golden Bough*, though the others have affinities too through their connection with the goddess and her lover.

Briefly put, Graves argues that certain medieval Welsh poems, notably "The Battle of the Trees" and "The Song of Taliesin" from *The Red Book of Hergest*, were deliberately confused so that their real significance—a symbolic and arcane statement of the name of the transcendent God—would not be detected by the authorities of the Christian church. The ultimate reason for the church's hostility is not only that the God named is a pagan one but, says Graves, that it is the Great Mother goddess of the original matriarchal age. She is hated and feared by those of the patriarchal age who have replaced her, for she embodies the mysteries of fertility and generation and demands man's "spiritual and sexual homage." To this they have retorted by exalting patrilinear institutions and reason or logic, both of which are calculated to expunge the power of the goddess.

Actually, the Welsh poems and their esoteric significance are but the vehicle on which Graves mounts his general thesis. He argues that the original language of poetry employed the grammar and vocabulary of myth, which in turn was based on a close knowledge and observation of the seasons and the various forms of vegetative life. This language was devoted to invoking, celebrating, and otherwise worshipping the primitive moon-goddess who is the true poet's true muse. This sense of the nature and function of myth was gradually driven underground where it survived in such disparate locations as the mystery cults at Eleusis, the ancient Celtic schools for poets, and the covens of witches in western Europe. But today there is no organized, disciplined study or worship of either the goddess or her poetic mode. Instead there is industrialism, patriarchalism, and classical poetry celebrating Apollo and reason, all enemies of the White Goddess and true poetry. Thus Graves claims to be concerned with rediscovering and expounding the lost rudiments of the magical principles that underlay the original forms of European poetic lore. In so doing, he will, he feels, be providing a nucleus of poetic education for those aspiring poets who are truly dedicated and prepared to make a total commitment to the craft of poetry.

Central to this education is the understanding of the true nature of poetic theme. Graves suggests that the determination of the true theme depends on the reaction of the reader, a fact which suggests the residual effects of his early involvement with psychoanalysis and W. H. R. Rivers. When a poem is perfectly rendering the "single yet infinitely variable Theme," the reader experiences "a strange feeling, between delight and horror." And yet one is not confined to the psychological determination. Graves also suggests a descriptive characterization of the theme:

> The Theme, briefly, is the antique story, which falls into thirteen chapters and an epilogue, of the birth, life, death and resurrection of the God of the Waxing Year; the central chapters concern the God's losing battle with the God of the Waning Year for love of the capricious and all-powerful Threefold Goddess, their mother, bride and layer-out. The poet identifies himself with the God of the Waxing Year and his Muse with the Goddess; the rival is his bloodbrother, his other self, his weird.

In short, the true poetic theme, the only real one for the serious poet, is life and death mediated by love whose archetypal form is the myth of the White Goddess. In it she imperiously and arbitrarily chooses a lover, bestows her favors on him, has a child by him, and then puts him to death before taking another lover.

These two ways of characterizing the theme of poetry combine shrewdly in Graves's poetic. The psychological explanation in terms of reader reaction suggests that whatever arouses the feeling compounded of delight and horror is a version of the theme. When this is taken in conjunction with the description of the theme in terms of the goddess and her consort, it becomes clear how Graves's mythopoeic interests merge with his fascination with contemporary concerns such as celebrating the love between individual human beings. For when the reader responds with delight and horror, he is, Graves can claim, responding to the powers of the goddess. By the same token, those poems that deal more explicitly with mythic topics already have defined for them the kind of response they should arouse so that in a sense Graves is very subtly preconditioning the audience. At the same time, of course, should such poems not arouse such a response, then this can be taken as evidence that while the subject is appropriate the treatment is not.

In this way he has a check against automatically assuming that the mythological poem is a good one, and at the same time he extends the notion of the range of poetic myth. For if the effect is the same and due to the same cause, then poems ostensibly personal and contemporary in subject are also aspects of the myth of the goddess and her lover. The effect of this is to suggest that the distinction frequently drawn between Graves's mythic poems and his others is misplaced; they really all form part of one infinitely various and developing story. What Graves is doing, then, is to restore to "myth" not only its original function as "grave records of ancient religious customs and events" but also a good deal of its original form and meaning as a word. That is, his contemporary poems dramatize for us the fact that the original sense of the word *myth* was simply that of *story*, and stories of human situations, emotions, and events are precisely what his poems supply in abundance.

II

Since this study does not purport to be a full-scale examination of Graves's poetry, this and similar matters must be set to one side. Nor can we even hope to examine in anything like the detail it demands *The White Goddess* itself. The central issue is to what extent that book is shaped by *The Golden Bough* and in what distinctive ways. It has been shown that Graves exhibited an early and considerable poetic interest in anthropology and comparative religion. It might be thought, however, that a work that deals with medieval Welsh poems, Celtic Ogham alphabets, Essene beliefs, and biblical symbology is one that has left the relative sobriety of *The Golden Bough* for headier areas of exploration. Even a casual reading (if such a thing is possible) of *The White Goddess* will dispel this notion. In all there are approximately twenty explicit references or quotations from Frazer as well as several others to Jane Harrison. In addition, there are almost thirty other passages which can with varying degrees of confidence be regarded as using *The Golden Bough* or other of Frazer's works as sources for the ideas advanced or as evidence or authority for the opinions expressed.

While such elementary statistics do not themselves establish the centrality of Frazer to Graves's study of myth, they do count for something. If nothing else they document both Graves's conversancy with *The Golden Bough* and his willingness to draw on it. But they do more. The tenor of his remarks about Frazer have a threefold emphasis. First, as he suggests in his interpretation of the myth of Uranus-Cronus-Zeus as "the annual supplanting of the old oak-king by his successor, . . . the theory of Frazer's *Golden Bough* is familiar enough to make this point unnecessary to elaborate at length." Second, he assumes the essential correctness of many of Frazer's interpretations; for example, he draws directly on *The Golden Bough*'s discussion of the corn spirit as an animal to support his claim that cat, pig, and wolf were particularly sacred to the Celtic goddess Cerridwen, the moon-goddess in her aspect as death-goddess. At the same time, Graves is not slavishly reliant on Frazer, and this takes us to the third aspect of his remarks about Frazer.

Running through *The White Goddess* is an attitude toward Frazer which can best be described as the critical impatience of a descendant. This is best typified by two instances. In the first, after mentioning Frazer's point about the similarity of words for *door* in Indo-European languages, Graves then goes on to say that "as usual, however, he [Frazer] does not press his argument far enough." The second instance is a more extended criticism of Frazer for having preserved his academic position by exercising considerable discretion in discussing the primitive and pagan origins of Christianity. As Graves puts it, Frazer retained his position "by carefully and methodically sailing all around his dangerous subject, as if charting the coastline of a forbidden island without actually committing himself to a declaration that it existed." Like Lawrence, Graves is unwilling to use Frazer and *The Golden Bough* without also affirming his independence. Indeed, there is more than a suggestion in his criticisms of Frazer that he is rebuking Frazer less for his views than for his not having a temperament and attitude more like that of Robert Graves. After *The White Goddess* and *The Nazarene Gospel Restored*, no one is likely to accuse Graves of not having carried his argument far enough or of not stating his position unequivocally.

From these three points of emphasis—familiarity, correctness, and incompleteness—we can chart with remarkable accuracy the character of Graves's use of *The Golden Bough*. Because he assumes Frazer's theories are well known, Graves mentions them without elaborating on them in detail. And because he thinks many of Frazer's individual statements and observations are undeniably true, he cites or alludes to them for corroboration of his own vastly more elaborate and ingenious theories. As a result, there is considerably more use of points drawn from *The Golden Bough* than there is exposition of its central theses. At the same time, since his own views about the nature and dissemination of myths are more involved and speculative than those of Frazer, and since he is not a professional scholar but rather a gifted amateur—a unique cross between Lord Raglan and Ezra Pound—he feels temperamentally impelled to declare the inadequacies of the author of *The Golden Bough*.

Partially qualifying these strictures, however, is the substantial evidence of his extensive knowledge of Frazer's works. In *The White Goddess* alone Graves's quotations from or allusions to *The Golden Bough* range from early volumes like *Taboo and the Perils of the Soul* to the very last ones entitled *Balder the Beautiful*. Other works of Frazer that he has drawn on here or elsewhere are *Totemism and Exogamy*, *Folk-Lore in the Old Testament*, the editions of Apollodorus's *Bibliotheca*, Ovid's *Fasti*, and Pausanias's *Graeciae Descriptio*. And the probability is very great that he is well acquainted with still other lesser known works by Frazer, not only because of his intimate knowledge of *The Golden Bough*, but also because of his awareness of many other authors in the field such as Bronislaw Malinowski, Jane Harrison, A. M. Hocart, Sir Flinders Petrie, Lord Raglan, A. B. Cook, W. H. R. Rivers, and Sir John Rhys.

In general terms we have seen the extent and kind of influence *The Golden Bough* exerted on Graves and *The White Goddess*. More specific examination, however, indicates that Frazer is not simply a source of evidence or a basis for extrapolations in *The White Goddess*. Actually, Graves's book is a kind of displacement and complication of the central themes of *The Golden Bough*. The centrality of the goddess and her consort to Graves's thesis is obvious, but it is precisely here in this myth that Graves is most receptive to Frazer's impact. In *The Golden Bough* Frazer focuses the central phenomenon in the development of man's religious consciousness. Thus, while he gives due attention to Isis, Ishtar, Aphrodite, and the others, the bulk of his discussion centers on gods like Adonis, Attis, Osiris, and Balder, who suffer the critical experience of sacrificial death and whose restoration to the full vigor of life is essential to the perpetuation of their worshippers. For the most part, their consorts are cast in the secondary role of compliant lovers and devoted mourners who, like Isis, wander desolate over the earth after his death and ultimately have their faithfulness rewarded by the god's revival and triumph over his adversary and death.

In essence, Graves deals with the same myths but from an inverted perspective: he concentrates on the goddess as the central figure responsible for the fertility and flourishing of all living things. In this he echoes Frazer's stress upon such Asiatic mother goddesses as the personification of all reproductive energies in nature. At the same time, what allows him to do so with such ease is the copious evidence provided by Frazer that originally the goddess was more important than her spouse. *The Golden Bough* explains this in, among other places, a crucial chapter entitled "Mother-Kin and Mother Goddesses." This chapter is of vital importance in pointing up Graves's response to Frazer. The latter says that the goddess's superiority over the god is best explained "as the result of a social system in which maternity counted for more than paternity, descent being traced and property handed down through women rather than through men."

Graves accepts this view but extends it to mean that originally women as representatives or embodiments of the goddess were politically preeminent and ruled society. Such a thesis flatly contradicts Frazer's argument that mother-kin or the custom of matrilineal descent does not imply that the government is in the hands of women. Indeed, Frazer goes so far as to say that "the theory that under a system of mother-kin the women rule the men and set up goddesses for them to worship is so improbable in itself, and so contrary to experience, that it scarcely deserves the serious attention which it appears to have received." The explanation for this divergence in views is perhaps that Graves is concerned with pushing his argument further than Frazer. The latter argues that all available evidence points away from the idea of a thoroughgoing matriarchy, while Graves feels that there was an earlier stage in society when such a mode of organization existed.

In this, Graves is possibly indebted to Laura Riding, though not in the fashion some critics have suggested. At one point in *Claudius the God* he acknowledges her aid on matters of what he calls "literary congruity," by which he means logical consistency applied to the construction of literary works. It is, quite possibly, this sense of literary congruity that impels him to infer a matriarchal state from the considerable evidence for the preeminence of goddesses in certain societies at certain periods in history. The neatness of this hypothesis also squares with Graves's penchant for standing accepted views of historical incidents on their heads, as he has in such novels as *Sergeant Lamb's America* and *Wife to Mr. Milton*. Frequently he shows that the truth about a character or event is not significantly different from but diametrically opposite to the received opinion.

If the White Goddess is Frazer's fertility goddesses exalted in her religious centrality, her character also owes a good deal to the same personages. Actually what Graves has done is to make a composite goddess out of those figures discussed by Frazer. He augments Frazer's remarks with information from other sources, both ancient and modern, as well as with his own speculative inferences based on highly imaginative readings of the available documents and evidence. Thus, *The Golden Bough* stresses the vegetative aspect of these goddesses, their human embodiment of that form of fertility on which primitive peoples depended for their sustenance. Frazer traces in considerable detail the precise plants, trees, and flowers held sacred to the individual goddesses. Graves does the same thing when he makes the White Goddess a goddess of trees and specifies which ones are linked with the goddesses of various peoples. His linking of the Sumerian goddess Belili with the willow is of precisely the same order as Frazer's ascribing corn to Isis. And like Frazer he sees deities who have the same kinds of vegetation sacred to them as being identified with one another.

The chief difference is again one of degree. Frazer is content to link Isis, Ceres, and Demeter as corn goddesses and devoted wives and mothers. Graves goes beyond this to postulate a divine figure who embraces all the various forms of the fertility goddesses, from orgiastic tyrant to serene helpmate. It is she whom he calls the White Goddess. In so doing he carries the Frazerian comparative method a step beyond its use in *The Golden Bough*, though in a way that is inherent in its pages. Frazer orders the myths and rituals of the deities in a steady succession of chapters. Long before he is done this conveys to us an overwhelming sense of their similarity and of their all being in some sense versions of the same hopes, fears, and needs. The recurring pattern creates a perspective of identification which is also one of identity.

Graves does the same thing though more by direct assertion than indirection. Rhetorically his is the order of anticlimax whereas Frazer's is the order of climax. Thus, the White Goddess is a conceptual myth founded on ritual and functional similarities in deities whose worship is historically veridical. No one except Graves ever worshipped her though many peoples may have worshipped goddesses one of whose attributes was that of whiteness. In substance she holds the same position in Graves's thought as the Dying God does in Frazer's. The only difference is that Frazer, the professional scholar and historian, is content to regard his concept as just that while Graves is inclined to see in his a historical reality.

In the process of formulating this composite figure, Graves does more, however, than merely assemble an amalgam of the fertility goddesses discussed in *The Golden Bough*. He recognizes clearly that they possess contradictory and unreconcilable qualities. Isis and Astarte, for example, embody opposite poles of the female temperament and behavior. What he does is to present the White Goddess as a creature of almost infinitely metamorphic nature who changes her guises, roles, and qualities, as well as names. These changes are not capricious but rather correlated to the phases of the moon, the time of year, and the various functional relationships obtaining between her and man. In this way he is able to make her simultaneously a vital figure throughout the entirety of human life and also a single, enduring, archetypal creature. What is striking here, apart from the symmetrical ingenuity exercised by Graves in working out her paradigmatic development, is the extent to which material and clues for such an orientation are traceable to *The Golden Bough*.

As the human image of the changing moon, she has, according to Graves, the following pattern: "the New Moon is the white goddess of birth and growth; the Full moon, the red goddess of love and battle; the Old Moon the black goddess of death and divination." Nowhere in *The Golden Bough* is there a comparably explicit statement of the moon pattern; Frazer does, however, devote considerable attention to the role of the moon in primitive religion. Included in his treatment are such points as the identification of certain goddesses and women with the moon, either in its new or harvest phases; the likening of the moon, in its waxing or waning phases, to a white cow and to "a coy or wanton maiden"; the primitive distinction between light and dark phases of the moon; and the correlation held to exist by many primitive peoples between human and lunar development. What Graves does is to codify and sharpen these points of Frazer's so that a clear imaginative pattern emerges.

It is also possible that Frazer aids in the selection of color symbolism employed. The use of white and black is obvious and natural, but the ascription of red to the full moon is less so. In the passage just quoted Graves is altering Suidas's term *rose* and this obviously is the primary source in this particular instance. At the same time there is a curious parallel to this color symbolism in the final chapter of *The Golden Bough*. In the penultimate paragraph of his monumental study Frazer discusses what he calls the web of thought, the pattern human thought has revealed in the course of its development. He likens it to "a web woven of three different threads—the black thread of magic, the red thread of religion, and the white thread of science, if under science we may include those simple truths, drawn from observation of nature, of which men in all ages have possessed a store." These concepts qua concepts may at first sight seem alien to the thought of *The White Goddess*, but when we look closely at the passage, its affinities with Graves's pattern increase. In both cases, black is associated with magic, divination being one form of it; white is connected with growth, though to be sure in somewhat different though still analogous senses; and red as emblematic of religion may well be thought to entail both love and battle. Also, the goddess who possesses these three forms often seems to represent for Graves the entire chameleonlike relationship obtaining between man and his environment. Thus, Frazer's web of thought is matched by a complex of fate and response that defines the destiny of man whatever the ground and character of his actions. The White Goddess is both the natural and psychological worlds in which the individual must live subject to forces other than his own untrammeled will.

The lunar trinity of the natural world has a parallel in the social world as well through which the functional relationships between goddess and man are defined. She also corresponds to what Graves considers as the three primary roles of woman, namely, maiden, mother, and old woman. The full complexity with which Graves sees her triple role is clear from the following passage:

> As Goddess of the Underworld she was concerned with Birth, Pro-
> creation and Death. As Goddess of the Earth she was concerned with

the three seasons of Spring, Summer and Winter: she animated trees and plants and ruled all living creatures. As Goddess of the Sky she was the Moon in her three phases of New Moon, Full Moon and Waning Moon. This explains why from a triad she was so often enlarged to an ennead. But it must never be forgotten that the Triple Goddess, as worshipped for example at Stymphalus, was a personi-fication of primitive woman—woman the creatress and destructress. As the New Moon or Spring she was girl; as the Full Moon or Summer she was woman; as the Old Moon or Winter she was hag.

Though these roles are part of life itself, it is interesting to note the extent to which they are emphasized in *The Golden Bough*; it seems likely the pattern owes more than a little to Graves's steeping himself in Frazer's work. Particularly apposite here is the first of the two volumes called *Spirits of the Corn and of the Wild*. It deals at length with Demeter and Persephone and their relationship, with the preeminent role of women in agricultural rituals, and with the meta-morphic and sacrificial character of corn spirits. Not only are Demeter and Persephone seen as mother and maiden, respectively, but they are also regarded as successive forms of the same thing, the corn at different stages in its growth. By presenting a continuity of nature coupled with transformation of appearance and role, *The Golden Bough* gave him not only images of fertility but also the rationale with which to coalesce them into a unified emblem of female power viewed as a religious phenomenon. Graves even continues to exploit its vegetative emphasis when he remarks that the goddess was also worshipped "in her triple capacity of white raiser, red reaper and dark winnower of grain." Similarly, though he is not wholly consistent in titling the roles, he follows Frazer in designating the youthful goddess as "maiden" and the aged one as "hag." Further aid for his symbolic schematizing is Frazer's information that the spring was called Persephone and the summer Aphrodite, while ceremonies connected with winter represented it as both aged and deformed, that is, as a hag.

From the foregoing we have seen something of the way Graves links the White Goddess to temporal periods, both monthly and annual, lunar and solar. There is, however, another pattern of development that is at least partly tem-poral. It is a progression that represents biological and psychological rather than astronomical or vegetative reality. There are "five stations of the year, typified by the five petals of the Lotus-cup—Birth, Initiation, Marriage, Rest from Labour, and Death." This explains, he says, why the apple has been given "such immense mythic importance" because "if an apple is halved cross-wise each half shows a five-pointed star in the centre, emblem of immortality, which represents the Goddess in her five stations from birth to death and back to birth again." *The*

Golden Bough has no such clear-cut delineation of seasonal or biological stages as this, it is true. Nevertheless, it contains much material to suggest this kind of pattern. All the stations save "Rest from Labour" are exhaustively explored in manifold dimensions by Frazer. The various rituals and beliefs associated with birth, initiation, marriage, and death help shape this pattern in Graves's thought.

Similarly, though the linking of the apple with the sequential movement of life itself is Graves's own, Frazer makes a number of points which bear out the apple's mythic importance. And these points may well have started Graves looking for an explanation of its significance. Thus, he shows that it was a sacrificial offering to Hercules, whom Graves not only regards as "the most perplexing character in Classical mythology" but as the preeminent instance of the sacred king whose story is that of the ritual course of life itself. It is Hercules who is seen to progress through the several stations described in the above passage. That the apple can be regarded as symbolizing the goddess may also have been suggested by its emblematic use at the festival of Diana in the summer, its employment as a fertility charm for barren women, its use in divination when sliced, and its tree serving as an index of the life expectancy of male children. Even without detailed study it is clear from these items that the apple was symbolically identified with fertility, with birth, marriage, and death, which comprise three of Graves's five stations of the year.

Such a series of stages emphasizes, even as it orders, the metamorphoses undergone by the goddess both in the course of a year and in the life of the individual worshipper. It corresponds in large measure to the cyclical pattern that *The Golden Bough* enunciates for the dying and reviving god. Both possess a mysterious birth, marvellous experiences of multiple initiation including that of the sacred marriage with a divine woman, and death by accident or design from which there is a resurrection to renewed glory. This does not mean, however, that Graves's goddess is merely a female version of Frazer's deity. Rather, she is Frazer's fertility goddess who shares in the god's cyclic movement through annual stations but as originator and spectator, not participant. In Graves as in Frazer, "it is always the god rather than the goddess who comes to a sad end, and whose death is annually mourned." For both, the divinity of the male lies in his capacity for resurrection, while that of the female stems from her immortality the proof of which is the continued existence of mankind.

According to Graves, the central functions of the goddess in relation to man are mother, wife or lover, and layer-out. The first two, as we have seen, are amply represented in *The Golden Bough*, where they probably provided Graves with the archetypes and images necessary to the creation of the White Goddess. The layer-out, however, is not nearly so prominent in Frazer's work. There seems to be no fully individualized goddess of the order of Persephone the maiden or Isis the wife-mother to lend significance to the one who prepares the body for burial. And yet if Graves is not simply filling out the sequence in logical fashion and recalling as do Lawrence and Joyce the folk custom of his youth, there is some material in *The Golden Bough* that might have proven stimulating. One of Frazer's central theses, heavily documented, is that fear of the dead played a prominent part in primitive life. So powerful and thoroughgoing was it that a number of taboos surrounded those persons who had come in contact with death or the dead. These taboos were of such stringency that the layer-out and other members of the burial party were "cut off from all intercourse and almost all communication with mankind." Consequently, such individuals were reduced to the haglike state Graves equates with the death-goddess. In one of his typically graphic descriptions, Frazer presents a prototype of such persons:

> Clad in rags, daubed from head to foot with red ochre and stinking shark oil, always solitary and silent, generally old, haggard, and wizened, often half crazed, he might be seen sitting motionless all day apart from the common path or thoroughfare of the village, gazing with lack-lustre eyes on the busy doings in which he might never take a part. . . . at night, huddling his greasy tatters about him, he would crawl into some miserable lair of leaves and refuse, where, dirty, cold, and hungry, he passed, in broken ghost-haunted slumbers, a wretched night as a prelude to another wretched day.

Admittedly such figures seem remote from Graves's layer-out, who is the human form of the death-goddess. Nevertheless, Frazer's account does focus on those elements of age, ugliness, insanity, and silence which epitomize the meeting with the death-goddess. Transposed to the female, they might well define her appearance for Graves. Her loathsome and ferocious nature Graves indicates clearly in his heavily Frazerian discussion of her sacred animals, who are she in beast disguise. Like Frazer, he explains myth as an extrapolation from natural history when he links the goddess with cat, wolf, and pig by virtue of their all feeding on corpse-flesh. Other qualities that intensify their foulness are the habits of mating openly and eating their own young. Clearly the layer-out as the human version of the death-goddess would have to be equally repugnant in appearance and behavior. Like Yeats's black pig and Joyce's "cold mad feary father," she is the emblem of the triumphant antagonist, of the power that survives our personal decease and indifferently prepares our corpse for its final dissolution.

It is true that Graves does work out a cyclical pattern and a series of forms for the White Goddess. It is equally true, however, that he is not generally inclined to give each stage or guise the same amount of attention. He lavishes most of his efforts, particularly in his poetry, on exploring the goddess as temptress-mistress-destroyer. It is in this form that he describes her, in what apparently is her quintessential appearance: "The Goddess is a lovely, slender woman with a hooked nose, deathly pale face, lips red as rowan-berries, startlingly blue eyes and long fair hair." All her other forms are but metamorphic versions of this archetypal image and so subordinate to it, for above all she is "the ancient power of fright and lust—the female spider or the queen-bee whose embrace is death." Why he should have focused on this image as central rather than that of the benevolent mother Demeter, or the dutiful wife Isis, or the serene virgin whether Persephone or Mary is uncertain. There may be personal reasons or it may be more simply because she is the earliest form in which the image of woman captured his imagination. As early as 1922 he was responding to Keats's "La Belle Dame Sans Merci" in substantially the same fashion as he does in chapter 24 of *The White Goddess*, some of which is composed of the last chapter from *The Meaning of Dreams* (1924). It is clear at any rate that from virtually the beginning of his career Graves thought of love and poetry as related not so much through beauty as through their both being dangerous enterprises demanding daring and devotion in equal measures. When to this complex is added, as World War I and its nightmare-haunted aftermath did for Graves, death in all inexplicable horror, the nucleus of the Keatsian and Gravesian White Goddess is formed.

The notion of the beautiful woman who is whimsical, capricious, cruel, and tyrannical, and, nonetheless, passionately desired and sought after has a long literary tradition of which the medieval court of love portion is perhaps the best known. For such a figure the poet need not look beyond poetry or personal experience, but in Graves's case it is clear, from her name alone, that he has. His analogical imaginative habit impels him to link things that seem similar, whether they are literary, natural, or human in character. So, sharing in the early Keatsian vision of La Belle Dame and perhaps giving Graves a clue to understanding the most haunting of poems is *The Golden Bough*'s accounts of the great orgiastic fertility goddesses. Virtually all of these emphasize the awesome honor and responsibility of cohabiting with the divine woman. A number also stress the fertile mother aspect, but this belongs to that stage of the goddess following the one we are presently considering. By far the most pertinent treatment of her as the imperious sexual ruler of man is that provided by the discussion of the legend of Semiramis, queen of Assyria. Here Frazer describes a woman whose beauty won her the honor of becoming the king's wife even though she was a courtesan. Then, according to Frazer's account, "she won the king's heart so far that she persuaded him to yield up to her the kingdom for five days, and having assumed the sceptre and the royal robes she made a great banquet on the first day, but on the second day she shut up her husband in prison or put him to death and thenceforward reigned alone." Thereafter, to avoid sharing her political power with a husband, she remained single. But since chastity was not her metier, she "admitted to her bed the handsomest of her soldiers, only, however, to destroy them all afterwards." This was done by burying them alive.

Such a creature has all the identifying characteristics of the White Goddess as ruthless monarch of men. What makes her even more clearly a central shaping force in Graves's image is the fact that Frazer suggests that she is both an embodiment of the Babylonian goddess of love and fertility Ishtar or Astarte and also "a real queen of Assyria." To fuse in herself both the archetypal dimensions of myth and the ceaseless variety of quotidian reality, to be both goddess and flesh-and-blood woman—when coupled with the aforementioned traits—is to provide Graves with a model for his own multinamed goddess and beloved. In addition to the evidence of the poems, which will be discussed later, there is a final indication of the closeness of the relationship between anthropologist and poet. Frazer links Semiramis and her lovers with the Babylonian epic of Gilgamesh, who avoids the fatal embraces of Ishtar whom Frazer in an adumbration of Graves calls "the cruel goddess." In *The White Goddess* Graves too identifies her as the betrayer of Gilgamesh and likens her to Blodeuwedd in *The Mabinogion*, Delilah in the Bible, and Deianira in classical myth, all of whom are regarded as the third or love-goddess aspect of the pentad of roles played by the White Goddess.

Gilgamesh is, as Graves suggests and Frazer implies, a later version of Tammuz, the original Babylonian lover of Ishtar, who died and was reborn annually. The chief difference between them is that Gilgamesh rejects the love of the goddess while Tammuz reciprocates it. In the myth of the White Goddess as Graves elaborates it, the latter is correct. To avoid the goddess in order to remain safe, to retain tranquility and life, is to be guilty of masculine self-sufficiency. Out of this stems the passion for rational logic and patriarchal social institutions both of which serve to all but obliterate the goddess as a figure of public veneration. Graves does not devote any significant amount of attention to mythological versions of such evasions in *The White Goddess*. He does, however, have a good deal to say about the dereliction of manly duty practiced by what he calls classical poets (poets of all eras who follow reason and Apollo rather than passion and the White Goddess) and most of the modern age. The theme—the importance of submission to the goddess and her ritual of the seasons and life—is clearly central to Graves's mythopoeic pattern. But for its clearest and most significant cultural (as opposed to personal) delineation we must turn from *The White Goddess* to its dialectical counterpart, *King Jesus*.

III

This novel was published two years after *Hercules, My Shipmate* and two before *The White Goddess*, which places it right at the heart of Graves's burgeoning myth. The crux of the novel is the historical role Graves adduces for Jesus together with the intellectual and cultural climate in which he places his tragic hero. Jesus is said to be the son of Miriam or Mary, the daughter of Joachim and Hannah, and Antipater, the son of Herod King of Israel. By marriage with Miriam, Antipater acquired a true title to rule in Israel which even his father Herod did not possess. According to his father's will, the succession to the throne was to move from Antipater to Herod Philip and then back to Antipater's heirs. With the death of Herod, the execution of Antipater, the abdication of Herod Philip, and the murder of Antipater the Younger, Antipater's other son, Jesus, is left possessing the right of succession. That this is both resolutely opposed in the novel and unrecorded in scriptural or other documents is explained as due to Antipater's marriage being a secret one. The central dramatic line of the novel, then, is Jesus' attainment of the secret of his birthright and his attempt to claim the spiritual power attendant upon it while rejecting the temporal.

His clash with the White Goddess and many of the reasons for it can be gleaned from the following passage which represents the opinions of the narrator, Agabus, an Alexandrian scholar purporting to write around A.D. 90.

> As a sacred King, the last legitimate ruler of an immensely ancient dynasty, his avowed intention was to fulfil all the ancient prophecies that concerned himself and bring the history of his House to a real and unexceptionable conclusion. He intended by an immense exercise of power and perfect trust in God the Father to annul the boastful tradition of royal pomp—dependent on armies, battles, taxes, mercantile adventures, marriages with foreign princesses, Court luxury and popular oppression—which King Solomon had initiated at Jerusalem; and at the same time to break the lamentable cycle of birth, procreation, death and rebirth in which both he and his subjects had been involved since Adam's day. Merely to resign his claim to temporal power was not enough. His resolute hope was to defeat Death itself by enduring with his people the so-called Pangs of the Messiah, the cataclysmic events which were the expected prelude to the coming of the Kingdom of God; and his justification of this hope was the prophecy in the twenty-fifth chapter of Isaiah: "He shall destroy Death forever." In the Kingdom, which would be miraculously fertile and perfectly pacific, all Israelites would be his subjects who acknowledged him in his threefold capacity as king,

prophet and healer, and under his benignant rule would live wholly free from error, want, sickness or fear of death for no less than a thousand years.

One of the more important ways in which he contradicts the goddess's ritual is ignoring the fact that as a sacred king, he was her consort and subject to her authority. Breaking the cycle of birth-death-rebirth was the grossest violation of the stations of her year and of the pattern of existence she represented. To destroy Death was to annihilate the ultimate phase of her cycle. Similarly, his denial of "royal pomp," of material factors external to the individual human soul, is in essence a denial of the natural world itself on which the worship of the goddess is grounded. And finally, by assuming a threefold capacity capable of producing a paradisiacal and virtually immortal existence for his subjects, he is clearly parodying the trinity of her functions and the cyclic nature of her reign.

The most flagrant contradiction of her rule, however, comes with Jesus' enjoining chastity on all Israel as the price for destroying Death and entry into the Kingdom of God. As his wife Mary, the daughter of Cleopas, is told:

> Desire for progeny in marriage is an ancient error implanted in men and women by God's Adversary. . . . He has persuaded them that by this means they are staving off the ultimate victory of Death over mankind. . . . But the truth is that by performing the act of death they are yielding Death the victory.

In assuming that this course of sexual abstention is generally possible for and desirable to the faithful of Israel, Jesus is guilty either of confusing a spiritual with a temporal reality or of trying to hasten a state for which the moment had not yet come. The former seems to be Graves's own view as expressed through the texture and tone of the novel, while the latter is suggested by one of the characters, Mary the Hairdresser, who represents the goddess as the crone.

It is Jesus' confrontation with this Mary Magdalene at the Terebinth Fair which renders the clash between sacred king and fertility goddess, male and female religious principles, in its most dramatic and imagistic form. They engage in a ritual combat by way of offering rival and contradictory interpretations of the pictures on two tablets. These pictures render, Mary says, "the story of the ancient covenant from which the Ark takes its name; the covenant sworn between my Mistress and the twin Kings of Hebron; that she will share her love and her anger equally between them both so long as they obey her will." Their struggle to assert the superiority of their respective deities culminates in a victory of the moment for Jesus when he expels the evil spirits from her and leads her out into the starlight and the land of life. Yet even at the moment of his apparent triumph there are forebodings that the goddess is not so easily thwarted. For one thing, Mary recites a prophetic poem which picking up their earlier identification with Adam and Eve also associates Adam-Jesus with Frazer's Hanged God, the sacrificial victim. And for another, even after she is divested of the evil spirits, her final words to Jesus are to the effect that "the end is not yet, and when the Mother summons me to my duty, I will not fail her."

In delineating the character and origins of latter-day Christianity's regimen of ascetic chastity, Graves is not reflecting views or attitudes explicit in *The Golden Bough*. He may, however, be adapting its habit of showing the falsity of currently received views about the nature of Christ and Christianity. Frazer explodes the idea of the historical purity of Christianity by showing how much it derives from pagan religions that center on a dying and reviving god. In his discussion of the crucifixion of Christ he also provides Graves with a model for reinterpreting the event in terms that square with known rituals as well as with the demands for historical and documentary consistency. The reasons for Jesus' crucifixion adduced by Frazer and Graves are startlingly at odds with the traditional view; they are centered in rituals observed for the dying and reviving god of still earlier times. Frazer suggests Jesus was cast in the role of Haman in the Jewish festival of Purim, which in turn derived from the Babylonian festival of the Sacaea, both of which were Saturnalia involving a mock king and his ritual death. Graves does substantially the same thing, though he compounds the irony by stressing the orthodoxy of Jesus' Jewry while underscoring that his death takes the form of a ritual sacrifice to the heathen goddess he had opposed.

What makes *King Jesus* a reflection of the impact of *The Golden Bough* is not simply its hero's role as sacrificial scapegoat but the extent to which the cultural ambience in which he moves is suffused by the belief, customs, and images of the great fertility goddess. The impression created by the novel is that of the ancient Hebrew world being seen beneath a palimpsest composed of patterns elaborated in *The Golden Bough*. Frazer's concern is largely with the Mediterranean religious world, and when he deals with its Semitic extensions, it is from a distance and with a certain measure of simplicity. Graves, on the other hand, gives us through names, genealogies, idiom, and customs a sense of the distinctively Hebraic caste of his world in much the same way as Thomas Mann does in *Joseph and His Brothers*. But to this he adds also a lively and vigorous impression of the extent to which this world was a part of the whole Mediterranean complex. He lets us see, in effect, Judaism growing out of earlier primitive religions and then standing at the verge of the origin of Christianity. And what one is impressed by is precisely what strikes one in *The Golden Bough*, the ways and the extent to which these religions have common grounds, however altered their symbols and displaced their rituals.

In the opening pages of *King Jesus* Graves quickly establishes the preeminence of the female deity as the hero's antagonist in several ways. The narrator, who has the same cool detached tone of the outsider as Frazer, reports that the Jews believed "they never owed any duty either to the Great Triple Moon-Goddess who is generally reputed to have mothered the Mediterranean races, or to any other goddess or nymph whatsoever." But then he proceeds to claim that their own sacred stories of their heroes disprove this belief. Another and perhaps the most prominent way Graves emphasizes her importance is by the sheer proliferation of references to her worship, its customs, emblems, and forms. Elements of this order appearing at the outset and reminding us strongly of *The Golden Bough*'s stress are such things as premarital prostitution as a religious rite, self-castration on the same ground, ritual fornication to ensure flourishing crops, the rule of kings based on matrilineal succession and ultimogeniture, and the reddening of the god's face. These references continue throughout the book and by so doing achieve several ends.

One is the saturating of the novel's background in the myths of the fertility goddess enunciated in *The White Goddess*. At the same time it adds highly detailed, concrete scenes of specific human beings who either believe in her and her powers or else whose minds and habits of behavior are saturated by the residue of her earlier position in Israel. As a result, the novel, unlike the equivalent essay or critical study, gives us a clear sense of the dynamics of the goddess's religion and worship. Instead of unfamiliar mythical figures like Blodeuwedd or Cerridwen we encounter a talking, breathing woman named Mary the Hairdresser (Magdala), whose appearance of "a tall blue-eyed hag, her nose crooked like a falcon's beak" reveals the goddess as crone. From such details multiplied many times we see that for Graves, history is a record, often confused and distorted, of life lived mythically and ritualistically. Therefore, the historical novel is an accurate imaginative re-creation of that life, a re-creation that both records and interprets by the use of what he calls the analeptic method.

To grasp the wide-ranging and intricate relationships and meanings provided by the mythic details that are both dramatized and analyzed in the novel is to see another goal they achieve. The concentration on the mother goddess and the extent to which her religion underlies that of Israel in Jesus' day bears in on the reader that the whole career of Jesus and virtually the entire dramatic action of the novel conforms to the ritual pattern of the sacred king, her consort. Central to this pattern is the fact that, according to Graves, "in every country around the Mediterranean Sea, crucifixion was a fate reserved for the annual Sacred King" who was always "regarded as a sacrifice made on behalf of the tribe to its Goddess Mother."

This directly entails the third end achieved by the novel's extensive reliance on mythic detail. For the ultimate point of the material is ironic, as Graves makes quite explicit. Jesus' rejection of the goddess is symbolized intellectually by his battle of wits with the hag and emotionally by his sexual abstention with his bride. Both women significantly have the same name, as does his mother. Nevertheless he is ultimately subjected to her power of death and resurrection and to playing the role in which he was cast by birth. To this irony of event Graves adds another by the tone with which he invests Jesus' story. Instead of the traditional tragic caste, he gives it an ironic perspective through his narrator. Agabus writes religious history with as strong a comparative bent as Frazer himself and with as keen an eye as that master ironist for the incongruities between human aspirations and achievements, beliefs and realities. Graves makes Jesus not only Frazer's dying and reviving god who ritualistically sacrifices himself that his people may be redeemed from a world of death, but also the sacred king who is the consort and ritual victim of the White Goddess. In effect, the irony is achieved by making the hero a myth within a myth, of which the ritual actions are identical in form and antithetical in purpose. The function of such irony, of course, is to validate dramatically the thesis enunciated in *The White Goddess*, namely, that she can be flouted only at the individual's peril because her ritual embodies the fundamental and ineluctable course of life itself.

PAUL FUSSELL

The Caricature Scenes
of Robert Graves

Of all memoirs of the war, the "stagiest" is Robert Graves's *Good-bye to All That*, published first in 1929 but extensively rewritten for its reissue in 1957. Like James Boswell, who wrote in his journal (October 12, 1780), "I told Erskine I was to write Dr. Johnson's life in scenes," Graves might have said in 1929 that it was "in scenes" that he was going to write of the front-line war. And working up his memories into a mode of theater, Graves eschewed tragedy and melodrama in favor of farce and comedy, as if anticipating Friedrich Dürrenmatt's observation of 1954 that "comedy alone is suitable for us," because "tragedy presupposes guilt, despair, moderation, lucidity, vision, a sense of responsibility," none of which we have got:

> In the Punch-and-Judy show of our century . . . there are no more guilty and also, no responsible men. It is always, "We couldn't help it" and "We didn't really want that to happen." And indeed, things happen without anyone in particular being responsible for them. Everything is dragged along and everyone gets caught somewhere in the sweep of events. We are all collectively guilty, collectively bogged down in the sins of our fathers and of our forefathers. . . . That is our misfortune, but not our guilt. . . . Comedy alone is suitable for us.

And in Graves's view, not just comedy: something close to Comedy of Humors, a mode to which he is invited by the palpable character conventions of the army,

From *The Great War and Modern Memory*. © 1975 by Oxford University Press.

with its system of ranks, its externalization of personality, its impatience with ambiguity or subtlety, and its arcana of conventional "duties" with their invariable attendant gestures and "lines." "Graves," says Randall Jarrell, "is the true heir of Ben Jonson." Luxuriating in character types, Graves has said few things more revealing about his art than this: "There is a fat boy in every school (even if he is not really very fat), and a funny-man in every barrack-room (even if he is not really very funny).

In considering *Good-bye to All That*, it is well to clear up immediately the question of its relation to "fact." J. M. Cohen is not the only critic to err badly by speaking of the book as "harshly actual" and by saying, "It is the work of a man who is not trying to create an effect." Rather than calling it "a direct and factual autobiography," Cohen would have done better to apply to it the term he attaches to Graves's Claudius novels. They are, he says, "comedies of evil." Those who mistake *Good-bye to All That* for a documentary autobiography (Cohen praises its "accurate documentation") should find instructive Graves's essay "P.S. to *Good-bye to All That*," published two years after the book appeared. Confessing that he wrote the book to make "a lump of money" (which he did—he was able to set himself up in Majorca on the royalties), he enumerates the obligatory "ingredients" of a popular memoir:

> I have more or less deliberately mixed in all the ingredients that I know are mixed into other popular books. For instance, while I was writing, I reminded myself that people like reading about food and drink, so I searched my memory for the meals that have had significance in my life and put them down. And they like reading about murders, so I was careful not to leave out any of the six or seven that I could tell about. Ghosts, of course. There must, in every book of this sort, be at least one ghost story with a possible explanation, and one without any explanation, except that it was a ghost. I put in three or four ghosts that I remembered.
>
> And kings. . . . People also like reading about other people's mothers. . . . And they like hearing about T. E. Lawrence, because he is supposed to be a mystery man. . . . And, of course, the Prince of Wales.
>
> People like reading about poets. I put in a lot of poets. . . . Then, of course, Prime Ministers. . . . A little foreign travel is usually needed; I hadn't done much of this, but I made the most of what I had. Sport is essential. . . . Other subjects of interest that could not be neglected were school episodes, love affairs (regular and irregular),

wounds, weddings, religious doubts, methods of bringing up children, severe illnesses, suicides. But the best bet of all is battles, and I
had been in two quite good ones—the first conveniently enough a
failure, though set off by extreme heroism, the second a success,
though a little clouded by irresolution.

So it was easy to write a book that would interest everybody. . . .
And it was already roughly organized in my mind in the form of a
number of short stories, which is the way that people find it easiest
to be interested in the things that interest them. They like what they
call "situations."

Furthermore, "the most painful chapters have to be the jokiest." Add "the best
bet of all is battles" to "the most painful chapters have to be the jokiest" and
divide by the idea of "situations" and you have the formula for Graves's kind of
farce. The more closely we attend to Graves's theory and practice, the more we
can appreciate the generic terminology used by "Odo Stevens," in Anthony
Powell's *Temporary Kings*. Stevens was one who "hovered about on the outskirts
of the literary world, writing an occasional article, reviewing an occasional book.
. . . [He] had never repeated the success of *Sad Majors*, a work distinguished, in
its way, among examples of what its author called 'that dicey art-form, the war
reminiscence.' "

"Anything processed by memory is fiction," as the novelist Wright Morris
has perceived. In *Leviathan*, Thomas Hobbes puts it this way: "Imagination and
memory are but one thing, which for divers considerations hath divers names."
And in *An Apology for Poetry*, Sir Philip Sidney apprehends the "poetic"—that
is, fictional—element not just in all "history" but specifically in history touching
on wars and battles:

Even historiographers (although their lips sound of things done, and
verity be written in their foreheads) have been glad to borrow both
fashion and perchance weight of poets. . . . Herodotus . . . and all
the rest that followed him either stole or usurped of poetry their
passionate describing of passions, the many particularities of battles,
which no man could affirm, or . . . long orations put in the mouths
of great kings and captains, which it is certain they never pronounced.

We expect a memoir dealing with a great historical event to "dramatize" things.
We have seen Sassoon's memoir doing just that. But with Graves we have to
expect it more than with others, for he is "first and last," as Jarrell sees, "a poet:
in between he is a Graves." A poet, we remember Aristotle saying, is one who

has mastered the art of telling lies successfully, that is, dramatically, interestingly. And what is a Graves? A Graves is a tongue-in-cheek neurasthenic farceur whose material is "facts." Hear him on what happens to the wives of brilliant mathematicians:

> Mathematic genius is . . . notoriously short-lasting—it reaches a peak at the age of about twenty-three and then declines—and is as a rule colored by persistent emotional adolescence. Since advanced mathematicians are too easily enticed into the grey political underworld of nuclear physics, a remarkably high percentage of mental breakdowns among their wives is everywhere noted.

Asked by a television interviewer whether his view that homosexuality is caused by the excessive drinking of milk is "based on intuition or on what we would call scientific observation," Graves replies: "On objective reasoning." His "objective reasoning" here is as gratuitously outrageous as the anthropological scholarship of *The White Goddess*, the literary scholarship of his translation (with Omar Ali Shah) of *The Rubáiyát of Omar Khayyám*, or the preposterous etymological arguments with which he peppers his essays.

But to put it so solemnly is to risk falling into Graves's trap. It is to ignore the delightful impetuosity, the mastery, the throw-away fun of it all. Graves is a joker, a manic illusionist, whether gaily constructing flamboyant fictional anthropology, rewriting ancient "history," flourishing erroneous or irrelevant etymology, overemphasizing the importance of "Welsh verse theory," or transforming the White Goddess from a psychological metaphor into a virtual anthropological "fact." And the more doubtful his assertions grow, the more likely he is to modify them with adverbs like *clearly* or *obviously*. Being "a Graves" is a way of being scandalously "Celtish" (at school "I always claimed to be Irish," he says in *Good-bye to All That*). It is a way—perhaps the only way left—of rebelling against the positivistic pretensions of non-Celts and satirizing the preposterous scientism of the twentieth century. His enemies are always the same: solemnity, certainty, complacency, pomposity, cruelty. And it was the Great War that brought them to his attention.

Actually, any man with some experience and a bent toward the literal can easily catch Graves out in his fictions and exaggerations. The unsophisticated George Coppard explodes one of the melodramatic facilities in *Good-bye to All That* with simple common sense. Graves asserts—it is a popular cynical vignette—that machine-gun crews often fired off several belts without pause to heat the water in the cooling-jacket for making tea. Amusing but highly unlikely—Coppard quietly notes that no one wants tea laced with machine oil. Another of

Graves's machine-gun anecdotes collapses as "fact" upon inquiry. At one point he says,

> There was a daily exchange of courtesies between our machine-guns and the Germans' at stand-to; by removing cartridges from the ammunition belt one could rap out the rhythm of the familiar prostitutes' call: "MEET me DOWN in PICC-a-DILL-Y," to which the Germans would reply, though in slower tempo, because our guns were faster than theirs: "YES, with-OUT my DRAWERS ON!"

Very nice. But the fact is that if you remove cartridges from the belt the gun stops working when the empty space encounters the firing mechanism. (These stories are like the popular legend that in a firing squad one man is given a rifle secretly loaded with a blank so that no member of the squad can be certain that he has fired one of the fatal bullets. But attractive as this is as melodrama, there's something wrong with it: the rifle containing the blank is the only one that will not recoil when fired, with the result that every man on the squad will end by knowing anyway. The story won't do.)

But we are in no danger of being misled as long as we perceive that *Good-bye to All That* is no more "a direct and factual autobiography" than Sassoon's memoirs. It is rather a satire, built out of anecdotes heavily influenced by the techniques of stage comedy. What Thomas Paine says of Burke's *Reflections on the Revolution in France* applies exactly: Burke, says Paine, makes "the whole machinery bend to produce a stage effect." No one has ever denied the brilliance of *Good-bye to All That*, and no one has ever been bored by it. Its brilliance and compelling energy reside in its structural invention and in its perpetual resourcefulness in imposing the patterns of farce and comedy onto the blank horrors or meaningless vacancies of experience. If it really were a documentary transcription of the actual, it would be worth very little, and would surely not be, as it is, infinitely rereadable. It is valuable just because it is not true in that way. Graves calls on paradox to suggest the way it is true:

> The memoirs of a man who went through some of the worst experiences of trench warfare are not truthful if they do not contain a high proportion of falsities. High-explosive barrages will make a temporary liar or visionary of anyone; the old trench-mind is at work in all over-estimation of casualties, "unnecessary" dwelling on horrors, mixing of dates and confusion between trench rumors and scenes actually witnessed.

In recovering "the old [theatrical] trench-mind" for the purposes of writing the book, Graves has performed a triumph of personal show business.

He was in an especially rebellious mood when he dashed off the book in eight weeks during May, June, and July of 1929 and sent the manuscript to Jonathan Cape. His marriage with Nancy Nicolson had just come apart, he owed money, he had quarreled with most of his friends, his view of English society had become grossly contemptuous, and he was still ridden by his wartime neurasthenia, which manifested itself in frequent bursts of tears and bouts of twitching. His task as he wrote was to make money by interesting an audience he despised and proposed never to see again the minute he was finished. Relief at having done with them all is the emotion that finally works itself loose from the black humor which dominates most of the book.

The first nine chapters detail his prewar life. He was, he says, a perceptive, satiric, skeptical infant, from the outset an accurate appraiser of knaves and fools, including Swinburne, "an inveterate pram-stopper and patter and kisser." His Scotch-Irish father was a school inspector, but also a composer, collector, and anthologist of Anglo-Irish songs. In addition, he was a popular dramatist, one of whose plays ran for two hundred performances. His first wife, who was Irish, died after bearing five children, and he then married a German woman who bore him five more, including Robert, born in 1895. The family lived at Wimbledon in ample, literate middle-class style while Robert attended a succession of preparatory schools and spent summers roaming through the romantic castles near Munich belonging to relatives of his mother's. At fourteen he entered Charterhouse School, which he despised. He was humiliated and bullied, and saved himself only by taking up boxing. He mitigated his loneliness by falling in love with a younger boy, "exceptionally intelligent and fine-spirited. Call him Dick." (The name *Dick* was becoming conventional for this sort of thing. Sassoon's *Memoirs of a Fox-Hunting Man*, with its "Dick Tiltwood," had appeared a year before Graves wrote this.) Graves's devotion to Dick and his friendship with one of the masters, the mountaineer George Mallory, were about all he enjoyed at Charterhouse. Before he could go on to Oxford, the war began, and he enlisted immediately. He was nineteen.

In this nine-chapter prologue Graves practices and perfects the form of the short theatrical anecdote or sketch which he will proceed to impose upon the forthcoming matter offered by the war. His wry anecdotes take the shape of virtual playlets, or, as he is fond of calling them, especially when he is one of the players, "caricature scenes." They are "theatrical" because they present character types entirely externally, the way an audience would see them. The audience is not vouchsafed what they are or what they think and feel or what they were last Thursday, but only visible or audible signs of what they do and say, how they dress and stand or sit or move or gesture. Their remarks are not paraphrased or rendered in indirect discourse: they are presented in dialogue. Many of these playlets have all the black-and-white immediacy of cartoons with captions, and, indeed, Graves's skill at writing pithy "lines" will suggest the dynamics of the standard two-line caption under a cartoon in *Punch*. It is a model that is always before him. In 1955, ridiculing Yeats's shrewd irrationalism, he dramatizes Yeats's reliance on his wife as a medium whose maunderings can be turned into salable poems:

> UNDERGRADUATE: Have you written any poems, recently, Sir?
> YEATS: No, my wife has been feeling poorly and disinclined.

One can see it as on a stage and hear the burst of laughter at the end.

Whatever material they embody, the effect of Graves's "caricature scenes" is farcical, and they rely on a number of techniques associated with comic writing for the theater. Some depend upon astonishing coincidences. Some deploy the device of climactic multiple endings — the audience thinks the joke is over and is then given an additional one or sometimes two even funnier lines. Some expose the disparity between the expected and the actual. Some offer bizarre characters borrowed from what would seem to be a freak show. Some, like sketches in music hall, present comic encounters between representatives of disparate social classes. Some involve the main character's not knowing some crucial fact. And some, more melodramatic, depict rescues or salvations in the nick of time. All operate by offering the audience a succession of little ironies and surprises. By the time we have reached the fifth paragraph of *Good-bye to All That*, we are convinced that we are in the hands of a master showman who is not going to let us down. "My best comic turn," says the author, "is a double-jointed pelvis. I can sit on a table and rap like the Fox sisters with it." Indeed, so extraordinary is this puppet master that, as he says proudly, "I do not carry a watch because I always magnetize the main-spring."

Graves had been in the Officers Training Corps at Charterhouse, and when he presented himself at the regimental depot of the Royal Welch Fusiliers at Wrexham, he was commissioned after a few weeks' training. His account of his early days in the Army is full of caricature scenes. One of the funniest, the grave judicial inquiry into the "nuisance" deposited by Private Davies on the barrack square, Graves introduced into the book only in 1957. In 1929 he said, "I have an accurate record of the trial, but my publishers advise me not to give it here." It is a perfect Jonsonian comic scene, each man in his humor, and it is ready to be staged by a cast of six:

> SERGEANT-MAJOR (*offstage*): Now, then, you 99 Davies, "F" Com-
> pany, cap off, as you were, cap off, as you were, cap off! That's
> better. Escort and prisoner, right *turn!* Quick *march!* Right

wheel! (*Onstage*) Left wheel! Mark time! Escort and prisoner, *halt!* Left *turn!*

COLONEL: Read the charge, Sergeant-Major.

SERGEANT-MAJOR: No. 99 Pte. W. Davies, "F" Company, at Wrexham on 20th August: improper conduct. Committing a nuisance on the barrack square. Witness: Sergeant Timmins, Corporal Jones.

COLONEL: Sergeant Timmins, your evidence.

SERGEANT TIMMINS: Sir, on the said date about two p.m., I was hacting Horderly Sar'nt. Corporal Jones reported the nuisance to me. I hinspected it. It was the prisoner's, Sir.

COLONEL: Corporal Jones! Your evidence.

CORPORAL JONES: Sir, on the said date I was crossing the barrack square, when I saw prisoner in a sitting posture. He was committing excreta, Sir. I took his name and reported to the orderly-sergeant, Sir.

COLONEL: Well, Private Davies, what have you to say for yourself?

99 DAVIES (*in a nervous sing-song*): Sir, I came over queer all of a sudden, Sir. I haad the diarrhoeas terrible baad. I haad to do it, Sir.

COLONEL: But, my good man, the latrine was only a few yards away.

99 DAVIES: Colonel, Sir, you caan't stop nature!

SERGEANT-MAJOR: Don't answer an officer like that! (*Pause*)

SERGEANT TIMMINS (*coughs*): Sir?

COLONEL: Yes, Sergeant Timmins?

SERGEANT TIMMINS: Sir, I had occasion to hexamine the nuisance, Sir, *and it was done with a heffort, Sir!*

COLONEL: Do you take my punishment, Private Davies?

99 DAVIES: Yes, Colonel, Sir.

COLONEL: You have done a very dirty act, and disgraced the regiment and your comrades. I shall make an example of you. Ten days' detention.

SERGEANT-MAJOR: Escort and prisoner, left *turn!* Quick *march!* Left wheel! (*Offstage*): Escort and prisoner, *halt!* Cap on! March him off to the Guard Room. Get ready the next case!

Despite such moments, Graves was proud to be in so self-respecting a regiment as the Royal Welch Fusiliers, a mark of whose distinction was the "flash," a fanlike cluster of five black ribbons attached to the back of the tunic collar. The Army Council had some doubts about permitting the regiment this irregular privilege, but the Royal Welch resisted all attempts to take it away.

Graves's pride in it is enacted in this little bit of theater, warmly sentimental this time, set in Buckingham Palace:

> Once, in 1917, when an officer of my company went to be decorated with the Military Cross at Buckingham Palace, King George, as Colonel-in-Chief of the Regiment, showed a personal interest in the flash. . . . The King gave him the order "About turn!," for a look at the flash, and the "About turn!" again. "Good," he said, "You're still wearing it, I see," and then, in a stage whisper: "Don't ever let anyone take it from you!"

That is typical of Graves's theatrical method: the scene is a conventional, almost ritual confrontation between character types representative of widely disparate classes who are presented externally by their physical presence and their dialogue. We feel that the King would not be playing the scene properly if his whisper were anything but a *stage-whisper*: after all, the audience wants to hear what he's saying.

Posted to France as a replacement officer in the spring of 1915, Graves disgustedly finds himself assigned to the sad and battered Welsh Regiment, consisting largely of poorly trained scourings and leavings. His platoon includes a man named Burford who is sixty-three years old, and another, Bumford, aged fifteen. These two draw together with a theatrical symmetry which might be predicted from the similarity of their names: "Old Burford, who is so old that he refuses to sleep with the other men of the platoon, has found a private doss in an out-building among some farm tools. . . . Young Bumford is the only man he'll talk to." We are expected to credit this entirely traditional symmetrical arrangement with the same willing suspension of disbelief which enables us to enjoy the following traditional turn. Two men appear before the adjutant and report that they've just shot their company sergeant major.

> The Adjutant said: "Good heavens, how did that happen?"
> "It was an accident, Sir."
> "What do you mean, you damn fools? Did you mistake him for a spy?"
> "No, Sir, we mistook him for our platoon sergeant."

Punch again.

After some months in and out of the line near Béthune, Graves finally joins the Second Battalion of his own regiment near Laventie, and his pride in it suffers a sad blow. He is horrified to find the senior regular officers bullies who forbid the temporary subalterns, or "warts," whiskey in the mess and ignore them socially for a period of six months except to rag and insult them whenever possible. He is humiliated by the colonel, the second-in-command, and the adjutant just as he had been humiliated by the "Bloods" at Charterhouse. But he finds one man to respect, Captain Thomas, his company commander. It is he who must direct the company's part in a preposterous attack, which begins as farce and ends as Grand Guignol.

The operation order Thomas brings from battalion headquarters is ridiculously optimistic, and as he reads it off, Graves and his fellow officers—including a subaltern called "The Actor"—can't help laughing.

> "What's up?" asked Thomas irritably.
> The Actor giggled: "Who in God's name is responsible for this little effort?"
> "Don't know," Thomas said. "Probably Paul the Pimp, or someone like that." (Paul the Pimp was a captain on the Divisional Staff, young, inexperienced, and much disliked. He "wore red tabs upon his chest, And even on his undervest.")

Thomas reveals that their attack is to be only a diversion to distract the enemy while the real attack takes place well to the right.

> "Personally, I don't give a damn either way. We'll get killed whatever happens."
> We all laughed.

The attack is to be preceded by a forty-minute discharge of gas from cylinders in the trenches. For security reasons the gas is euphemized as "the accessory." When it is discovered that the management of the gas is in the hands of a gas company officered by chemistry dons from London University, morale hits a comic rock-bottom. "Of course they'll bungle it," says Thomas. "How could they do anything else?" Not only is the gas bungled: everything goes wrong. The storeman stumbles and spills all the rum in the trench just before the company goes over; the new type of grenade won't work in the dampness; the colonel departs for the rear with a slight cut on his hand; a crucial German machine gun is left undestroyed; the German artillery has the whole exercise taped. The gas is supposed to be blown across by favorable winds. When the great moment proves entirely calm, the gas company sends back the message "Dead calm. Impossible discharge accessory," only to be ordered by the staff, who like characters in farce are entirely obsessed, mechanical, and unbending: "Accessory to be discharged at all costs." The gas, finally discharged after the discovery that most of the wrenches for releasing it won't fit, drifts out and then settles back into the British trenches. Men are going over and rapidly coming back, and we hear comically contradictory crowd noises: " 'Come on!' 'Get back, you bastards!' 'Gas turning on us!'

'Keep your heads, you men!' 'Back like hell, boys!' 'Whose orders?' 'What's happening?' 'Gas!' 'Back!' 'Come on!' 'Gas!' 'Back!' " A "bloody balls-up" is what the troops called it. Historians call it the Battle of Loos.

(A word about the rhetoric of "Impossible discharge accessory." That message falls into the category of Cablegram Humor, a staple of Victorian and Georgian comedy. Graves loves it. Compare his 1957 version of Wordsworth's "The Solitary Reaper" in Cable-ese: "SOLITARY HIGHLAND LASS REAPING BINDING GRAIN STOP MELANCHOLY SONG OVERFLOWS PROFOUND VALE.")

As the attack proceeds, farce gradually modulates to something more serious but no less theatrical. One platoon officer, attacking the untouched German machine gun in short rushes, "jumped up from his shell-hole, waved and signalled 'Forward!' "

> Nobody stirred.
> He shouted: "You bloody cowards, are you leaving me to go on alone?"
>
> His platoon-sergeant, groaning with a broken shoulder, gasped: "Not cowards, Sir. Willing enough. But they're all f——ing dead." The . . . machine-gun, traversing, had caught them as they rose to the whistle.

At the end of the attack Graves and the Actor were the only officers left in the company.

After this, "a black depression held me," Graves says. And his worsening condition finds its correlative in the collapse of his ideal image of Dick, at home. The news reaches him that sixteen-year-old Dick has made "a certain proposal" to a Canadian corporal stationed near Charterhouse and has been arrested and bound over for psychiatric treatment. "This news," says Graves, "nearly finished me. I decided that Dick had been driven out of his mind by the War. . . . with so much slaughter about, it would be easy to think of him as dead." (The real Dick, by the way, was finally "cured" by Dr. W. H. R. Rivers, Sassoon's and Owen's alienist at Craiglockhart.) This whole matter of Dick and his metamorphosis from what Graves calls a "pseudo-homosexual" into a real one lies at the heart of Good-bye to All That. Its importance was clearer in the first edition, where Graves says,

> In English preparatory and public schools romance is necessarily homosexual. The opposite sex is despised and hated, treated as something obscene. Many boys never recover from this perversion. I only recovered by a shock at the age of twenty-one. For every one born homo-sexual there are at least ten permanent pseudo-homo-sexuals

made by the public school system. And nine of these ten are as honorably chaste and sentimental as I was.

In 1957 Graves deleted one sentence: "I only recovered by a shock at the age of twenty-one." The shock was his discovery that he had been deceived by pleasant appearances: a relation he had thought beneficially sentimental now revealed itself to have been instinct with disaster. It was like the summer of 1914. It makes a telling parallel with Graves's discovery—"Never such innocence again" —that the Second Battalion of the Royal Welch Fusiliers, a few company-grade officers and men excepted, is a collection of bullies, knaves, cowards, and fools.

He is delighted to find himself transferred to the more humane First Battalion in November 1915. There he meets Sassoon, as well as Sassoon's "Dick," Lieutenant David Thomas. The three become inseparable friends while the battalion begins its long rehearsals for the breakout and open warfare it assumes will follow the Somme attack in the spring. Life in billets offers opportunities for numerous caricature scenes. One takes place in the theaterlike setting of a disused French schoolroom, where the officers of the battalion are addressed by their furious colonel. He has noticed slackness, he says, and as he designates an instance of it, he falls naturally into the Graves mode of theatrical anecdote, complete with a consciousness of social distinctions and the "lines" appropriate to different social players:

> I have here principally to tell you of a very disagreeable occurrence. As I left my Orderly Room this morning, I came upon a group of soldiers. . . . One of these soldiers was in conversation with a lance-corporal. You may not believe me, but it is a fact that he addressed the corporal by his Christian name: *he called him Jack!* And the corporal made no protest. . . . Naturally, I put the corporal under arrest. . . . I reduced him to the ranks, and awarded the man Field Punishment for using insubordinate language to an N.C.O.

Listening to this as a member of the "audience," Graves is aware of the "part" he himself is playing in this absurd costume drama:

> Myself in faultless khaki with highly polished buttons and belt, revolver at hip, whistle on cord, delicate moustache on upper lip, and stern endeavor a-glint in either eye, pretending to be a Regular Army captain.

But "in real life" he is something quite different, "crushed into that inky desk-bench like an overgrown school-boy."

Back in the line again in March 1916, the battalion has three officers killed in one night, including David Thomas. "My breaking-point was near now," Graves recognizes, and he speculates on the way his nervous collapse, when it comes, will look to spectators. His view of it is typically externalized, the telltale gestures visualized as if beheld by someone watching a character on stage: "It would be a general nervous collapse, with tears and twitchings and dirtied trousers; I had seen cases like that." His transfer back to the hated Second Battalion is hardly a happy omen, and in early July 1916, he finds himself in incredible circumstances near High Wood on the Somme. On July 20, his luck runs out: a German shell goes off close behind him, and a shell fragment hits him in the back, going right through his lung. He is in such bad shape at the dressing-station that his colonel, assuming he's dying, kindly writes his parents, informing them that he has gone. As a result his name appears in the official casualty list: he has "Died of Wounds."

A few days later Graves manages to write home and assure his parents that he is going to recover. There is some discrepancy about dates here: for symbolic and artistic reasons, Graves wants the report of his death to coincide with his twenty-first birthday (July 24), although his father remembers the date as earlier. "One can sympathize with Graves," says George Stade, "who as a poet and scholar has always preferred poetic resonance to the dull monotone of facts; and to die on a twenty-first birthday is to illustrate a kind of poetic justice.

Back in hospital in London, Graves is delighted by the combined comedy and melodrama of a clipping from the Court Circular of the *Times*: "Captain Robert Graves, Royal Welch Fusiliers, officially reported died of wounds, wishes to inform his friends that he is recovering from his wounds at Queen Alexandra's Hospital, Highgate, N." Almost immediately, he quotes another funny document, the infamous propaganda pamphlet containing a letter by "a Little Mother" reprehending any thought of a negotiated peace and celebrating the sacrifice of British mothers who have "given" their sons. It is sentimental, blood-thirsty, complacent, cruel, fatuous, and self-congratulatory, all at once, and ("of course," Graves would say) it is accompanied by a train of earnest illiterate testimonials from third-rate newspapers, noncombatant soldiers, and bereaved mothers, one of whom says: "I have lost my two dear boys, but since I was shown the 'Little Mother's' beautiful letter a resignation too perfect to describe has calmed all my aching sorrow, and I would now gladly give my sons twice over."

It is at this point in *Good-bye to All That* that we may become aware of how rich the book is in fatuous, erroneous, or preposterous written "texts" and documents, the normal materials of serious "history" but here exposed in all their farcical ineptitude and error. Almost all of them—even Sassoon's "A Sol-dier's Declaration"—have in common some dissociation from actuality or some fatal error in assumption or conclusion. Their variety is striking, and there are so many that Graves felt he could cut one entirely from the 1957 edition, the priceless letter at the end of chapter 2 from an amateur gentlewoman poet, instinctively praising Graves's very worst poem and at the same time slyly begging a loan with a long, rambling, self-celebrating paranoid tale of having been cheated of an inheritance. There is the "question and answer history book" of his boyhood, which begins

QUESTION: Why were the Britons so called?
ANSWER: Because they painted themselves blue.

There are the propaganda news clippings about the priests of Antwerp, hung upside down as human clappers in their own church bells. There is the laughable Loos attack order, and the optimistic orders, all based on false premises, written on field message forms. There is the colonel's letter deposing not merely that Graves is dead but that he was "very gallant." There is the erroneous casualty list and the Letter of the Little Mother. There is the farcical mistransmission in Morse code that sends a battalion destined for York to Cork instead. There is an autograph collector's disoriented letter to Thomas Hardy, beginning

Dear Mr. Hardy,
    I am interested to know why the devil you don't reply to my request.

There are the lunatic examination-papers written by three of Graves's students of "English Literature" at the University of Cairo. And in the new epilogue, written in 1957, there is the news that one reason Graves was suspected of being a German spy while harboring in South Devon during the Second War is that someone made a silly, lying document out of a vegetable marrow in his garden by surreptitiously scratching "HEIL HITLER!" on it. The point of all these is not just humankind's immense liability to error, folly, and psychosis. It is also the dubiousness of a rational—or at least a clear-sighted—historiography. The documents on which a work of "history" might be based are so wrong or so loathsome or so silly or so downright mad that no one could immerse himself in them for long, Graves implies, without coming badly unhinged.

The Letter from the Little Mother is the classic case in point and crucial to the whole unraveling, satiric effect of *Good-bye to All That*. One of Graves's readers, "A Soldier Who Has Served All Over the World," perceived as much and wrote Graves:

You are a discredit to the Service, disloyal to your comrades and typical of that miserable breed which tries to gain notoriety by belittling others. Your language is just "water-closet," and evidently your regiment resented such an undesirable member. The only good page is that quoting the beautiful letter of The Little Mother, but even there you betray the degenerate mind by interleaving it between obscenities.

A pity that letter wasn't available to be included in *Good-bye to All That*. It is the kind of letter we can imagine Ben Jonson receiving many of.

By November 1916, Graves is well enough to put on his uniform again—the entry and exit holes in the tunic neatly mended—and rejoin the Depot Battalion for reposting. He is soon back with the Second Battalion on the Somme, where he is secretly delighted to find that all his enemies, the regular officers, have been killed or wounded: it makes the battalion a nicer place and fulfills the angry prophecy Graves had uttered when he first joined and had been bullied in the Officers' Mess at Laventie: "You damned snobs! I'll survive you all. There'll come a time when there won't be one of you left in the Battalion to remember this Mess at Laventie." But the weakness in Graves's lung is beginning to tell, and he is returned to England with "bronchitis." He finds himself first in the hospital at Somerville College, Oxford, and then recuperating anomalously and comically at Queen Victoria's Osborne, on the Isle of Wight.

It is while at Osborne that he sees Sassoon's Declaration. He is appalled at the risk of court martial Sassoon is taking and distressed by Sassoon's political and rhetorical naïveté: "Nobody would follow his example, either in England or in Germany." The public temper had already found its spokesman in the Little Mother: "The War would inevitably go on until one side or the other cracked." Graves gets out of Osborne, rigs Sassoon's medical board, and testifies before it. He bursts into tears "three times" and is told, "Young man, you ought to be before this board yourself." His dramaturgy is successful, and Sassoon is sent to Craiglockhart for "cure." Graves tells us that there Sassoon first met Wilfred Owen, "an idealistic homosexual with a religious background." At least that is what he wanted to tell us in the American edition (the Anchor Books paperback) of the 1957 reissue. The phrase was omitted from the British edition at the request of Harold Owen, and it was subsequently canceled in the American edition. It does not now appear in any edition of *Good-bye to All That*. Just as Graves always knew they would, respectability and disingenuousness have won. Just as Graves learned during the war, written documents remain a delusive guide to reality.

He is now classified B-1, "fit for garrison service abroad," but despite his hope to be sent to Egypt or Palestine, he spends the rest of the war training troops in England and Ireland. In January 1918, he married the feminist Nancy

Nicolson: "Nancy had read the marriage-service [another funny document] for the first time that morning, and been so disgusted that she all but refused to go through with the wedding":

> Another caricature scene to look back on: myself striding up the red carpet, wearing field-boots, spurs and sword; Nancy meeting me in a blue-check silk wedding dress, utterly furious; packed benches on either side of the church, full of relatives; aunts using handkerchiefs; the choir boys out of tune; Nancy savagely muttering the responses, myself shouting them in a parade-ground voice.

The news of the Armistice, he says, brought him no pleasure; rather, it "sent me out walking alone . . . , cursing and sobbing and thinking of the dead."

Demobilized, he instantly catches Spanish influenza and almost dies of it. He recovers in Wales, where for almost a year he tries to shake off the war:

> I was still mentally and nervously organized for War. Shells used to come bursting on my bed at midnight, even though Nancy shared it with me; strangers in daytime would assume the faces of friends who had been killed. When strong enough to climb the hill behind Harlech . . . , I could not help seeing it as a prospective battlefield. I would find myself working out tactical problems, planning . . . where to place a Lewis gun if I were trying to rush Dolwreiddiog Farm from the brow of the hill, and what would be the best cover for my rifle-grenade section.

Some legacies of the war ran even deeper, and one, perhaps, has had literary consequences: "I still had the Army habit of commandeering anything of uncertain ownership that I found lying about; also a difficulty in telling the truth." His experience of the Army had ratified his fierce insistence on his independence, and he swore "on the very day of my demobilization never to be under anyone's orders for the rest of my life. Somehow I must live by writing." In October 1919, he entered Oxford to study English Literature, living five miles out, at Boar's Hill, where he knew Blunden, Masefield, and Robert Nichols. There he and Nancy briefly ran a small general store while he wrote poems as well as his academic thesis, brilliantly titled—the war had certainly handed him the first three words—*The Illogical Element in English Poetry*.

"The Illogical Element in the Experience of Robert Graves" might be the title of the episode that closes *Good-bye to All That*. He takes up the position of Professor of English Literature at the ridiculous Royal Egyptian University, Cairo. The student essays are so funny and hopeless that as an honest man he can't go on. After saying that "Egypt gave me plenty of caricature scenes to look back on," he approaches the end of the book in a final flurry of anecdotes and vignettes, most of them farcical, and concludes with a brief paragraph summarizing his life from 1926 to 1929, which he says has been "dramatic," with "new characters [appearing] on the stage." All that is left is disgust and exile.

Compared with both Blunden and Sassoon, Graves is very little interested in "nature" or scenery: human creatures are his focus, and his book is built, as theirs are not, very largely out of dialogue. And compared with Sassoon, who is remarkably gentle with his characters and extraordinarily "nice" to them, Graves, who had, as Sassoon once told him, "a first-rate nose for anything nasty," sees his as largely a collection of knaves and fools. Almost literally: one can go through *Good-bye to All That* making two lists, one of knaves, one of fools, and the two lists will comprise ninety per cent of the characters. As a memoirist, Graves seems most interested not in accurate recall but in recovering moments when he most clearly perceives the knavery of knaves and the foolishness of fools. For him as for D. H. Lawrence, knavery and folly are the style of the war, and one of the very worst things about it is that it creates a theater perfectly appropriate for knavery and folly. It brings out all the terrible people.

If Graves, the scourge of knaves and fools, is the heir of Ben Jonson, it can be seen that Joseph Heller is the heir of Graves. And the very theatricality of *Catch-22* is a part of what Heller has learned from *Good-bye to All That*. *Catch-22* resembles less a "novel" than a series of blackout skits, to such a degree that it was an easy matter for Heller to transform the work into a "dramatization" in 1971. Another legatee of Graves is Evelyn Waugh, whose *Sword of Honor* trilogy does to the Second War what Graves did to the First. Waugh's book is made up of the same farcical high-jinks, the same kind of ironic reversals, all taking place in the Graves atmosphere of balls-up and confusion. Indeed, both Graves and Waugh include characters who deliver the line, "Thank God we've got a Navy." If Loos is the characteristic absurd disaster to Graves, Crete is Waugh's version. Waugh's sense of theater is as conspicuous as Graves's, although it tends to invoke more pretentious genres than farce. During the rout on Crete, a small sports car drives up: "Sprawled in the back, upheld by a kneeling orderly, as though in gruesome parody of a death scene from grand opera, lay a dusty and bloody New Zealand officer." Both Graves and Waugh have written fiction-memoirs, although Graves's is a fiction disguised as a memoir while Waugh's is a memoir disguised as a fiction. To derive Waugh's trilogy, one would superadd the farce in *Good-bye to All That* to the moral predicament of Ford's Tietjens in *Parade's End*: this would posit Guy Crouchback, Waugh's victim-hero, as well as establish a world where the broad joke of Apthorpe's thunder-box coexists harmoniously with messy and meaningless violent death. And both Waugh and Heller would be as ready as Graves to agree with the proposition that comedy alone is suitable for us.

PATRICK J. KEANE

A Wild Civility

One of the very few poems of his own that Graves admits into *The White Goddess*, "On Portents" is used in that context to illustrate an extension of the doctrine of proleptic thought: that, "in the poetic act, time is suspended and details of future experience often become incorporated in the poem, as they do in dreams." Beginning with this markedly Yeatsian precursor of the theme poems, [this] section will move toward those poems in which the Goddess makes her major appearances.

> If strange things happen where she is,
> So that men say that graves open
> And the dead walk, or that futurity
> Becomes a womb and the unborn are shed,
> Such portents are not to be wondered at,
> Being tourbillions in Time made
> By the strong pulling of her bladed mind
> Through that ever-reluctant element.

The "she" of "On Portents" reflects the Isis of Apuleius and of Plutarch, whose "On Isis and Osiris" Graves was reading during the period of the poem's composition (1929–31). She also, as J. M. Cohen has observed, "shares with Yeats's Maud Gonne the capacity for disturbing history." This will draw no argument from readers of, say, "No Second Troy," where Yeats's Helen—no more "to be wondered at" than Graves's Goddess—is absolved of all blame for

From *A Wild Civility*. © 1980 by the Curators of the University of Missouri. University of Missouri Press, 1980.

her "violent ways" in a passage that may have suggested one element of the
weaponlike mind, and perhaps even Graves's syntactical construction pivoting on
"Being":

> What could have made her peaceful with a mind
> That nobleness made simple as a fire,
> With beauty like a tightened bow, a kind
> That is not natural in an age like this,
> Being high and solitary and most stern?

But "On Portents" may be still more Yeatsian. Graves's curious image of
gyrelike "tourbillions" made by cutting through time recalls a curious image
employed by Yeats in another of his celebrations of a strong woman, in this case
Augusta Gregory. Yeats describes, as a less violent but equally irresistible strong
pulling, the capacity of that "woman's powerful character" to keep her literary
acolytes in concentrated formation, so that, seeming "to whirl upon a compass-
point," they found

> certainty upon the dreaming air,
> The intellectual sweetness of those lines
> That cut through time or cross it withershins.

The possibility that Graves may have been familiar with the poem (first
published in 1931) is enhanced by the presence of what seems to be a variation
on the Yeatsian image in Graves's "The Felloe'd Year," the thematic twin of "On
Portents." There, the poet, admitting that he is caught up in the "creak and
groan" of the painfully turning wheel of the seasons in which all still move,
prays that "the twelve spokes of this round felloe'd year / Be a fixed compass,
not a turning wheel."

Though it is an "ever-reluctant element," time is of a most equivocal
nature. It can be suspended—fixed upon a compass point—by the poet in the
act of creation, the poet's work being done, as Blake says, in the momentary
pulsation of an artery, in what Wordsworth calls a spot of time. More violently,
it can be cut through by the propellerlike mind of the "woman genius" or of the
Muse Goddess herself, whose symbol is the double-bladed ax. Or it can be
crossed in a contrariwise direction—"withershins," in Yeats's word, a word
known to Graves, who tells us of a witch charged with "dancing widdershins"
around men's houses while stark naked, a tourbillion that "portended ill-luck."
And, thanks to a book that both poets studied closely in 1931, time can be
demonstrated to be "not the stable moving-staircase that prose-men have for
centuries pretended it to be, but an unaccountable wibble-wobble" (to quote
Graves's synopsis of J. W. Dunne's *Experiments with Time* in support of what is
said about time in "On Portents"). The Mad Hatter's tea party still goes on.

This conception of time as a wibble-wobble—an unsteady, alternating zigzag—accords with Graves's penchant for flying crooked. Yet in "The Felloe'd Year" (a strong poem unaccountably never reprinted after its first appearance), he acknowledges his Ixion-like bondage and is reduced to "praying" that he be exempted from the inexorable turning of the temporal wheel, that the seasonal and zodiacal spokes of the year might radiate inward to a fixed compass point rather than outward to the wheel's necessarily restricting rim. In romantic poetry, the shattering of the prose-men's conception of time as stable often takes the form of a radical conflation. We hear of "the Bard who present, past, & future sees" (Blake); of "Ancestral voices prophesying war" (Coleridge); of "what is past, or passing, or to come" (Yeats). In "On Portents," Graves's analeptic and proleptic methods of thought coalesce in a suspended present in which "graves open / And the dead walk," while, simultaneously, "futurity / Becomes a womb and the unborn are shed." Complete triumph over time, in occult and romantic texts alike, tends to take the form of an inward whirling to a centripetal center. In the hero's initiatory purification in Graves's "Instructions to the Orphic Adept," one of his most rhythmically compelling performances, we return to such a still point. Completion of the ritual takes man "Out of the weary wheel, the circling years, / To that still, spokeless wheel:—Persephone."

For both Graves and Yeats, the power to make her chosen men "perne in a gyre" is possessed only by woman—in Graves's case, the Muse Goddess, in her various mythological forms or as incarnate in a mortal woman; for Yeats, as resident in the tourbillion Maud Gonne (or, as in "Coole Park, 1929," in the sweet disciplinarian Augusta Gregory). Always present are the elements of discipline, compulsion, and the devotee's persistent effort throughout the exacting ordeal. The Orphic initiate must, for example, be able to answer the climactic question by emphasizing his own effort in the required submission: "My feet have borne me here." Above all, man must submit to woman's judgment. In the "fundamental relation," which is between male and female mind, "the female mind is the judge, and the male mind the subject of judgment." Thus spake Laura Riding, the "woman genius" Graves had in mind when he wrote "On Portents." This seems tyrannous; but then, as Lucius says of Isis in *The Golden Ass* (which Graves thinks the fullest depiction of the Goddess in literature), "Her service is perfect freedom." Resenting St. Augustine's Christian cribbing from Apuleius and his application of the phrase to "the ideally benign Father-god," Graves has made Lucius's address his motto and transformed Isis into his own Goddess.

It is significant that "On Portents," so proleptic of Graves's future direction, was placed in the fifth and final section of the 1938 *Collected Poems*, part of a small group of lyrics that, according to Graves's foreword, express "a more immediate sense of poetic liberation"—though it is a liberation "achieved,"

Graves adds, "not by mysticism but by practical persistence." In "On Portents," that persistence takes the form, first, of the Goddess's own efforts to overcome resistance. But it is the poet-lover who is caught up in the turbulence made by the strong pulling of her bladed mind. Clearly, service to the Goddess—then incarnate in Laura Riding, who had as bladed a mind as even Graves could wish—must take the form of a freedom to be achieved only after considerable difficulty, and pain, on the part of her acolyte.

The more-than-metaphoric significance of that "bladed" mind is stressed in the final stanza of "End of Play," in this same concluding section of the 1938 *Collected Poems*. At the end of "pastime" (presided over by a "foolish smiling Mary-mantle blue" sky), childish illusions are put away by those who have ceased idling and—that familiar imperative—"tell no lies now." Gone is the shallow faith of weaklings who, "on their knees / Call lugubriously upon chaste Christ." So much for Christianity, including Mariolatry, about which Graves is usually less severe; that it is St. Paul who is echoed in this putting away of the things of a child is, of course, a typically Gravesian irony. Gone too are both "hypocritic pomp" and "bestial sensuality," with its "frantic laceration of naked breasts."

> Yet love survives, the word carved on a sill
> Under antique dread of the headsman's axe;
> It is the echoing mind, as in the mirror
> We stare at our dazed trunks at the block kneeling.

The awestruck, and imaginatively posthumous, affirmation of love's survival even of the block seems very different in tone from the brusque dismissal of the Christian order with its sentimentalities and dichotomies. Yet the final stanza gathers up the echo-and-mirror imagery of stanza 2—"a mirror and an echo / Mediate henceforth with vision and sound"—and the final effect is one of change within a deeper continuity. The old faith and the old self (equally deluded, childish, idling, mendacious, "romantic") have died; the new, more "mettlesome" faith and self are born—only to be instantly subjected to the ax of an unsentimental, fiercer romanticism. Though this constitutes a new vision, it is revealed, like most things ostensibly new, to be "antique," the adjective Graves later reserves for the "antique story" told in *The White Goddess*. In the imaginative mirror that now mediates that newly reconstructed vision of martyrdom, we stare at our own dazed trunks, victims kneeling in adoration. In Graves as in Yeats, "stare" is part of the vocabulary of the sublime, a verb expressing stunned wonder and, as here, pulsing with daemonic, bloody potential. The primal scene established in these lines will become standard in Graves's mythology; for this is decapitation by a headsman proleptic of the White Goddess: that archetypal axwielder whose bladed mind pulls strongly deep in our own, or at least in Robert Graves's, "echoing mind."

The replacement of the childish viewpoint, again reduced to delusion ("These were all lies"), by a now austere vision is most dramatically embodied in "A Love Story," the masterful opening poem of Graves's next volume. The delusive spring and relentless winter of that poem are then transformed to a genuine midwinter spring in a poem in which the Muse Goddess revives her poet from hibernation ("Mid-Winter Waking," 1939). And the Goddess herself finally appears in all her terrible beauty in three of Graves's most hypnotic, resonant hymns: "To Juan at the Winter Solstice," "Darien," and the quest poem entitled "The White Goddess," where, recalling the mirror and echo of "End of Play," she is called "Sister of the mirage and echo."

"A Love Story" opens theatrically on a symbolic winter moonscape, introduces a reflexively urbane note, then returns to the sublime and a "shiver" as complex as the "shivering glory" of "Sick Love."

> The full moon easterly rising, furious,
> Against a winter sky ragged with red;
> The hedges high in snow, and owls raving—
> Solemnities not easy to withstand:
> A shiver wakes the spine.

The double nature of that shiver, compounded of terror and longing, is developed in the rest of the poem: a fantasia of recollection that moves from boyhood fear through illusory fulfillment of longing to the revelation that the speaker has been the victim of a dangerous deception, fundamentally self-deception. The poem ends on a note that, precisely because it is so perfectly disciplined, suggests temporary quietude rather than permanent paralysis:

> In boyhood, having encountered the scene,
> I suffered horror: I fetched the moon home,
> With owls and snow, to nurse in my head
> Throughout the trials of a new Spring,
> Famine unassuaged.

> But fell in love, and made a lodgement
> Of love on those chill ramparts.
> Her image was my ensign: snows melted,
> Hedges sprouted, the moon tenderly shone,
> The owls trilled with tongues of nightingale.

> These were all lies, though they matched the time,
> And brought me less than luck: her image

Warped in the weather, turned beldamish.
Then back came winter on me at a bound,
The pallid sky heaved with a moon-quake.

Dangerous it had been with love-notes
To serenade Queen Famine.
In tears I recomposed the former scene,
Let the snow lie, watched the moon rise, suffered the owls,
Paid homage to them of unevent.

The stage properties and the final inaction suggest a reworking of an earlier poem we have already glanced at. "Full Moon" also has owl and nightingale and a moon that, "attained to her full height," presides over the "defeat" of lovers who "held the tyrannous moon above / Sole mover of their fate." Both "queens" adumbrate the archetype, Queen Famine being the White Goddess in her malevolent, ravenous aspect. Just as the young man's sexual and emotional hunger is "unassuaged," so the incarnate queen, in satisfying her need to seduce, whets her appetite for vengeance on the deluded lover whose ensign was her image, bringing him, in Graves's marvelous meiosis, "less than luck."

The vengeance is cruel but, in part at least, justified by his mixture of naiveté and presumption, and by his subsequent complaining. He has been, as Graves would later say, "party to his own betrayal and has no just cause for complaint." The young man's folly in making a "lodgement / Of love on those chill ramparts" is revealed not only in the difficult, precarious, and frigid nature of such a lodgement, but in the insipidity and unnaturalness of snow melting in winter, hedges sprouting, and owls trilling. This, as Kirkham says, is "the poet's sardonic judgment" on the lover's "mistaking a temporary phase of sanguine romanticism for the full reality" of the man-woman relationship, which is in truth a "constantly changing cycle of situations." The Gravesian speaker should admit, as he does in a related poem ("To Sleep"), "Loving in part, I did not see you whole."

When her image, warping in the weather, "turned beldamish" (that is, like a hideous old woman, but with a play on *"La Belle Dame sans Merci"*), the winter that the lover dreamed transformed by love comes "back" on him at a predatory "bound." In his tearful recomposition of the former scene, the tragic wintry bleakness is restored: he let the snow "lie" (unmelted, truthfully inert), "watched the moon rise" ("furious," as it had been at the outset, not domesticated and shining "tenderly"), and "suffered the owls" (enduring their screech, rather than imagining it changed to the romantic song of the nightingale).

In the middle phase, her lunar image had been his ensign; now the "homage" paid to moon, owls, and snow (earlier "nursed" and sentimentally softened in his head) is the passivity of "unevent." It may seem that the death of love in the present (the first and last stanzas) has returned the man, regressively, to the stage of boyhood with its horror of love. But in fact he has advanced, attaining a sort of Wordsworthian sober maturity. In the final lunar phase, coming again to the terrifying scene he encountered as a boy, he knows the place for the first time. He has moved beyond inexperienced dread, delusion, and the hubristic serenading of Queen Famine with facile love notes. Now the poet-lover simply submits, chastened and resigned to his fate as vassal of the moon goddess whose service, Graves will soon announce, is perfect freedom. His homage is of unevent; but there is such a thing as wise (if sad) passiveness, and of course they also serve who only stand and wait. The readiness is all: Graves, examining his own aging face in the mirror, is soon to ask himself why "He still stands ready, with a boy's presumption, / To court the queen in her high silk pavilion" ("The Face in the Mirror"). But the man knows what the boy didn't: the precariousness of that courtship of the Muse.

The compensation and reward for waiting in readiness, one eye open, come in the revivification of "Mid-Winter Waking," a beautiful love lyric and Muse-poet poem with Keatsian echoes:

> Stirring suddenly from long hibernation,
> I knew myself once more a poet
> Guarded by timeless principalities
> Against the worm of death, this hillside haunting;
> And presently dared open both my eyes.

The ambiguity of the syntax allows us to read "this hillside haunting" as referring to either the speaker or "the worm of death." Either way, we are reminded of Keats's dreaming knight-at-arms who, guarded by "pale kings and princes," "awoke and found me here / On the cold hill's side." But in Graves's "waking" (quite different from the knight's, and from the shiver that "wakes" the spine in "A Love Story"), there is union, not abandonment, and, rather than isolated "unevent," the shared event of a true love story.

The remaining two stanzas are gratefully addressed to the mysterious powers of inspiration at the back of the mind and to their external manifestation in "sudden warm airs," winter's harbingers of the fruitful spring to come:

> O gracious, lofty, shone against from under,
> Back-of-the-mind-far clouds like towers;
> And you, sudden warm airs that blow
> Before the expected season of new blossom,
> While sheep still gnaw at roots and lambless go—

> Be witness that on waking, this mid-winter,
> I found her hand in mine laid closely
> Who shall watch out the Spring with me.
> We stared in silence all around us
> But found no winter anywhere to see.

For the conclusion of his poem "Her Triumph," with its sudden revelation and liberation brought by love—"And now we stare astonished at the sea / And a miraculous strange bird shrieks at us"—Yeats turned to the conclusion of the sonnet in which Keats, on first looking into Chapman's Homer, felt like Cortez

> when with eagle eyes
> He stared at the Pacific—and all his men
> Looked at each other with a wild surmise—
> Silent, upon a peak in Darien.

Graves, who took the name of his Goddess's son, Darien, from this sonnet, also alludes to these lines—to better effect than Yeats—in the conclusion of "Mid-Winter Waking": "We stared in silence all around us / But found no winter anywhere to see."

Later in this section of *Collected Poems*, in an exquisite short lyric that combines eternally springing hope and plangent elegy, Graves offers his unimprovable final word on signs of spring in winter:

> She tells her love while half asleep,
>   In the dark hours,
>   With half-words whispered low:
> As Earth stirs in her winter sleep
>   And puts out grass and flowers
>   Despite the snow,
>   Despite the falling snow.

The poem first appeared, as a song Orpheus sings of the dead Eurydice, in Graves's *The Golden Fleece*, the novel he was working on when he was suddenly overwhelmed by the figure of the White Goddess. We turn now to the poems in which she appears, the poems specifically designated by Graves as "Magical."

Randall Jarrell finds these "mythical-archaic" pieces Graves's "richest, most moving, and most consistently beautiful poems—poems that almost deserve the literal *magical*. . . . The best of these are different from anything else in English" (*The Third Book of Criticism*). Before discussing the three most representative of these poems, it may be useful to have Graves's own synopsis of his Muse and her myth.

Whatever her roots in, and reflections of, Graves's own biography and psyche, his Goddess seems essentially an extension of two romantic concerns.

One is the sublime. "The function of poetry," writes Graves, "is religious invocation of the Muse; its use is the experience of mixed exaltation and horror that
her presence excites." The other is the submission to the femme fatale: a poet,
even the nineteenth-century romantic, was, says Graves, "a true poet only in his
fatalistic regard for the Goddess as the mistress who commanded his destiny."
That Graves has in mind particularly the author of "La Belle Dame sans Merci"
and his Muse, Fanny Brawne, is suggested in the conclusion of his most succinct
synopsis of the theme:

> The Theme, briefly, is the antique story . . . of the birth, life, death
> and resurrection of the God of the Waxing Year; the central chapters
> concern the God's losing battle with the God of the Waning Year for
> love of the capricious and all-powerful Threefold Goddess, their
> mother, bride, and layer-out. The poet identifies himself with the
> God of the Waxing Year and his Muse with the Goddess. . . . All
> true poetry—true by Housman's practical test—celebrates some in-
> cident or scene in this very ancient story.

Housman's famous test of a true poem was that the hair bristles if one repeats it
while shaving. Housman didn't explain *why*; Graves does:

> The reason why the hairs stand on end, the eyes water, the throat is
> constricted, the skin crawls and a shiver runs down the spine when
> one writes or reads a true poem is that a true poem is necessarily an
> invocation of the White Goddess, or Muse, the Mother of All Liv-
> ing, the ancient power of fright and lust—the female spider or the
> queen-bee whose embrace is death. Housman offered a secondary
> test of true poetry: whether it matches a phrase of Keats's, "every-
> thing that reminds me of her goes through me like a spear." This is
> equally pertinent to the Theme. Keats was writing under the shadow
> of death about his Muse, Fanny Brawne; and the "spear that roars
> for blood" is the traditional weapon of the dark executioner and
> supplanter.

Execution and supplanting are the inevitable denouement; but Graves,
counting the beats of his single theme, covers a considerable spectrum. The
Goddess is at her most terrible in "The Destroyers" and the even more sardonic
"Dethronement" (dropped in 1965), in which the lover's "true anguish / Is all
that she requires." She is at her most winning, for me, as Ariadne, in that
splendid exposure of male egotism and self-deception, "Theseus and Ariadne,"
which ends with the deserted woman a triumphant moon goddess, "Playing the
queen" to the "nobler company" of the lover who succeeded ignorant Theseus
when he abandoned her on Naxos: the god Dionysus.

In between are those central demonstrations of Graves's wild civility, the poems in which the Goddess is both terrible and beautiful. It is not necessary to reproduce the elaborate glosses, by Graves and others, that have accumulated around the best known of these—the best known, indeed, of all Graves's poems. The critic's function in discussing "To Juan at the Winter Solstice" is, in fact, largely reduced to annotation, a flaw in the poem if judged by Graves's own criterion: plain expression requiring no "learned" glosses. As an epitomization of *The White Goddess*, the poem provides a remarkable synopsis of its "antique story" of the solar hero's relationship with the Triple Goddess, his union with her, and his inevitable death at her hands or by her command. Whatever stories his newborn son Juan may eventually tell—whether of trees, or beasts, or birds, or stars; of the Virgin compounded of Aphrodite and Rahab, or of Ophion, the "undying snake from chaos hatched"—it will always be the same story, to which

> all lines or lesser gauds belong
> That startle with their shining
> Such common stories as they stray into.

Like the son to whom the poem is addressed, we are preempted from originality. It's all in *The White Goddess*, with everything *not* there reduced by definition to the "common," brightened only by the fortuitous intermixture of stray threads from the monomyth. The truly "magical" thing about "To Juan at the Winter Solstice" is that, despite Graves's exclusive claim-staking and thematic reductiveness, the poem itself is a triumph of incantatory resonance. I will be suggesting that what the poem gains in the awestruck power of the sublime, it pays for in human terms. But first that power must be granted. Even the grimmest cyclical determinism, that governing the life-and-death cycle of the Goddess's consort, is made exultant, shot through as it is with the constellated light of the turning zodiac:

> Water to water, ark again to ark,
> From woman back to woman:
> So each new victim treads unfalteringly
> The never altered circuit of his fate,
> Bringing twelve peers as witness
> Both to his starry rise and starry fall.

To appreciate these lines it is not really necessary to know that solar heroes, traditionally born at the winter solstice, reappear in reincarnated form at that time, floating on a waterborne ark; nor that the "twelve peers"—like Christ's apostles and like knights Arthurian and French—personify the months of the year and the signs of the zodiac. Nor do we need glosses from *The White*

Goddess on owl, elder tree, and Yule log in order to respond to the eerie power of the penultimate stanza:

> Much snow is falling, winds roar hollowly,
> The owl hoots from the elder,
> Fear in your heart cries to the loving-cup:
> Sorrow to sorrow as the sparks fly upward.
> The log groans and confesses:
> There is one story and one story only.

Following these death-haunted lines—their acceleration resolved in the finality of the repetition, "There is one story and one story only"—we are left to ponder the imponderable: the ambivalent threefold nature of the Goddess herself:

> Dwell on her graciousness, dwell on her smiling,
> Do not forget what flowers
> The great boar trampled down in ivy time.
> Her brow was creamy as the crested wave,
> Her sea-grey eyes were wild
> But nothing promised that is not performed.

Though Graves denied Eliot the right to mythopoeic conflation, taking him to task for inaccurately locating Agamemnon's death in a bloody wood in "Sweeney Among the Nightingales," he does some conflating of his own here. The boar that killed so many solar heroes, among them Aphrodite's beloved, Adonis, is set trampling flowers at "ivy time"—that is, during October, which is both the boar-hunting season and the time of the revels of the Maenads. Frenzied priestesses of Dionysus, they chewed ivy as an intoxicant and would tear to pieces any man who interrupted their autumnal rites. No one who has read *The Bacchae*, and is here asked to "dwell on her graciousness, dwell on her smiling," is likely to forget the fate of Pentheus or Euripides' emphasis on the ever-smiling, inscrutable, destructive Dionysus.

Nevertheless, Juan is to dwell on this graciousness and smiling. The equivalent Yeatsian text is "A Prayer for My Daughter," in which the newborn child is advised to cultivate a kindlier beauty and to concentrate upon the gentler, more benign aspects of life. In both cases, the admonishing fathers acknowledge, implicitly or explicitly, their own fatal attraction to the fiercer aspects of that terrible beauty they join in celebrating. But where Yeats ends, as Coleridge does in "Frost at Midnight," with a prayer that his child enjoy a very different and serene fate, Graves's inexorable myth presses him to warn his son that whatever aspect of the Goddess he may concentrate on, she will inevitably turn as murderous as the Maenads. Yet, at the same time, she remains beautiful—creamybrowed and with eyes that, like la belle dame's, "were wild." "But" (and this is the final turn in the poem) everything that has been promised will be performed. During the time of allotted union, she shall bring her devotee love and inspiration —until the time comes for the ax to fall, as fall it must. Hence the negative construction of the final affirmation: "nothing promised that is not performed."

The Goddess is exacting, but just. She is also irresistible—an Aphrodite holding forth the promise both of sensuous bliss and of an experience that can end in only one way. There are no surprises, in either the myth or the poem: her graciousness and smiling are marked as ambivalent and fatal back in the central stanza. There, after being depicted both as a virgin, pure in her celestial "silver beauty," and as promiscuously sublunar, even subhuman ("all fish below the thighs"), she appears in an iconographic pose, gesturing, "her lips curved" (to quote "Rhea," another Goddess-poem) "In a half-smile archaic":

> She in her left hand bears a leafy quince;
> When with her right she crooks a finger, smiling,
> How may the King hold back?
> Royally then he barters life for love.

If we let the poem do its work, the bargain with the Goddess seems worth it; we may suspend disbelief in the myth and allow Graves's architectural skill, the magnificence of his imagery and hypnagogic rhythms, to persuade us that he has made the vicissitudes of the man-woman relationship into "something like a Mystery play, which gives ritual shape to the varied incidents of a love story"; that "all the painfulness of love is here but impersonalized by its association with the full conception of love's meaning embodied in the Myth—of which suffering is only a necessary part." This is to see the sacred drama as, ultimately, a divine comedy in which individual agony is subsumed. Just such a ritual shaping and distancing occur in stanza 4 of the "Ode on a Grecian Urn." But Keats never forgets that what he is describing is a "sacrifice." He depicts the protesting victim (though it is merely a heifer) as "lowing at the skies," and makes the stanza end in full recognition of the "desolate" human consequences of participation in the sacrificial rite.

Similarly, in a poem no less dependent on the mythology behind it than "To Juan at the Winter Solstice," Yeats's "Byzantium," the ritualistic "dying into a dance" is yet described as "an agony." And the poem ends in emotional perplexity. The golden smithies of the Emperor and marbles of the dancing floor—emblems of the endorsed ritual of Byzantine "simplicity" and of the artifice of eternity—are twice said to "break" the flood of blood-begotten, un-purged spirits surging into the Holy City. They

> Break bitter furies of complexity,
> Those images that yet
> Fresh images beget,
> That dolphin-torn, that gong-tormented sea.

Ostensibly, chaos is broken by the taming power of art; but the governing power of the verb "break," as Helen Vendler has observed, "is spent long before the end of the stanza is reached, and the last three lines stand syntactically as absolutes." In short, the literally overwhelming climactic sentence pours back into the poem all the turbulent, spawning images—and all the human torment —its marmoreal scenario had ostensibly left behind.

In these examples, Keats and Yeats, for all their ritualistic distancing and impersonalizing of pain, never lose sight of the reality of human suffering. Graves does—even though "To Juan at the Winter Solstice" is addressed to his own son. To clarify the difference, we might cite the nineteenth century's three chief theoreticians of the tragic. In Keats and Yeats, one senses the vision of Kierkegaard, with his emphasis upon the particular individual, rising up to counter that of Hegel, for whom the private grief of the sacrificial victim is absorbed into the all-reconciling universal order. In "To Juan," Graves is the most Hegelian of the three poets. But perhaps all might be brought together under the aegis of Nietzsche, who, while fully aware of the irreplaceability of individuals, wistfully longs to circumscribe suffering within a fuller glory—a "higher, overmastering joy" and order so transforming terror that "lamentation itself becomes a song of praise" (*The Birth of Tragedy*).

Lamentation becomes a song of praise, though not without an admixture of uncertainty, in another mythological love poem, "Darien." The poem begins in the present tense:

> It is a poet's privilege and fate
> To fall enamoured of the one Muse
> Who variously haunts this island earth.

The next line shifts tenses and reveals the poem to be, like "To Juan," a quasi-dramatic monologue: "She was your mother, Darien." The direct address of father to son is surprising here given the burden of what follows: the sacrificial death of the father in order to bring his (and her) son into the world. Before encountering that paradox, however, let us have Graves's elaborate description of the Muse Goddess:

> She was your mother, Darien,
> And presaged by the darting halcyon bird

> Would run green-sleeved along her ridges,
> Treading the asphodels and heather-trees
> With white feet bare.
>
> Often at sunrise I had watched her go,
> And a cold shudder shook me
> To see the curved blaze of her Cretan axe.
> Averted her set face, her business
> Not yet with me, long-striding,
> She would ascend the peak and pass from sight.
> But once at full moon, by the sea's verge,
> I came upon her without warning.
>
> Unrayed she stood, with long hair streaming,
> A cockle-shell cupped in her warm hands,
> Her axe propped idly on a stone.
>
> No awe possessed me, only a great grief;
> Wanly she smiled, but would not lift her eyes
> (As a young girl will greet the stranger).

His reaction is ambivalent. Does his grief reflect hers, that of a shy young girl deterministically trapped (like Coleridge's Geraldine or one of Hardy's "Subalterns") in her cruel, archetypal role? Or was he grieved essentially because he realized his time was at hand? Or because she had not yet marked him for her own? She too was uncertain. When he spoke to her (" 'See who has come,' I said"), she answered: " 'If I lift my eyes to yours / And our eyes marry, man, what then? / Will they engender my son Darien?' " She shares the procreant urge of Yeats's swan-god, but the issue, though named, remains occult, the sense of concealed mystery extending to her final description of that son as "Guardian of the *hid* treasures of the world."

One thing, however, is certain. Observing the anticipatory trembling of the Goddess's hands, the man recognized, and accepted, his fate: I knew then . . . / For whom that flawless blade would sweep: / My own oracular head, swung by its hair." He had no need then to ask for whom the bell tolled. But as her chosen man, he became the Goddess's prophet as well as her victim. " 'Mistress,' I cried, 'the times are evil / And you have charged me with their remedy.' " In this spirit of apocalyptic romanticism, he pleads only that she "look up, so Darien may be born!"

That request would seem to seal his fate. But the unmistakable implication of the imagery he employs in describing the prophesied son as "deathless," the "topless branch" of the Muse's "unfellable tree," and (climactically) "The new green of my hope" is that in embracing death he is really choosing a new, and rejuvenated, life; praying that, all autumnal foliage gone, he may shoot into a newly greened, vernal joy. That resurrection beyond martyrdom is implicit in the ecstatic final plea, an exclamation both doom-eager and hungry for renewal: " 'Sweetheart,' said I, 'strike now, for Darien's sake!' "

That the poet-lover should be more than half in love with death, that he has such celerity in dying, can be explained only if, reborn phoenixlike from his own sacrifice, he is able to continue singing after his decapitation by the Goddess. This extends the conclusion of "End of Play," where "We stare at our dazed trunks at the block kneeling," and looks forward to Orpheus's question in the later poem "Eurydice": "Is ours a fate can ever be forsworn / Though my lopped head sing to the yet unborn?" The "oracular head" of "Darien" is clearly to be connected with the prophetic head of Orpheus, which recalls for Graves as well the singing head of the decapitated Welsh god Bran (*The Greek Myths* 1:113-14). And all of this bizarre material links up with the ritual sacrifices of mortal man to immortal queen in Yeats's late dance-plays, *The King of the Great Clock Tower* and its revised version, *A Full Moon in March*, in which severed heads also sing on in an oracular strain.

If there is an element here of sadomasochistic savagery parading as mythology, Yeats seems more guilty than Graves. In "Darien," the mythological paradigm supports the poetic theme. Just as the old king, surrogate of the departing year, must be slain to make way for the new, so the middle-aged poet (wrinkled, but, like Darien, "grey-eyed") must willingly yield up his old self in order to create the vital new poetry inherent in his visionary marriage with the Muse—a promise embodied in the living form of their son. Graves's parable is part of that genre so typical of romantic and post-romantic poetry: works about the relationship between the poet and his poem, the sacrifice he makes in order to create. As in Hart Crane's "The Broken Tower," it is the poet's self-sacrifice that liberates his music.

"Only look up, so Darien may be born!" When poet and Muse look at each other it can only be with what Keats calls, in his sonnet of eagle-eyed discovery and wonder, "a wild surmise." For whatever the certitude resident in the deterministic theme, mystery persists at the heart of the actual poem: "What then? / Will [our joined eyes] engender my son Darien?" Though the answer is apparently Yes, this embedded caveat, this element of uncertainty, adds at least some dramatic tension to the narrative. One thing about which there can be little or no doubt is that Keats's poem, the last word of which is "Darien," stands behind Graves's. The new planet that swims into the speaker's ken is Darien himself, the star-son of the Goddess: "the northern star, the spell of knowledge," as his father-to-be calls him in breathless anticipation.

The Goddess's own description of Darien as "Swifter than wind, . . . Untameable," links the poem as well with Shelley's "Ode to the West Wind." That wind, a pestilence-cleansing harbinger of the apocalyptic spring to come, is, like its prophet, "tameless, and swift, and proud," though he is admittedly "less free / Than thou, O uncontrollable." Like Shelley, Graves, his own leaves falling and in sore need, is invoking, *incorporating*, a renovating power capable of driving his dead thoughts over the universe "Like withered leaves to quicken a new birth!" As Graves has put it in prose, "the pre-Celtic White Goddess was Death, but she granted peotic immortality to the victim whom she had seduced by her love-charms. . . . For though she loves only to destroy, the Goddess destroys only to quicken." The purpose of that destruction of "whatever is over-blown, faded, and dull" is "to clear the way for a new sowing." The Gravesian speaker in this poem, in effect, says to Darien, "Be thou me." That swift, un-tameable child will be at once the speaker's re-created self and the apocalyptic "remedy" in an evil time; in both cases, he is "The new green of my hope." For if winter comes, can spring be far behind?

In "The White Goddess," originally published as the dedicatory poem to the volume of that title, the promise of fecund spring sustains the true quester in bleakest winter. The seeker (singular in the dedicatory poem, a plural "we" in *Poems and Satires 1951* and in *Collected Poems*) acts in defiance of the conventional world: the saints and sober men who, "Ruled by the God Apollo's golden mean," revile the Goddess. In predictable "scorn" of the life- and imagination-denying Apollonians,

> we sailed to find her
> In distant regions likeliest to hold her
> Whom we desired above all things to know,
> Sister of the mirage and echo.

Though she seems hopelessly remote and tenuous in the extreme, there *is* the fascination of what's difficult. The sea expedition is undertaken with infectious confidence, a confidence rewarded with the imaginative fleshing out of the mirage:

> It was a virtue not to stay,
> To go our headstrong and heroic way
> Seeking her out at the volcano's head,
> Among pack ice, or where the track had faded

Beyond the cavern of the seven sleepers:
Whose broad high brow was white as any leper's,
Whose eyes were blue, with rowan-berry lips,
With hair curled honey-coloured to white hips.

Though full appreciation of her sensuous beauty is troubled and confused by the traditional and Coleridgean leper comparison, the rich alliteration and assonance of the final lines sweep most doubt away. These lines, and the final stanza as a whole, reveal, as Kirkham says, a "romanticism more full-bodied" than that of any previous Graves poem:

Green sap of Spring in the young wood a-stir
Will celebrate the Mountain Mother,
And every song-bird shout awhile for her;
But we are gifted, even in November
Rawest of seasons, with so huge a sense
Of her nakedly worn magnificence
We forget cruelty and past betrayal,
Heedless of where the next bright bolt may fall.

The Gravesian incantation is as magnificent as his Goddess, whose nakedness is that of the whole truth and nothing but the truth. "Truth has been represented by poets as a naked woman: a woman divested of all garments or ornaments that will commit her to any particular position in time and space. The Syrian Moon-goddess was . . . represented so, with a snake head-dress to remind the devotee that she was Death in disguise." This poem's romanticism is as "full-bodied" as it is precisely because it incorporates the full paradox of death in disguise: the truth that beyond the longed-for spring we glimpse in raw winter there still lurks the "curved blaze" of her Cretan ax—here, the "bright bolt" that, balancing the green sap that rises in the spring, shall fall *in* the fall. For in ivy time, just as the flowers shall once again be trampled down by the great boar, the quester must die at the hands of she whom he desired above all things to "know." Indeed, emphasis is placed on knowledge. The birds and flowers celebrate her in season; "we," who have struggled through hardship to find her and are alone conscious of what is to come, hail the Goddess proleptically, with expectancy of both her generosity and her ultimate destructive blow.

Instead of masochism, however, there is a wonderful recklessness in the final alleged suspension of memory. Though in fact the lines look before and after, the acknowledged "cruelty and past betrayal" are, if not quite forgotten, absorbed; "we" are caught up in the spirit of headstrong and heroic *sprezzatura*,

"Heedless of where the next bright bolt may fall." This is the "wasteful virtue," the nonchalant gesture in the face of danger and death, that so enraptured Yeats when he encountered it in that strong enchanter, Nietzsche. Here it is caught perfectly by Graves, who finds—in sound and majestic cadence—the bravura adequate to his great theme.

The White Goddess poems seem "major." And, indeed, Graves has done almost all those things major poets do. He has written a great deal of poetry and, through revision and winnowing (judicious until recent years), has established a canon. An occasionalist in many modes and tones, he eventually sought a central, focusing theme. He found it, for both his mythological studies and his practice of poetry, in love. Love is the main theme and origin of true poems, he believes, and the true poet writes *with* love, treating poetry with a single-minded "devotion" that may be called "religious." Graves's religion is his myth of the White Goddess and, since 1959, her Black sister. The neolithic and Bronze Age religious faith in the Triple Goddess has survived among what are called the Romantic poets, and Graves is convinced that his studies have shown that the imagery of the authentic Romantics was drawn, either consciously or unconsciously, from the cult of the Goddess and that the "magic" their poems exert largely depends on an intimacy with her mysteries.

What for Graves is a central theme will seem to others merely eccentric; what to him is the persistent survival of a timeless motif is for others an atavistic aberration. And yet, despite his obsession with the ancient world—with love magic and poetic magic, with dragons and dreams and rites of blood, with ancient Welsh prosody, Sufi mysticism, and Celtic romance—Graves is a man of the modern world. He fought in that war which has itself come to seem a zigzag trench cutting through this century, dividing the old from the "modern" consciousness; and he has lived long enough to see both his island retreat and his most esoteric speculations domesticated by cultural tourists. He may find little to admire in the modern world, but he is certainly aware of what it is he spits from his mouth.

There is, then, a considerable body of work—much, though by no means all, of it now conveniently available in *New Collected Poems*. There is a central theme: that "one story and one story only / That will prove worth your telling." There is an elaborate mythography and a vital poetic tradition to buttress the theme, to provide a larger sustaining context for the hundreds of skillfully crafted lyrics that make up Graves's poetic corpus. And there is Graves himself: soldier, scholar, craftsman he; a figure larger than life, yet a man whose sophisticated primitivism, whose characteristically modern double-mindedness, makes him our contemporary.

But Graves remains an anomaly. We seldom think of him as a "major" poet, certainly not as a major *modern* poet. A case can be made (and has, by Kirkham) for his modernity on the basis of sensibility and awareness rather than of themes, images, and advanced techniques; and certainly the author of *Good-bye to All That* is aware of twentieth-century chaos and brutality and of the modern patriarchy and mechanarchy he repudiates. He also repudiates "Franco-American modernism" with its "major poems of truly contemporary malaise" written for "an aggregate public." While he denies opposing innovations in poetic technique, he is clearly wary of them and of the often extreme explorations of sensibility we associate with Eliot, Pound, and the later Yeats. The problems of sensibility and awareness in Graves have to do, not with his experience of the modern world, but with his failure to consistently translate that experience into poetry.

There is something at once heroic and perverse in Graves's stance. Yeats, a poetic traditionalist too, felt himself to be a man "flung upon this filthy modern tide" ("The Statues"); but he entered, however quirkily, the waters of poetic modernism and so was reborn after midlife. Graves has never ceased regarding the "foul tidal basin of modernism" as a stagnant deviation from the mainstream of tradition. For him, the genuine poet, independent of fashion and of public service, is a servant only of the true Muse, committed on her behalf to "continuous personal variations on a single prehistoric, or post-historic, poetic theme." Writing in 1949 (in the introduction to *The Common Asphodel*), and by then persuaded that he was himself such a Muse-poet, he tells us, in a most revealing metaphor, that he has "ceased to feel the frantic strain of swimming against the stream of time."

Actually, Graves had largely reconciled himself to swimming in his own way, against the modern mainstream, by the early thirties. And, with characteristic pride and cunning, he had turned his "limitations" into a claimed advantage. "Flying Crooked" is perhaps the best of his anecdotes on the theme, a poem in which he chooses an image emblematic for Yeats as well: the butterfly. The older poet, who associated "zigzag wantonness" and the "crooked road of intuition" with the eccentric flight of that insect, wore a ring depicting butterfly and hawk and liked to autograph books with the explanatory lines: "wisdom is a butterfly / And not a gloomy bird of prey." At the same time, of course, Yeats was attracted to straight-flying predatory birds of war and chose as his central hero Cuchulain, that "clean hawk out of the air." In "Rocky Acres," Graves too identified with the unburgherly predator who, hovering in the air, rocking on his wings, "scans his wide parish with a sharp eye." But in more whimsical, and more persuasive, moods he adopts as his own the zigzag crooked path:

> The butterfly, a cabbage-white,
> (His honest idiocy of flight)
> Will never now, it is too late,
> Master the art of flying straight,
> Yet has—who knows so well as I?—
> A just sense of how not to fly:
> He lurches here and here by guess
> And God and hope and hopelessness.
> Even the aerobatic swift
> Has not his flying-crooked gift.

Behind the precision of observation (even the species is identified) the parallel with Graves's own idiosyncratic strategy as a poet ("who knows so well as I?") is obvious. If Graves's flight is eccentric, even "idiotic," it is also—and, here again, we must read in the contrast with the other modern idols, especially Yeats—"honest." And whatever he lacks to qualify as a "master" of the "art of flying straight" he makes up for in the possession of good sense and a mysterious "gift" in comparison with which that dubious mastery seems well lost. It is a variation on a recurrent paradox in Graves's "interaction" with his contemporaries: his recognition not merely that it is "too late" to teach an old aeronaut like himself the new tricks of the hawks, the alleged masters of mainstream modernist poetry, but also that his "flying-crooked gift" is actually superior to their "straight" but, by implication, *dis*honest (and therefore *morally* "crooked") aerobatic skills.

In "Flying Crooked," Graves typically celebrates his chosen crookedness in a craftsmanlike way—here, in impeccably metrical couplets (iambic tetrameters rather than pentameters; that they were the choice of Jonathan Swift in the age of the heroic couplet opens the possibility of a pun in Graves's penultimate line). As usual, too, the Romantic-intuitive is in balance with the Classical-rational aspect of double-minded Graves. Like the butterfly (and like the bat in Richard Wilbur's poem "Mind"), Graves "lurches" about "by guess" yet has a "just sense" of how *not* to fly, of what to avoid. And though, like other honest idiots, he is a child of "God," he seems directed less by that male divinity than by the "hope and hopelessness" associated with a Muse Goddess who, however deterministic, is no less wanton and wayward than the flight of a butterfly and whose power will eventually be epitomized in the crooked (*cur-vus*), "curved blaze of her Cretan axe" ("Darien").

In a thematically related poem of the same period, "In Broken Images,"

Graves contrasts the quick, confident, linear rationalist who thinks in clear images with himself, "slow, thinking in broken images." But in mistrusting his images and questioning their relevance, he becomes "sharp" as the clear-thinker grows "dull." And whereas when "fact fails" the logician he can only "question" his physical senses and instincts, Graves can "approve" his. So both continue, "He in a new confusion of his understanding; / I in a new understanding of my confusion." No images, clear or broken, appear in the poem. Yet even so abstract an exercise in verbal gymnastics demonstrates Graves's skill, the poem's construction (propositions in couplets) parodying as it does the discourse of Apollonian logicians. It also demonstrates, and exemplifies, Graves's ability to turn acknowledged limitations into an occasion for triumph: another instance of Goliath being toppled by underdog, "minor" David.

One way to pull off such triumphs is to claim to be part of the "true" mainstream. If modernist poetry was bogus, complex, ambiguous, stylistically idiosyncratic, dislocated, and pretentiously "major," then true poetry, consisting of personal variations on a single timeless theme, must be lucid, ecstatic, traditionalist, and—deliberately, aggressively—"minor." Graves, who has been called "the most prideful poet writing in the world today," has dismissed not only Auden and Thomas, but Yeats, Eliot, Pound, and Wallace Stevens as well: it has been observed that "if it is true Graves won't suffer fools gladly, it is even truer he suffers his betters not at all." At the same time, he himself eschews all claim to being a major poet. "Minor poetry, so called to differentiate it from major poetry, is the real stuff," he insists, pride characteristically mingling with that sense of limitation.

At this point, critics tend to become either consciously playful or annoyed with the distinction as an extrinsic or wrongfully applied standard. George Stade opens his monograph on Graves by declaring him "a minor poet of major proportions"; David Bromwich, concluding his brief review of *New Collected Poems*, asks, "Is Graves a minor poet? A major poet? A major minor poet? A minor major poet?" and concludes by understandably passing the buck: "There are those who will enjoy deciding." The real enjoyment, of course, comes in reading the best of Graves's poetry. In his full-scale study, Kirkham avoids throughout the classification of Graves's work as either major or minor on the ground that these are "vague categories usually implying standards extrinsic to literary judgment." Thom Gunn, a poet influenced by Graves, has suggested that professional critics, confronted with Graves's versatility, have taken refuge in the formula that, though he is admittedly accomplished, he is minor. Somebody's standards are wrong, Gunn concludes, and that somebody isn't Graves (*Shenandoah* symposium).

Graves himself treats the distinction as critical shoptalk and, more significantly, as an Apollonian conspiracy against the Muse and her poets. In his essay "Sweeney among the Blackbirds," he declares all "magic poems" to be the work of young people. But the poet, as he grows "old and reasonable," tends to lose his power of falling in love, or even of remaining in love.

> The Literary Establishment has a bright label for what he then produces, if he follows the right models energetically enough. It is "Major Poetry"—which casually consigns the magical poems of his early manhood to the category "Minor Poems." Having by this time graduated as a solid member of society, the new major poet transfers his allegiance from the White Goddess of Inspiration to Apollo, the god of musical and artistic achievement—the all-too-reasonable upstart godling who dethroned the great Ninefold Muse-goddess of Greece, reduced her to nine little obedient Muses.

The transfer of allegiance from the White Goddess to Apollo, from ecstatic Muse poetry to nonecstatic, architectural, "major" Apollonian poetry, is the Gravesian sin against the spirit. "Nothing," he has said in a lecture on the legitimate criticism of poetry, "is better than the truly good, not even the truly great. . . . Good poets are exceedingly rare; 'great poets' are all too common. The poet who accepts his limitations but works to the point of exhaustion on getting every word of a poem into place, may yet fail, for one reason or another, to be as good as he intends." Nevertheless, such an honest worker shall

> mount and keep his distant way
> Beyond the limits of a vulgar fate:
> Beneath the Good how far—but far above the Great.

Even if we grant (I do) the partial validity of Graves's distinction, we yet pull up short of full assent—both to the general proposition and to its application to Graves himself: an idiosyncratic but perhaps major mythographer and a dedicated craftsman who, to alter his own distinction, stands firmly among the Good, but *beneath* the Great how far.

The Great I have had in mind throughout much of the present study are the Great Romantics, Graves's precursors both in devotion to the Muse and as mythmakers. While there is truth in Harold Bloom's observation that, unlike the "First Romantics," the "Last Romantics" (Yeats, Lawrence, and Graves) have succumbed to "shamanism" and "phantasmagoria," with the darkest phantasmagoria Graves's masochistic insistence on "the mutual rendings of poet and Muse as being true love," it is equally true that Gravesian wildness is tempered by stoicism and a stress on limitation. For Graves, true poetry is by definition minor poetry. The chief popular impact of the Great Romantics, too, has been achieved with short lyrics rather than with their attempted or accomplished epics. But even if those precursor-poems for Graves—"The Mental Traveller," "The Ancient Mariner," and the most condensed of these epical ballads, "La Belle Dame sans Merci"—were to be considered minor, the fact remains that the ambition of Blake, Coleridge, and Keats (one shared by Wordsworth and Shelley) was to create major poetry, specifically to out-Milton Milton. In contrast to these titanic overreachers and failed questers, Graves is teleological. His reach seldom if ever exceeds his grasp. Though surprise was a notable element in his earlier poems, the later ones seem sometimes so predictable that their end is in their beginning. And his vision, for all his abandonment to the vagaries of the Goddess, remains stoic rather than apocalyptic.

I am not arguing with Graves's dualistic temperament, a double-mindedness that has provided one of my main themes. But if we are reminded of Hardy and Frost, stoic traditional poets whom Graves admires, we must also remember not only that they are "major" poets compared to him, but also that they share little of his mythopoeic extravagance, his phantasmagoria. And yet, for all his attunement to archetypal mysteries, Graves is even more obsessed than they with the minutiae of craftsmanship and the need for poems to make "good sense." It is not necessary to endorse shoddy craftsmanship or perverse obscurity to observe the inherent dangers in such a program as Graves's. As he himself admitted in a preface to a reading, some of his later poems are so "cunning" that they lack exuberance (Steps).

To adapt T. E. Hulme's celebrated distinction between the Romantic and the Classic, Graves seems a poet who, while fully conscious of the vast ocean around him, prefers to dip his bucket in a limited well. And this Romantic-Classic distinction may be applied to that between major and minor poetry. In one unreprinted poem that clarifies the poet-Muse relationship, the ephebe is advised:

> Never sing a song clean through,
>   You might disenchant her,
> Venture on a verse or two
> (Indisposed to sing it through),
> Let that seem as much as you
>   Care, or dare, to grant her.

The jaunty rhythms of light verse embody the problem. For it seems less a fear of the Muse that inhibits Graves than his own sense of limitation and the precariousness of that bond with her that provides enchanted inspiration. One "dare" not press too far: to be disposed to "sing a song clean through" is to be willing both to penetrate to the experiential sources of creativity and to take the ambitious risks that separate major poetry from a modest verse or two. "Indisposed," "seem," and "care" slyly suggest that the effort is actually being made under a defensive show of laconic wit and nonchalance. But in fact Graves is rarely willing to "venture" into either length of conceptual depth. It may be true, as he says, that "all Muse poetry is minor poetry, if length be the criterion," but it seems suspiciously convenient that his Muse should prefer brief finger exercises to ambitious odes.

This is an uncharitable way to put it, and unfair to Graves, who has after all produced an impressive and well-wrought body of work. His poetry—characterized by a lucid, tempered awe in face of the phantasmagoria he himself evokes—is poetry of the British middle ground, its climate of thought generally located in the temperate zone, content to be native and traditional in both technique and theme. "*Vers libre* could come to nothing in England," Thomas Hardy assured an admiring Graves in the twenties. "All we can do is to write on the old themes in the old styles, but try to do it a little better than those who went before us" (*Good-bye to All That*). Graves has from the beginning maintained a traditionalist belief that certain principles cannot be violated without poetry turning into something else, and though his distillation of Hardy's "old themes" into the "one story" of his monomyth may seem idiosyncratic, that theme is, in Graves's eyes, even more traditional than his conservative poetic technique.

And he is proud of his old-fashioned virtues. An American critic recently complained in the *New York Times Book Review*: "Robert Graves, the British veteran, is no longer in the poetic swim. He still resorts to traditional metres and rhyme, and to such out-dated words as *tilth*; withholding his 100 percent approbation also from contemporary poems that favor sexual freedom." It is hard not to be won over by the veteran's response:

> Gone are the drab monosyllabic days
> When "agricultural labour" still was *tilth*;
> And "100% approbation," *praise*;
> And "pornographic modernism," filth—
> Yet still I stand by *tilth* and *filth* and *praise*.

Here as elsewhere, craft triumphs over crankiness. This little poem, which might have been no more than a bit of reactionary grumbling, is manipulated so that the last line not only scoops up the three operative terms but concludes resonantly, its final word, "praise," elevating the poem well above its germinal anger. Reading "Tilth," one feels no inclination to take issue with an arrogance that on other occasions can be monstrous. The stubborness of "Yet still I stand" here seems admirable. Like Swift and Yeats, Graves feels himself a man appointed to guard a position. "Stand we on guard oath-bound," Yeats defiantly asserted in his deathbed poem "The Black Tower"; those banners of materialistic modernism "come not in."

Graves's stubborn "stand" is also the final position of an old man ("Tilth" was written in the seventies). At the end of the story as at its beginning, Graves's soldierly stance is both perverse and heroic, poignant and admirable. "The pride of 'bearing it out even to the edge of doom' that sustains a soldier in the field," he has written in a characteristic fusion of Shakespeare, war, and poetry, "governs a poet's service to the Muse."

> It is not masochism, or even stupidity, but a determinism that the story shall end gloriously: a willingness to risk all wounds and hardships, to die weapon in hand. For a poet this defiance is, of course, metaphorical: death means giving in to dead forces, dead routines of action and thought. The Muse represents eternal life and the sudden lightning-flash of wisdom.

If pride, determination, length of dedicated service, and courage in the field were the only criteria, Robert Graves would be second to no poet of this century, not even to Yeats. But they are not the only criteria; and Graves, for all his indisputable achievement and valiant refusal to give in to dead forces, remains a poet whose story ends honorably rather than gloriously.

Above all, it ends, Graves insists, with poetic integrity and commitment to that truthfulness he denied in Yeats. Yet as Pindar, Nietzsche's Zarathustra, and Zarathustrian Yeats have acknowledged, a poet's very skill can make him a liar. Auden once called Graves's natural facility for writing verse a valuable but dangerous gift, for the poet who possesses it "can all too easily forsake the truth for verbal display" (*Shenandoah* symposium). The source is as significant as the substance of the criticism. What has been said of Auden's employment of Skaldic meters and of the verbal tricks of late Norse poetry (that it can produce a verse that, in Goethe's phrase, "does the poet's thinking for him," and so can become a "substitute for any deeper movement and expansion of the poet's mind") might be said of Graves's employment of Welsh and Anglo-classical prosodic "tricks," particularly his use of *cynghanedd* and allied techniques of alliteration, assonance, and internal rhyming. There is, after all, no guarantee that an intricately "crafted" poem will not be trivial.

It was precisely this charge—technical skill concealing a nullity of thought and "truth"—that, as we've seen, Graves leveled against later Yeats, who had "a new technique, but nothing to say," and who, bereft of a true Muse, employed "a ventriloquist's dummy." Perhaps with that example in mind, Graves declared in the Oxford lectures that "technique takes one no farther than articulating the skeletons [in Ezekiel's valley of dry bones] with wire, and plumping them up with plastic limbs and organs," whereas when poetry is treated in the true spirit, "the notion of technique falls away"; all that remains is the acolyte's service to the Muse, "his unwavering love of whom, for all her unpossessibility, assures that his work will be truthful." Will the preserved poems of the dedicated poet "figure as durable records of blessedness," or merely "convey, truthfully, the darkness of his self-deception?" That seems to double-minded Graves a philo-sophical, and therefore "irrelevant," question. "A poet's destiny is to love."

Despite the lesser, thinner work of recent years, much of which sacrifices passionate intensity to a love-"magic" and "togetherness" more tedious than serene, Graves is a craftsman rather than a mere technician. His poems may be said to succeed or fail insofar as they fulfill the implications of the marvelous concluding line of his most celebrated lyric: "But nothing promised that is not performed." Beyond the bittersweet fruit of the votary's pact with his Goddess— ecstasy shadowed by the inevitable ax—the line implies that the poet puts on *something* of the power and knowledge of the Muse: that nothing is numinously conceived that is not executed by the devotee as man and craftsman. Though there are exceptions (of which "To Juan at the Winter Solstice" is among the most obvious), Graves's most ambitious work falls short of its promise when it fails, in performance, to memorably and dramatically embody the myth. Even in poems with few if any mythopoeic pretensions, failure results when Graves is too rationally reined in or when he succumbs to abstraction. Too often he tells rather than shows—and despite his deserved reputation as a love poet, the later lyrics only sporadically make us feel the passion Graves asserts.

But then there are the poems in which Graves succeeds. There are many of these; and the qualities that make them admirable—clarity, flexibility of tone and diction, syntactical and verbal precision, ironic wit and a genuine balance between wildness and civility—ought to recommend them to a wider audience. This is especially true at a time when the "common reader" of poetry, who still hankers after sense and meaning, has virtually nowhere to turn; when poetry itself has dwindled to a province largely restricted to practitioners and academi-cians. In Graves's tradition—though he sometimes grandly announces that he writes poems only for poets—the poet is still a man speaking to others. Poets who "serve the Muse" must wait for the "inspired lightning flash of two or three words that initiate composition and dictate the rhythmic norm"—what later Graves calls *báraka*, an Islamic word meaning lightning, the "sudden divine rapture" that overcomes devotees. But the result, however "lightning-struck" its inception, must communicate. The doctrine and its imagery inform "Dance of Words" (1964), a poem that embodies the interaction of chance and discipline, puzzling magic and plain sense, individual rhythm and traditional form:

To make them move, you should start from lightning
And not forecast the rhythm: rely on chance,
Or so-called chance for its bright emergence
Once lightning interpenetrates the dance.
Grant them their own traditional steps and postures
But see they dance it out again and again
Until only lightning is left to puzzle over—
The choreography plain, and the theme plain.

In two loosely formal quatrains (alternating between feminine and masculine endings, rhyming on the even lines, prosodically a Gravesian variation on
iambic), "Dance of Words" traces poetic genesis to the inexplicable mysteries of
báraka but insists that the product of that private inspiration make good public
sense, its form and content unembellished and comprehensible. The poem itself
is another instance of that wild civility characteristic of double-minded Graves at
his balanced best. He may not be a "major" poet, and he is certainly not in the
modernist swim, but Robert Graves's accomplishment—reflected, at its best, in
his ability to start from mystery and yet render the choreography plain and the
theme plain—makes him too good a poet to be politely dismissed, and considerably more than an archaic torso washed up at Majorca and out of the swing
of the sea.

MARTIN SEYMOUR-SMITH

Claudius

In the diary (written in England) "A Journal of Curiosities" included in *But It Still Goes On*, which covers the period August 23–September 30, 1929, the entry for September 5 reads:

> I had a dream that I had written a popular song hit called "You surely won't charge me for that." This is only one of dozens of winning ideas that attack me in my weaker moments of sleep or daydream, and are only with difficulty repulsed. It is not long since a complete historical romance or interpretative biography occurred to me—"The Emperor Pumpkin." I had been reading Suetonius and Tacitus. It was about Claudius, the emperor who came between Caligula and Nero. The *dramatis personae* were all ready. The only character who needed any serious enlargement was his physician and adviser Xerxes of Cos, in gratitude for whose services, it may be remembered, he gave the island its freedom from all Imperial imposts. Claudius has always been a puzzle to the historians, as indeed he was to his contemporaries. The Emperor Augustus was much surprised one day to hear his supposedly idiot grandson making a sensible speech. Claudius was to be presented in this story as an idealistic enemy of Caesardom; his father Drusus had made no secret of his own republican views and it was probably these that cost him his life. Claudius escaped both succession and assassination at the

From *Robert Graves: His Life and Work*. © 1982 by Martin Seymour-Smith. Holt, Rinehart & Winston, 1982.

hands of claimants to the succession by a parade of his physical
infirmities, an affected lowness of taste and a cultivated weak-
mindedness. But in spite of every precaution the soldiers forcibly
acclaimed him Caesar after their murder of Caligula. He demurred,
but they insisted. So he decided, the story would show, to do his
best to bring Caesardom into disrepute by playing the fool. Certainly
he did issue numerous ridiculous edicts—such as that mentioned by
Suetonius that no man should hesitate to break wind in his presence,
if he felt so inclined, because to hold it might be injurious to health.
And wrote ridiculous official letters like the one to the Alexandrians
which has survived. And allowed his wife Messalina, whom he dis-
liked, to cuckold him openly and make a laughing stock of him—
until he decided (in my reading) to carry the farce further and to
appear in the further ridiculous guise of the deceived jealous husband. He played the fool in the lawcourts and in the circus. He
allowed himself to be ruled (as it seemed) by millionaire eunuchs.
But when the city stood for all this, and more, and he saw that his
fun was wasted, he became bitter. He married as a second wife
Agrippina, the worst woman he could find, gave her a free hand in
affairs and chose, for his successor, Nero his step-son, whom he
knew to be mad, egotistical and degenerate. He was persuaded that
the sequence of Tiberius in his wicked old age, Caligula the monster,
himself the idiot and then Nero would be enough to bring back the
republic. It nearly was.

As for Britannicus, his son, whom he loved and therefore passed
over for the succession and to whom he is reported to have said, "He
that wounded thee will also heal thee," according to the story I
intended he was handed over to the care of Xerxes, who smuggled
him out to Cos and found a changeling to take his place and be
murdered, in due course, by Nero. I would have presented the death
of Claudius not as murder by his wife with Xerxes as accomplice,
but as suicide with Xerxes as accomplice. The satire of Seneca, *The
Pumpkinification of Claudius*, circulated after his death, would be
attributed to Claudius himself. I would have made it clear that
Claudius did not play his hand as well as he might have done. He
was too sincere a lover of his country to let his buffooneries prevent
him from undertaking many valuable public works, and too moral a
character to discredit the Imperial power by adding debauch to
buffoonery.

I reckon all this here to lay the ghost of an idea which otherwise
might continue to plead for execution.

As he says, Graves specifically recorded this sketch for a possible novel in order to avoid writing it. He had always expressed a dislike of ancient Rome and continued to do so after writing the *Claudius* books. But beneath his disdain for the period and the outline plot the idea had been working like yeast: it *was* "pleading for execution."

It was an unusual project. Most writers, especially those with Graves's gift for the grotesque, aiming to produce a popular book set in Rome, would have plumped for Nero, Caligula or at least Caesar as a central subject. The general public had heard of Claudius, if at all, as the Roman emperor who took a personal part in the invasion of Britain. Scholars tended to ignore him. At best he was a "problem": an American classicist, T. de C. Ruth, had entitled his 1924 book on him *The Problem of Claudius*. He was an odd fish: proclaimed as emperor in A.D. 41 largely by accident, unpopular with the senate because he pressed them to act responsibly, a victim of ill health—and yet, as is now generally conceded, a man "of profound common sense," with a greater grasp of Roman history than that of any other emperor, a learned writer—and the author of a lost autobiography (which, of course, Graves now supplied).

Now what had merely been "pleading for execution," and gently at that, became harsh necessity. When some years later Graves was asked whether he knew, when he set out on *Claudius*, that it would bring in large amounts of money, he replied: "I knew it had bloody well got to." He felt he had been let down over money he had borrowed for Laura's land-buying and building plans; now he could not pay it back. He said in 1955 that the proceeds from *Claudius* allowed him to "hold his head up."

He did much preparatory work for it. The books he used are still in Canelluñ, and they comprise most of the general scholarly works on ancient Rome then available. He steeped himself in the atmosphere of the Rome of Claudius's time: its sociology, its customs at all levels, its politics, its geography, its legal system, its trade and agriculture, its military practices, and, of course, its brutal, murderous and coarsegrained history. He knew as much as anyone, academic or otherwise, about conditions in ancient Rome. Having a "nose" (not the same as a taste) for what Sassoon had called the "nasty," he was well equipped to deal with the excessive nastiness of Rome with just as excessive a gusto.

But the result—*I, Claudius* and *Claudius the God*, which are really one book—is anything but academic or "historical" in the accepted sense. Graves applied his own highly idiosyncratic view to the facts he gleaned. Yet most classical students, even orthodox ones, have gained from this work a general picture of ancient Rome which they would not otherwise have had. The moral, or rather amoral, atmosphere is authentic. In certain ways Graves wanted, in fact needed, to escape from his predicament. His soaking of himself in the atmosphere of Rome served his purpose. Although this work was to be referred to—by Laura Riding, himself and everyone else under their instructions—as a potboiler, rubbish, and so forth, it is really nothing of the sort; and he sublimated his problems in the very hard work he put into it: not the least was the assumption of a bizarre role in life.

Randall Jarrell's view that *Claudius* is "a good book singular enough to be immortal" is shared by most critical readers—even by those who do not as a rule enjoy historical fiction, as Graves himself certainly does not. Recently the *Times Literary Supplement* referred to the work, quite casually, and in the context of a review of several historical novels none of which dealt with Rome, as the only successful historical novel of the century. Millions of TV viewers, when at last *Claudius* reached the screen, were so fascinated by it that they could not tear themselves away. Avidly discussed everywhere, it was the most successful major series ever put out by the BBC (although Graves's own financial reward for the series itself, if not for the new sales of the book thus generated, was shockingly meagre, partly owing to earlier contractual arrangements). But in 1934 *Claudius* was going to have a long wait before it reached a form other than its original one, between covers. And this despite the fact that it cries out for popular dramatic treatment.

What fascinated the mass television audience in Great Britain was by no means only the excellent acting and production, it was also, and in very large measure, the successful transference to a new medium of a certain ingredient of the original. That ingredient was the sense of immediacy, of actuality. Not all viewers believed that the events they were witnessing week by week really took place in history. But they were convinced of their essential truth. *Claudius* satisfies Aristotle's dictum that fiction (in the sense of something that is not historically true) may be more satisfying than the real: he stated, and *Claudius* is a case in point, that fiction could present the *general* truth about something more effectively—indeed, more truthfully—than could some *particular* (or even unique) historical record.

Graves once puzzled Tom Matthews by telling him that he had no imagination. Matthews thought this a strange admission for a poet to make. And so it would have been, if the poet had made it in the context of poetry. But Graves was talking specifically about his capacity for the conventional novel: the novel set in the writer's own time. What Graves meant was that he lacked the kind of inventiveness shown by an Anthony Powell, a Graham Greene, a Simenon. At one time, when they still hoped to make money through conventional fiction, Riding and he entertained the notion that to write a successful novel all you had to do was to invent a lively or odd situation. Then, in the course of the writing, "things would happen of themselves." This may be the way in which certain competent novelists happen to work; but such novelists are interested in the outcome, whereas Graves and Riding weren't; the contemporary world was already rejected, goddawful, historical, and "all that."

Graves has tried his hand at one or two novels of the conventional variety; but they proved damp squibs, and he could not finish them. The nearest he came, in published work, was in *Antigua, Penny, Puce*—but in this he was satirizing family history, family nastiness (both of a specifically English type), and certain other things he found both comic and unlikeable, such as some traits in the character of his brother John. *Seven Days in New Crete*, the most neglected of his major novels, is set in the future, and is by no means conventional.

But give Graves a set of historical facts to make sense out of, and, if he is interested in them—if they set a puzzle—then you are likely to get at least a competent novel. *Claudius* is much more than competent. Under these circumstances he has plenty of "imagination," although he calls it "reconstruction."

But in 1933, settled at last in Canelluñ, he was telling himself that he was sitting down to turn out a potboiler. He was even more insistent on this than Riding: he needed to be. It was fortunate that the ingredients of the novel happened to be responses to the pressures he was under—though he was literally too busy to recognize this at the time (he does now). *I, Claudius* is an objective correlative for his situation, and all the more powerful a one because the pressure to write it appeared to him to be solely financial.

His poem of the mid-thirties, "The Devil's Advice to Storytellers," provides a description of his novelistic method. Part of it reads:

> my advice to storytellers is
> Weigh out no gross of probabilities,
> Nor yet make diligent transcriptions of
> Known instances of virtue, crime or love.
> To forge a picture that will pass for true,
> Do conscientiously what liars do—
> Born liars, not the lesser sort that raid
> The mouths of others for their stock-in-trade:
> Assemble, first, all casual bits and scraps
> That may shake down into a world perhaps.
>
> . . . .
>
> Sigh then, or frown, but leave (as in despair)
> Motive and end and moral in the air;
> Nice contradiction between fact and fact
> Will make the whole read human and exact.

The background against which Graves set his story of the supposed bumbling nonentity Claudius might have been tailored to match his especial, robust skills: it was one of brutality, deceit, treachery, sensuality, superstition. It was a caricature of the goddawful, and he could let himself go in his description of it without upsetting any of his readers' preconceptions. His misunderstood central character was an oblique caricature (but by no means a portrait) of himself— more particularly of his situation.

"My stutter, my cough, my unfinished sentences . . ." he began his fifties poem "The Second-Fated"; and he has recorded in many other places his sense, physical as well as mental, of being awkward, of not "fitting in"—even of being grotesque. Sassoon's picture of him as a soldier, not an unkind one, suggests that others felt this "differentness."

He does not like attention drawn, in conversation, either to this aspect of his character or to his absent-mindedness; and when his daughter Jenny Nicholson wrote a piece on him in *Picture Post* (in the early fifties), in which she said that he might well be found "with marmalade in his hair," he was distinctly annoyed—the day it arrived in the post he said, "I could be very annoyed," which meant he was.

The character of the historical Claudius is irretrievable, as the few scholarly non-fiction books about him make abundantly clear. So Graves's subtle and gripping psychological portrait has, so to say, taken over: this *is*, for millions of people, Claudius.

One feature of the real Claudius's personality is known, and it attracted Graves. He was, as a classical authority puts it, "incurably uxorious." The concentration of evil to be found in certain of the female characters of the book, particularly in Livia Drusilla, added yet another fascinating dimension to the novel.

Arthur Barker published *I, Claudius* in May 1934, in a jacket designed by John Aldridge; Harrison Smith (who had now gone into partnership with Robert Haas) followed suit in America in June. In England the book had reached a third impression before the end of its month of publication, and a ninth (large one) by October 1935. *Claudius the God* appeared in November 1934, again published by Barker. (When Barker wound up his affairs in 1939 the rights were taken over by Methuen.) The two volumes have since appeared in numerous editions, and have never been out of print—and when Penguin released their second edition to coincide with the television series in 1976, it was on the best-seller lists for over a year. *Claudius* has been translated into seventeen languages.

But in both his and Riding's terms the work was a potboiler, and its merits were not allowed to be discussed. One afternoon Graves was forcibly reminded of this.

Both partners subscribed to a press-cutting agency. Riding took up any mention of herself (or got Graves to), and was particularly sensitive to any attribution of their joint work to Graves alone (as she had every right to be). His

vitriolic letters complaining of this, a frequent habit of literary columnists, became something of a feature of thirties literary life.

When *Claudius* appeared it was hailed as a masterpiece by reviewers, and
eventually (1935) received both the James Tait Black and the Hawthornden
prizes. Press-cuttings poured in, and were duly filed. Perhaps he had been indulging in the universal authorial habit of secretly dwelling on the more lauda-
tory of them—for returning one afternoon from his customary swim he discovered that they had been torn up and scattered about the floor.

It was not long after the success of *Claudius* that Graves suggested to
Riding that she might write a historical novel of her own, about the fall of Troy.
Appeased, she took up this idea.

Apart from rewriting another book by Frank Richards—*Old Soldier Sahib*
(1936), published by Faber—and doing a translation (with Riding) of a book
by Georg Schwarz, a German neighbour, called *Almost Forgotten Germany*,
Graves's next venture would be the comedy of English manners and absurdities
Antigua, Penny, Puce (1936).

It is not surprising that Graves firmly believes in the anthropologically
untenable theory that before the state of patriarchy there existed a state of matriarchy. This is by no means owing to his study of Bachofen, or Engels, who also
believed it—but whose writings remain unread by Graves.

While he was working on *Claudius* there was established the absolute, the
carefully elaborated, "literal" rule of Laura Riding. Certainly, as everyone without exception who went there noted, she was effectively in charge by early 1932.
But by the next year and the occupation of Canelluñ the laws had been drawn
up. The constitution was partly written. Graves did what Laura told him to do,
and he believed in what she believed. He also enforced her wishes. She did not
initiate this state of matriarchy. They initiated it together. It is instructive to
know something of what it actually entailed.

First, as Riding explained to a correspondent, "quite frankly, it's not so
equal" in Canelluñ as all that: "we don't believe in equality":

> the apparatus is rather that there are certain laws of being and pro-
> cedure centralised in me on which Robert relies and which I am
> happy to realise cooperatively with him—and others who want the
> same security of mind.

Of Graves's condition she wrote:

> I don't think he regards his mind as poisoned [by celibacy]: it was
> much more poisoned when he was leading a non-celibate life, at any

rate. No doubt his mind has its brutal lapses; they are not important,
only psychologically interesting.

She thought that a woman might appear with whom Graves might have "brutal
lapses"; but these lapses would be only psychologically interesting anyway—
and "it doesn't occur to him to want anyone to appear" (it did, of course).

People "here," she wrote, "take the clue from me and Robert that we are
two very close friends, and not an establishment with a sexual definition."

She saw herself as a dispeller of darkness, though not quite as a magician,
because magicians work in the dark. "The many . . . behind me [are] probably
beings I was helping to clarify and therefore beings who were helping me to
dispel dark."

> As for Robert's knowing, or not knowing, whether I am a magician:
> Robert is very self-protective and on the whole doesn't let himself
> know more than he can absolutely help. And so it is satisfactory
> between us: I tell him what I am. He is perhaps the only one to
> whom I tell explicitly what I am. And I do not tell him that I am a
> magician.

And Graves, who did not allow himself to know more than he could absolutely
help, was gaining the energy from somewhere to write *Claudius*.

The stress which produced Graves's thirties poetry was that between his
worship of Riding and his own inclinations, instincts, beliefs, scepticisms—to
which must be added his resentment, however unconscious, of her treatment of
him. She was, it is true, very nice indeed to him—and often. But she continually
cancelled out such gestures by making him feel acutely unhappy. She handled
him with great skill when she was in control of herself; but when she lost control
it simply made him unhappy anyway. He could and did hand her his powerful
poem "Certain Mercies," as he handed all his poems to her, as testimony to his
willingness to be "lessoned"; but it may be read in another way:

> Now must all satisfaction
> Appear mere mitigation
> Of an accepted curse?
>
> Must we henceforth be grateful
> That the guards, though spiteful,
> Are slow of foot and wit?
>
> That by night we may spread
> Over the plank bed
> A thin coverlet?

That the rusty water
In the unclean pitcher
Our thirst quenches?

That the rotten, detestable
Food is yet eatable
By us ravenous?

That the prison censor
Permits a weekly letter?
('We may write: 'We are well.')

That, with patience and deference,
We do not experience
The punishment cell?

That each new indignity
Defeats only the body,
Pampering the spirit
With obscure, proud merit?

This was shown to Riding as a poem about the spirit as the prisoner of the body, and so it should—at the initial level—be read. But its occasion is suffering; suffering inflicted by Riding as well as by the goddawful world. The poem represents Graves's willingness to suffer. But those who interpret it as a straight body-spirit metaphor woodenly miss its robust, dismayed physicality. Clearly, as a certain kind of God(ess?) might say, physicality does postpone judgement. But judgement by whom? The worms? The angels? Riding?

"Certain Mercies" offers a perfect example of a poem whose true (though then unacknowledged) personal occasion is in direct opposition to its first-level meaning. Ultimately the poem is not dualistic: it is about the body–spirit's lack of freedom to find its true self, and we may infer that this lack stems from its inability to remain "unsplit," intact. Riding is a straightforward dualist: her post-1940 pseudoreligious system is an excellent example of poetry distorted into philosophy, and it lacks true coherence. Graves is subtler. The body ends, in "Certain Mercies," by being defeated by its indignities. But the spirit is nevertheless *pampered*; "obscure" and "proud" are contradictory, though "proud" is empirically justified. If Riding's best poetry has the quality of purity of utterance, his has that of stubborn, persistent acknowledgement of difficulties, of the sort of psychological truths unpalatable to philosophers because they spoil their theorizing.

But to hierophants difficulties become devils. If Graves had not been "patient and deferent" he might well have found himself a Severus being burned outside the boundaries of Deyá; but "playing safe," as he has very often said in conversation, is a strong instinct in him—even when he isn't absolutely sure what he is playing safe about. He played safe in this instance by quickly proving himself a golden goose: golden geese don't get roasted. He was never until old age absolutely lacking in shrewdness, and even then would tend to deviate into it.

But in spite of the atmosphere of unhappiness that underlay everything serious—Laura's dissatisfaction, and Graves's frustration at not being able to fulfil her wishes—there was plenty of fun and enjoyment, as well as much hard work, in the pursuit of which both partners temporarily forgot their miseries.

The sense of happiness then to be found in Deyá, though, was felt most strongly by those visitors who were not writers: those whom Laura did not consider as suitable for her ideal community. Towards these she (usually) behaved with an especially relaxed courtesy and light-heartedness—almost as though they provided her with a much needed excuse to drop, for the time being, the cares of the universe. There were parties—and dancing on the patio outside Canelluñ, visits to cafés, card-playing, joking conversations (many based on Aldridge's comic system of classification of human beings: his day- and night-slimers, and so on). On many of these occasions Gelat would be present.

Why Laura chose some people as "acceptable," and others as not, was puzzling to many. One retired couple, of distinctly right-wing disposition (they were Franco supporters when the Civil War began), and without any interesting conversation or knowledge of literature, or intelligence, were singled out as good friends—yet others, more interesting, were rejected with unnecessary rudeness. People who were not members of the intelligentsia afforded Laura a sense of relief. In their presence she lacked the strain and irascibility she showed in her dealings with writers, with the work of the Press, and with the relationships between her intellectual friends (with which she interfered as though she were God).

Yet the sense of lightness, of fun, of good humour, which she could induce in those around her was remarkable—and none of those who knew her has been able to forget it. It was a genuine gift. So the life in Deyá was one of strong contrasts. But she undoubtedly held sway, the others were a part of her court—and no one (witness Bronowski) who challenged her authority was allowed to stay long.

Graves's official role as poet during the years in Mallorca with Riding, during which time he "submitted" every one of his poems to her for approval, was that of a man putting himself into a state of purification so that he would be ready to be "judged." Thus he was "allowed" to confess his lusts, his feelings, and to retain his individual voice—diction, tone and so forth—because this was all in the interests of his redemption. ("Redemption" is not too strong a word; later Riding would claim, through Schuyler Jackson, that she had tried to "save his soul.") In the *Collected Poems* of 1938 Graves ended his foreword by saying that he had to thank her for her "constructive and detailed criticism" of his poems "in various stages of composition." Her detailed criticism was constructive, as other poets have testified; it had genius. She could often see, in a poem that was still in its draft stage, what was extraneous to its main theme. She could often tell a poet what he was really trying to say, when this eluded him. She helped to see many of Graves's poems of this time into more lively and exact expression. Fundamentally she did object, as she was later to tell him, to his poems "about himself"; but in Mallorca she hoped that he would come to be able to write poems directly about the uncovering of the truth, even if not poems which, as she claimed hers did, actually uncovered it. That she was not superior never occurred to her.

But his main achievement, though largely based on his experience of her, was entirely his own. She criticized him for manifesting his "poetic faith" in "a close and energetic study of the disgusting, the contemptible and the evil" (he uses these words deprecatingly of himself in the foreword to the 1938 collection), but did not expect more from him. It was a fortunate coincidence that his poetic development required him to make a close study of what he found most "evil" and "disgusting" in what he accurately called the "perfect confusion" of his times. There was, of course, confusion in Riding too.

"On Portents" (first published in *To Whom Else?*) was written about Riding as Muse, not about Riding as woman:

> If strange things happen where she is,
> So that men say that graves open
> And the dead walk, or that futurity
> Becomes a womb and the unborn are shed,
> Such portents are not to be wondered at,
> Being tourbillions in Time made
> By the strong pulling of her bladed mind
> Through that ever-reluctant element

This attributes qualities that are, in the Gravesian sense, "magical" to the poet's Muse, and is one of the earliest of the pure so-called "White Goddess" poems. The other side of the picture is given in "The Succubus" (*Poems 1930–1933*), another less immediately flattering—retrospective—"White Goddess" poem:

Thus will despair
In ecstasy of nightmare
Fetch you a devil-woman through the air,
   To slide below the sweated sheet
And kiss your lips in answer to your prayer
   And lock her hands with yours and your feet with her feet.

Yet why does she
Come never as longed-for beauty
Slender and cool, with limbs lovely to see,
   (The bedside candle guttering high)
And toss her head so the thick curls fall free
   Of halo'd breast, firm belly and long, slender thigh?

Why with hot face,
With paunched and uddered carcass,
Suddenly and greedily does she embrace,
   Gulping away your soul, she lies so close,
Fathering brats on you of her own race?
   Yet is the fancy grosser than your lusts were gross?

This deals specifically with the failure of erotic fantasy (or dream) to bring a "perfect lover" to the lust-heated imagination, but clearly refers to the reality of the human situation (which renders itself, distressingly, into the equivalent of fantasy in the very act) in which "unity" with the beloved is thwarted by lust. It ends by blaming the "fancy" on the unpurgeable grossness of lust. But, if only incidentally, it also shows another face of the White Goddess.

In "Ulysses" "flesh" had made the hero "blind": "Flesh had one purpose only in the act" and "set one purpose only in the mind"; "love-tossed / He loathed the fraud, yet would not bed alone."

Other poems record moods of pure despair, such as "Trudge, Body!," in which the body has no hope, nor regret: "Before each sun may rise, you salute it for set." Graves was aware that the course he was treading was an eccentric one, unlikely to put him in favour with readers of the poetry then currently fashionable. In "Flying Crooked" he bitterly—yet light-heartedly—criticized his own clumsy empiricism, which involved him in a continuously experimental, backwards-and-then-forwards-and-then-backwards-again way of living, rather than one impelled by some certainty of direction (Riding's life, on the contrary, seemed to be just that). At the same time he cleverly combined this with a satire on what he called (in a letter of the sixties which he neglected to post) "the ingenious routineness of poetry [of the fashionable kind]": scientists, he told his correspondent, "fail to understand that the cabbage-white's seemingly erratic flight provides a metaphor for all original and constructive thinking." He excepts Eratosthenes, Kekulé (the dreamer), Newton, Nils Bohr and Norbert Wiener from such scientists.

> The butterfly, a cabbage-white,
> (His honest idiocy of flight)
> Will never now, it is too late,
> Master the art of flying straight,
> Yet has—who knows as well as I?—
> A just sense of how not to fly:
> He lurches here and here by guess
> And God and hope and hopelessness.
> Even the aerobatic swift
> Has not his flying-crooked gift.

"Down, Wanton, Down!" is a humorous, Restoration-style treatment of the sexual problem: a poem in which a pure wit replaces the more familiar pained tension, and which demonstrates Graves's debt to Rochester very clearly:

> Down, wanton, down! Have you no shame
> That at the whisper of Love's name,
> Or Beauty's, presto! up you raise
> Your angry head and stand at gaze?
>
> Poor bombard-captain, sworn to reach
> The ravelin and effect a breach—
> Indifferent what you storm or why,
> So be that in the breach you die!
>
> Love may be blind, but Love at least
> Knows what is man and what mere beast;
> Or Beauty wayward, but requires
> More delicacy from her squires.
>
> Tell me, my witless, whose one boast
> Could be your staunchness at the post,
> When were you made a man of parts
> To think fine and profess the arts?
>
> Will many-gifted Beauty come
> Bowing to your bald rule of thumb,
> Or Love swear loyalty to your crown?
> Be gone, have done! Down, wanton, down!

But despite all his troubles and his bad dreams and his headaches and his sexual frustration and his other ailments, Graves cheerfully told himself that he enjoyed his life; and very often he did. He worked prodigiously, and, as Riding herself noted of him in her poem "Laura and Francisca,"

> Better a wrong day than none
> Would Robert to himself say
> Before thinking wrong to be wrong.

ANTHONY BURGESS

The Magus of Mallorca

Martin Seymour-Smith first met Robert Graves during the latter's enforced English exile: the Falangists had driven him from Deyá to Devon, and the Second World War postponed his reconciliation with the Franco regime. Seymour-Smith was only fourteen and "full of brash questions" about poetry. Graves gave succinct answers. Dylan Thomas was "nothing more, really, than a Welsh demagogic masturbator who failed to pay his bills." Stephen Spender was "a nice chap, but better as a greengrocer than a poet." T. S. Eliot was "a very decent chap, really," but had sold out to Anglicanism and published a detestable poetaster named Auden. Ezra Pound? "Yes, he had met Pound once: in T. E. Lawrence's rooms at All Souls. He'd had a wet handshake and was clearly crazy." Graves was glad that his future biographer was "getting to the stage of realising that there are hardly any poets or ever have been; this is the only decent excuse for writing poems oneself, because after all there *is* such a thing as poetry."

This kind of puerile dismissal of most of his contemporaries might have been excusable near closing time in the Wheatsheaf or Yorkminster, but there is something immoral in the spectacle of a grown man of proven poetic authority corrupting a youth with his own prejudices. On the other hand, Graves was entitled to write off poets in this manner because he knew what made a poet, or certainly a poem, bad. The essay on the Great English Lyric in *The Common Asphodel* is just and devastating. He and Laura Riding, in their *Survey of Modernist Poetry*, had pioneered the technique of dissecting a poem before pronouncing on it, a thing that only Dr Johnson and Coleridge seemed to have done

before. William Empson—who, of course, was no good—developed this technique in his *Seven Types of Ambiguity*, to, it is generally accepted, the benefit of
the art of criticism. It is generally accepted too, even among Graves's strongest
admirers, that the magus of Mallorca would have done well to apply to his own
work the informed rigour he brought to that of others.

For Graves's importance as a poet still seems to be in doubt. He has produced enough to ensure that (as with Wordsworth) at least ten percent of his
output has to be taken seriously, but there is not one stanza or even line of his
that has become a common quotation among the literary. Pound may have been
an impostor, Auden a plagiarist, Eliot a timeserver and Yeats (whom Graves
particularly despised) a poseur, but they have all modified our attitude to life and
implanted certain ineffaceable rhythms in our brains. Graves does not hug the
memory. He seems rhythmically flaccid and has never quite come to terms with
the movement of spoken English. His diction has a tendency to obsolete inver-
sion. There are many poems of his which one would not be without—this, for
instance, which astounded Eliot:

> Circling the circlings of their fish,
>   Nuns walk in white and pray;
>   For he is chaste as they,
>   Who was dark-faced and hot in Silvia's day,
> And in his pool drowns each unspoken wish.

But his extravagant rejection of the entire corpus of modern poetry in English—
with the exception of Hardy, Frost, Ransom and, of course, Riding—put him
into a position of dangerous eccentricity demanding from his readers a rehabilita-
tion of taste more appropriate to a cultus than to a decent catholicity.

Of the value of many of his prose writings there can be no doubt. Most of
the criticism is admirable and entertaining. The historical novels are very readable, and *I, Claudius* is compelling not only as a television series but as a Korda
film that never got itself completed. Of much of his prose output Graves has
been genially dismissive. His fine autobiography *Good-bye to All That* was written too fast and very carelessly. He essayed the novel not as a novelist but as a
needy hack, thus putting himself outside the canons of fictional art. So long as
the books paid the bills, the critics could be ignored. The scholars too could be
ignored when they complained about the false anthropology of *The White Goddess*. A lot of the prose was there to subsidize the poetry. Some of the prose was
a theoretical justification of poetic practice. The only thing that really mattered
was the poetry. Eliot never liked talk of "poets," preferring himself to be thought
of as a man who sometimes produced poems, but Graves took the title of poet

very seriously. He was a poet, and therefore he had to write poetry. It was never a matter of his having written poetry and therefore being entitled to the high title. Never was a literary life so loftily dedicated. But perhaps dedication, like patriotism, is not enough.

The life itself is of appalling interest. It is not merely fascinating but filmable. It has prolonged *sturm und drang* and ends with a hardly earned tranquillity. Seymour-Smith draws on *Good-bye to All That* and the memoirs of Graves's father (author of "Father O'Flynn") for the first part, filling in with details previously withheld and essaying psychological interpretations not available to the autobiographer. Graves was a chaste boy with a public-school education who tried, as we all do, to distinguish between love and lust. He loved a fellow-pupil who turned out to be homosexual. War neurasthenia, wrongly termed shell-shock, uncovered sexual guilt which had nothing to do with sexual enactment. At the end of the war (and nobody has given a better account of it from the infantry officer's angle), Graves, a virgin, married another virgin, Nancy Nicholson, a militant feminist who alleged that the sufferings of soldiers were nothing compared to the sufferings of women. She kept to her maiden name, thus rendering eventual divorce awkward, since the petition *Nicholson* v. *Graves* was not acceptable in law. Children were born, but there was not much love. Nancy was bossy, people felt sorry for Graves. A phrase used by Cantabile in Saul Bellow's *Humboldt's Gift*—pussywhipped—seems appropriate. Graves's postwar life begins with pussywhipping from one woman and continues with it from another.

Graves and his family, having made no money either from writing or from keeping a shop on Boar's Hill, went to Egypt, where there was a professor's job waiting. With them went Laura Riding. She, a young Jewish poet from Manhattan, had tried to boss the Fugitives in Nashville, Tennessee. One of the Fugitives was John Crowe Ransom, whom Graves admired. It was thought a good idea to send Laura Riding off to boss Robert Graves. She turned up in London on the eve of the Graveses' departure and attached herself to the family during the short-lived Cairo venture. Graves's account of his professorial troubles in *Good-bye to All That* is merely diverting: here we learn that he went through hell.

Really it was an anteroom to hell. The real hell began back in London, when the *ménage à trois* was turned into a foursome by the appearance of a certain Geoffrey Phibbs. Up to that point things had not been going too badly. Graves had earned £500 from a popular book on his friend T. E. Lawrence and had put the money into the Seizin Press, an enterprise designed to "actualize the new thinking, bring some of the right people together, and provide practical examples of how writing should be done. The implied precepts of *A Survey of*

Modernist Poetry (published in July 1927) required illustration." Then Phibbs, an Irish journalist, much impressed by Laura Riding's work, joined the group at what was known as "Free Love Corner" and helped to initiate hell.

Of Laura Riding, whose influence dominated Graves's life for so long, something must be said, since it is probable that she does not now have many readers. It is enough to examine the poems by which she is represented in Michael Roberts's *Faber Book of Modern Verse* (the first edition) to be made aware of her genuine power. The trouble with her as a person was that she was too conscious of her literary gifts and highly resentful of those who did not appreciate them. She was egoistical and damnably dogmatic. I remember her giving, in Manchester, a fifteen-minute lecture on the nature of poetry and refusing discussion, since she alone knew the meaning of words and her auditors could not be trusted to use them at all. When her *Collected Poems* appeared in 1938 I gave the book, apparently, the only review which she deemed intelligent. She wrote a long letter to my editor praising my appreciation of her "womanness" (her prose was always shocking) but demanding that her laudations be not published. When, in the same year, I thought rather less highly of Graves's first *Collected Poems*, I was subjected to a dual attack which she, not Graves, insisted be published. I was not merely illiterate, I was analphabetic. I was also ill-mannered. I had a notion that something very queer was going on in that, as it had now become, *ménage à deux*.

Laura Riding's womanness responded violently to Phibbs, whom she called an Irish Adonis. She tried to thrust Graves back into the arms of Nancy, who did not now want him. Then Phibbs announced that he wanted no more of Laura; he preferred Nancy. Laura's response was to drink Lysol, to no effect, and then to leap out of a fourth-floor window with the valediction "Goodbye, chaps!" Graves, more prudently, leapt out of a third-floor window. Phibbs ran away. A deformation of the spine, in evidence on her Manchester visit, and a prospect of deportation for attempted suicide were the fruits of the escapade. Phibbs lived in a houseboat with Nancy and Graves's and her four children, whom the father had to support. Graves and Laura Riding went off to Mallorca.

Graves loved her but was denied access to her bed. He put up meekly with her tyranny and probably for a good reason. Her poetic influence was wholly beneficial, even though her potboiling prose efforts were unpublishable, while Graves paid the bills. She resented this. She resented his becoming known while she remained unknown. She overestimated her personal magic and her capacity to arouse lust. She became a prophet and proposed reforming the world. When, with war imminent, she and Graves went to America she, perhaps all too explicably, fell in love with Schuyler Jackson, a man with little learning and no literary talent. She broke up his marriage and became tyrannically submissive to his physical advances. In *The White Goddess* Graves was to write:

> The archives of morbid psychology are full of Bassarid histories. An English or American woman in a nervous breakdown of sexual origin will often instinctively reproduce in faithful and disgusting detail much of the ancient Dionysiac ritual. I have myself witnessed it in helpless terror.

She ceased to be a poet. Mr and Mrs Jackson ended up running a citrus-fruit venture in Wabasso, Florida. It was said to be in a constant state of failure, but this did not prevent their keeping another house in New Mexico. Meanwhile Graves had fallen in love with Beryl, wife of his collaborator Alan Hodge (*The Long Week-End*, *The Reader over Your Shoulder*), and spent a happy war with her in Devon. It was long before Nancy consented to the onomastic adjustment which would permit the lovers to marry, but eventually things turned out all right. Back to Deyá with a wife, not a goddess who had registered with the villagers as a crazy chain-smoking harpy eccentrically dressed, the founding of a new family, a well-earned creative tranquillity.

The impact of femininity on Graves's life and thinking is clearly, as Seymour-Smith's book makes shockingly clear, not of a doctrinaire nature. He had lived simultaneously with two women of almost mythical assertiveness and had kept, for the sake of his art, his own well-developed masculinity in check. He knew the power of the goddess and submitted to it. Seymour-Smith, on the evidence of professional anthropologists, denies Graves's right to posit a primeval matriarchal system (though saying nothing of the *adat perpateh* in Negri Sembilan) but concedes its validity in terms of the poetic imagination. Laura Riding taught Graves to reject history, which is a masculine toy, but not the self-renewing cycle, which is altogether feminine. The error committed by the hero of *King Jesus* is the denial of the feminine, though his claim to kingship is based on female ultimogeniture. Graves's art, as practised in the pacific years at Deyá, depends on a dual concept of woman. His wife is his nearest and dearest, and the recipient of his best love poems, but she is merely Vesta. The goddess who disturbs into a different creative mode comes capriciously and may not be possessed. Graves's late strange adventures with young women in Deyá are not to be interpreted as senile lechery—though healthy rivalry has come into them, like having a fiancé shoved into the lock-up—but in terms of poetic need.

Meanwhile, on the subpoetic plane, Graves has had to go on earning a living, not merely to pay the bills but to subvent appointments like that as Oxford Professor of Poetry. It is consoling to read that he has suffered financially like the rest of us, maintaining an innocent trust in sharks. Tom Roe, for instance, who bought authors' copyrights and guaranteed them an income, though his real speciality was the floating of phantom companies like the infamous Cadco and passing forged dollar bills (the Swiss police found 200,000 false C-notes in the boot of his Mercedes). When Roe began to steal his authors' money Graves lost 65,000 Swiss francs, though Graham Greene and Northcote Parkinson, shrewder men, suffered too. Graves, again like the rest of us, has expected quick showbiz returns and trusted dipsomaniacs and rogues through personal loyalty. His admirable libretto for a musical on the Queen of Sheba (oversalted food in honour of Lot's wife, the only water pitcher in Solomon's bed chamber, Sheba's thirst leading her thither) was rejected by Lena Horne because she "didn't dig the lyrics." Graves was too old to express much satisfaction in the BBC's televisual adaptation of *I, Claudius*, and an earlier contractual screwing ensured that he got no money out of it. It is nearly every writer's sad story, but Graves has kept his primary vocation inviolate—or rather the very nature of that vocation has not tempted the world's bemerding fingers.

Still, his translation of the *Rubáiyát*, which may be taken as inviting the attention of Persian scholars and lovers of "Fitz-Omar" alike, as well as exhibiting the most mature phase of his pure verse craftsmanship, typified inveterate qualities—genial arrogance, innocence, unscholarliness, and a disturbing incompetence. The Cambridge manuscript provided by Omar Ali-Shah was said (in 1978) to be a forgery, and a literal prose translation was not, anyway, the best material with which to work. Graves, knowing no Persian, ventriloquized for Omar Ali-Shah, condemning Fitzgerald for inaccuracy and sentimentality, but producing himself a very dry paraphrase that could not, as Fitzgerald's version had done, accommodate the rhyme scheme of the original. Thus:

> Ah me, the book of early glory closes,
> The green of Spring makes way for wintry snow,
> The cheerful Bird of Youth flutters away—
> I hardly noticed how it came or went

which even I, who am no poet, can improve to

> I see the book of early glory close,
> The green of Spring make way for winter snows.
> The cheerful bird of Youth flutters away—
> I hardly notice how it comes or goes.

Martin Seymour-Smith has produced an admirable biography and a shrewd commentary on Graves's work. He goes wrong a little with his account of the

establishment of the Mediterranean Institute of Dowling College at Deyá in
1969–70. He says that the Institute had "a number of regular instructors, of
whom the least undistinguished and certainly the least drunken . . . was the over-
credulous but personally likeable Colin Wilson." I also was one of the instructors. I make no claim to distinction but I do to sobriety. I even gave a lecture in a
suit and collar and tie, a thing unheard of before in Deyá. Deyá I remember as
an overlax place with no garbage collection, a credulity about lunar magic,
hippies sick because they had to subsist on fish and red wine and could not get
Coca-Cola and hamburgers, a set of *Homage to Catalonia* for class study misdirected to Graves's house and sent, fearfully it was thought, back. That was
before the death of Franco. Things may be tougher now.

As a complement to the life, the letters, selected by Paul O'Prey, a young
man living in the Graves household in Deyá and working on the sorting of the
Graves archives. The poet has consistently cultivated the letterwriter's craft all
his long life, editing in a clear bold hand and Indian ink, whose virtue is that it
dries quickly, though too quickly (i.e. before it leaves the bottle) in the Mallor-
can sun. O'Prey provides biographical links but limits life and letters to the
periods of the two wars and the uneasy hagridden pax in the middle. Thus, we
have all of Graves the young infantry officer, far less mature than he is made to
appear with the hindsight of *Good-bye to All That*, and with that limitation of
poetic taste which, in one form or another, was to remain with him all his life.
Graves thought very highly of Rupert Brooke and very little of Ezra Pound. In
1915 he writes to Edward Marsh:

> A three days' spell in billets gives me the chance I have been wanting
> for some time, of writing to tell you how truly grieved I am about
> poor Rupert's death, for your sake especially and generally for all of
> us who know what poetry is: my Father (dear old man!) said this
> was a fitting end for Rupert, killed by the arrows of jealous Musa-
> getes in his own Greek islands; but fine words won't help; we can
> only be glad that he died so cheerfully and in such a good cause.
> What mightn't he have written had he lived?

In 1946 he writes to T. S. Eliot:

> I am in an unfortunate position about the Pound affair. I agree that
> poets should stick together in the most masonic way. . . . But since
> 1911 when I first read Pound in Harriet Monro's *Poetry* magazine;
> and since 1922 when I met him for the first time at All Souls in T. E.
> Lawrence's rooms, I could never regard him as a poet and have
> consistently denied him the title.

That early arrogance of "all of us who know what poetry is" is a theme developed, though often in the most amiable way, throughout the letters.

Denying the bays altogether to Pound, Graves is willing to find that Martin Tupper, best-selling Victorian figure of fun, is "a good bird at times." Writing to Siegfried Sassoon, he says: "Future literary historians will compare your antimajor complex:

When I am old and bald and short of breath

and elsewhere, with Tupper's sonnet on Army Caste:

> *Hard Routine*
> Sets caste and class each by itself aside.
> You fierce-lipped major, rich and well allied,
> To these poor privates hardly deigns to speak."

Whether Sassoon was or was not pleased at being compared with Martin Tupper is not recorded. What is recorded is the cooling of the friendship between two men who perhaps had little in common except a war and a talent for verse. Sassoon published in 1928 his *Memoirs of a Fox-Hunting Man*, unfavourably reviewed by Graves, and in 1930 his *Memoirs of an Infantry Officer*, where Graves, under the name of "David Cromlech," is presented as "a fad-ridden crank." *Good-bye to All That* has much to say about Sassoon, and very little of it was pleasing to the subject, who demanded changes from the publisher Cape, and, after some remarkable long letters to Graves, acquiesced in the closing of a friendship. Laura Riding, with her insistence on impossible perfection in both life and work, had a good deal to do with such closures. Here is Graves to "My dear Siegfried":

> I suppose my "talking through someone else's bonnet" is a reference to Laura. If you had said straight out that Laura was an obscurantist influence on my way of writing that could have passed as an ordinary ignorant remark, or if you had said that Laura herself wrote nonsense that could have been set against the testimony of other people that she is the most accurate writer there is. But you come out with a comic-postcard piece of vulgarity which is the counterpart of the lace-Valentine vulgarity of your *Heart's Journey*: and that ends it. So, for the last time,
> Yours
>
> Robert

Edward Marsh—"I am not angry with you Robert dear, because I never could be" (another indiscretion in *Good-bye to All That*)—maintains friendship. Basil Liddell Hart, after a break, resumes it. Graves deeply offends Eliot by alleging that the *Criterion* compromises its integrity for commercial reasons:

> I would not suggest that you vulgarize the *Criterion* to increase the sales and fill your pockets: obviously you are not that sort of person but I do think that you have compromised about it just as far as was necessary to keep it afloat and I think poetry has been compromised just to that extent.

That was in 1927. All correspondence between Eliot and Graves ceased until 1946. Graves reconciled himself to having no literary friends, except of course Laura Riding, but he does not emerge from his letters as being essentially a quarrelsome man. His great quality is innocence, expressed to the world as bumptiousness and indiscretion. These letters are, almost without exception, most engaging. It is a pity that there can be no Graves–Riding correspondence: they were too close to mingle souls with letters. But Gertrude Stein, Laura's literary aunt, writes cosily, and, at the end, we have an exchange with the doomed Alun Lewis, who seemed to Graves to be, as Lynette Roberts was, all right. O'Prey's title comes from the lines

> He continues quick and dull in his clear images;
> I continue slow and sharp in my broken images.
>
> He in a new confusion of his understanding;
> I in a new understanding of my confusion—

he being everybody else.

Chronology

1895	Robert Graves born July 26 in Wimbledon, England.
1910–14	Attends school at Charterhouse.
1914	Enlists in the Royal Welch Fusiliers.
1916	*Over the Brazier*. Writes first book of poems. Is seriously wounded and reported dead.
1917	Poems appear in *Georgian Poetry, 1916–1917*.
1918	Marries Nancy Nicholson.
1919–26	Attends St. John's College, Oxford. Publishes several volumes of poetry.
1926	Invites Laura Riding to England. Teaches at the Royal Egyptian University in Cairo for one year.
1927	Takes a flat with Riding not far from Nancy and their children. Founds Seizin Press and writes *A Survey of Modernist Poetry* with Riding.
1929	Graves and wife separate permanently. *Good-bye to All That*. Leaves for Majorca with Laura Riding.
1934	*I, Claudius*.
1936	Graves and Riding leave Majorca during the Spanish Civil War.
1938	*Count Belisarius*.
1939	Graves and Riding move to America. Riding leaves Graves for Schuyler Jackson. Graves returns to England and takes up with Beryl Hodge, while collaborating with her husband Alan on *The Long Week-End*.

1945   *Hercules, My Shipmate.*

1946   Returns to Majorca. *King Jesus.*

1948   *The White Goddess: A Historical Grammar of Poetic Myth.*

1953   *The Nazarene Gospel Restored* (with Joshua Podro).

1954   *The Greek Myths.*

1961–66 Professor of Poetry at Oxford.

1964   *The Hebrew Myths* (with Raphael Potai).

1965   *Mammon and the Black Goddess.*

1967   *Poetic Craft and Poetic Principle. The Rubáiyát of Omar Khay-
         yám* (translated with Omar Ali-Shah).

1972   *Difficult Questions, Easy Answers.*

1977   *New Collected Poems.*

1985   Robert Graves dies on December 8 in Deyá, Majorca.

Contributors

HAROLD BLOOM, Sterling Professor of the Humanities at Yale University, is the author of *The Anxiety of Influence*, *Poetry and Repression*, and many other volumes of literary criticism. His forthcoming study, *Freud: Transference and Authority*, attempts a full-scale reading of all of Freud's major writings. A MacArthur Prize Fellow, he is general editor of five series of literary criticism published by Chelsea House.

RANDALL JARRELL was Professor of English at Sarah Lawrence College. His books of essays and criticism include *Poetry and the Age*, *Poets, Critics, and Readers*, and *Kipling, Orwell, and Others*.

J. M. COHEN was a noted translator (of Montaigne and Cervantes, among others) and literary editor.

DOUGLAS DAY is Professor of English at the University of Virginia. He is the author of *Malcolm Lowry: A Biography* and *Swifter than Reason: The Poetry and Criticism of Robert Graves*.

DANIEL HOFFMAN is Professor of English at the University of Pennsylvania, as well as a practicing poet. His critical works include *Barbarous Knowledge: Myth in the Poetry of Yeats, Graves and Muir*, *The Poetry of Stephen Crane*, and *Paul Bunyan: Last of the Frontier Demigods*. He has also published several volumes of poetry, among which are *Broken Laws* and *The Center of Attention*.

MICHAEL KIRKHAM teaches English at the University of Toronto. He is the author of *The Poetry of Robert Graves*.

JOHN B. VICKERY is Professor of English at the University of California at Riverside. He is the author of *Robert Graves and the White Goddess*, *The Literary Impact of the Golden Bough*, and *Myth and Literature: Contemporary Theory and Practice*.

PAUL FUSSELL is Professor of English at the University of Pennsylvania. He is the author of studies of the eighteenth century and of *Poetic Meter and the Poetic Form*. His study *The Great War and Modern Memory* won a National Book Award.

PATRICK J. KEANE is Associate Professor of English at Le Moyne College. He has written on Yeats and Wordsworth, and is the author of *A Wild Civility: Interactions in the Poetry and Thought of Robert Graves*.

MARTIN SEYMOUR-SMITH is the author of *Robert Graves: His Life and Work*. He has also compiled selections of Shakespeare's sonnets, Elizabethan poems, and English sermons.

ANTHONY BURGESS is writer-in-residence at the Grimaldi Palace in Monaco. He is the author of *A Clockwork Orange*, *Earthly Powers*, and the Enderby novels. His criticism includes a study of D. H. Lawrence and two books on Joyce.

Bibliography

Adams, Hazard. "Whence and Whither?" *The American Scholar* 28 (1959): 226–38.

Auden, W. H. "A Poet of Honor." *Shenandoah* 13, no. 2 (1962): 5–12.

Bromwich, David. "Verse Chronicle." *The Hudson Review* 30 (1977): 277–92.

Cohen, J. M. *Robert Graves.* Edinburgh: Oliver & Boyd, 1960.

Cowan, Louise. *The Fugitive Group.* Baton Rouge: University of Louisiana Press, 1959.

Creeley, Robert. "Her Service is Perfect Freedom." *Poetry* 93 (1959): 395–98.

Dahlberg, Edward, and Herbert Read. "Robert Graves and T. S. Eliot." *Twentieth Century Literature* 166 (1959): 293–98.

Davie, Donald. "Impersonal and Emblematic." *Shenandoah* 13, no. 2 (1962): 38–44.

Day, Douglas. *Swifter than Reason: The Poetry and Criticism of Robert Graves.* Chapel Hill: University of North Carolina Press, 1963.

Enright, D. J. "Robert Graves and the Decline of Modernism." *Essays in Criticism* 2 (1961): 319–36.

Forster, Jean-Paul. "The Gravesian Poem, or Language Ill-Treated." *English Studies* 60, no. 4 (1977): 471–83.

Fraser, G. S. "The Poetry of Robert Graves." In *Vision and Rhetoric*, 135–48. London: Faber & Faber, 1959.

Gaskell, Ronald. "The Poetry of Robert Graves." *The Critical Quarterly* 3 (1961): 213–22.

Gregory, Horace. "Robert Graves: A Parable for Writers." *Partisan Review* 20 (1953): 44–54.

Gunn, Thom. "In Nobody's Pantheon." *Shenandoah* 13, no. 2 (1962): 34–35.

Hayman, Ronald. "Robert Graves." *Essays in Criticism* 5 (1955): 32–43.

Hoffman, Daniel. *Barbarous Knowledge: Myth in the Poetry of Yeats, Graves and Muir.* New York: Oxford University Press, 1967.

Jackson, Laura (Riding). "Some Autobiographical Corrections of Literary History." *Denver Quarterly* 8 (1974): 1–33.

Keane, Patrick J. *A Wild Civility: Interactions in the Poetry and Thought of Robert Graves.* Columbia: University of Missouri Press, 1980.

Kirkham, Michael. *The Poetry of Robert Graves.* New York: Oxford University Press, 1969.

Malahat Review, The, no. 35 (July 1975): Special Robert Graves issue.

Matthews, T. S. *Jacks or Better.* New York: Harper & Row, 1977.

Mehoke, James. *Robert Graves: Peace-Weaver.* The Hague: Mouton, 1975.

Musgrove, Sydney. *The Ancestry of The White Goddess*. Auckland, New Zealand: University of Auckland Press, 1962.

Nemerov, Howard. "The Poetry of Robert Graves." In *Poetry and Fiction: Essays*, 112–17. New Brunswick, N.J.: Rutgers University Press, 1963.

Pritchard, William H. "English Poetry in the 1920s: Graves and Lawrence." In *Seeing through Everything*, 114–23. London: Faber & Faber, 1977.

Schwartz, Delmore. "Graves in Dock: The Case for Modern Poetry." *The New Republic* 134, no. 19 (March 19, 1956): 20–21.

Seymour-Smith, Martin. *Robert Graves: His Life and Work*. New York: Holt, Rinehart & Winston, 1982.

Shenandoah 13, no. 2 (1962). Special Robert Graves issue.

Snipes, Katherine. *Robert Graves*. New York: Frederick Ungar, 1979.

Spears, Monroe K. "The Latest Graves: Poet and Private Eye." *The Sewanee Review* 73 (1965): 660–78.

Steiner, George. "The Genius of Robert Graves." *The Kenyon Review* 22, no. 2 (1960): 340–65.

Trilling, Lionel. "A Ramble with Graves." In *A Gathering of Fugitives*, 20–30. Boston: Beacon Press, 1956.

Vickery, John E. *Robert Graves and the White Goddess*. Lincoln: University of Nebraska Press, 1972.

Acknowledgments

"Graves and the White Goddess (Part I)" by Randall Jarrell from *The Yale Review* 45, no. 1 (September 1955) and "Graves and the White Goddess (Part II)" by Randall Jarrell from *The Yale Review* 45, no. 3 (March 1956), © 1955 and © 1956 by *The Yale Review*. Reprinted by permission.

"Autobiography, Historical Novels, and Some Poems" by J. M. Cohen from *Robert Graves* by J. M. Cohen, © 1960 by J. M. Cohen. Reprinted by permission of Barnes & Noble Books, Totowa, New Jersey.

"The Coming of the Goddess" by Douglas Day from *Swifter than Reason: The Poetry and Criticism of Robert Graves* by Douglas Day, © 1963 by the University of North Carolina Press. Reprinted by permission.

"Significant Wounds" by Daniel Hoffman from *Barbarous Knowledge: Myth in the Poetry of Yeats, Graves and Muir* by Daniel Hoffman, © 1967 by Daniel Hoffman. Reprinted by permission of the author and Oxford University Press.

"The Black Goddess of Wisdom" by Michael Kirkham from *The Poetry of Robert Graves* by Michael Kirkham, © 1969 by Michael Kirkham. Reprinted by permission of the Athlone Press Ltd.

"The White Goddess and King Jesus" by John B. Vickery from *Robert Graves and the White Goddess* by John B. Vickery, © 1972 by the University of Nebraska Press. Reprinted by permission.

"The Caricature Scenes of Robert Graves" by Paul Fussell from *The Great War and Modern Memory* by Paul Fussell, © 1975 by Oxford University Press. Reprinted by permission.

"A Wild Civility" by Patrick J. Keane from *A Wild Civility* by Patrick J. Keane, © 1980 by the Curators of the University of Missouri. Reprinted by permission of the University of Missouri Press.

"Claudius" (originally entitled "1933") by Martin Seymour-Smith from *Robert Graves: His Life and Work* by Martin Seymour-Smith, © 1982 by Martin Seymour-Smith. Reprinted by permission of Holt, Rinehart & Winston.

"The Magus of Mallorca" by Anthony Burgess from *But Do Blondes Prefer Gentlemen? Homage to Qwert Yuiop and Other Writings* by Anthony Burgess, © 1986 by Liana Burgess. Reprinted by permission of McGraw-Hill Book Company.

Index